RESEARCH BIBLIOGRAPHIES & CHECKLISTS

40

Clément Marot: an Annotated Bibliography

RESEARCH BIBLIOGRAPHIES & CHECKLISTS

R_CB

General editors

A.D. Deyermond, J.R. Little and J.E. Varey

CLÉMENT MAROT

An Annotated Bibliography

H.P. CLIVE

Grant & Cutler Ltd
1983

ISBN 0 7293 0147 8

I.S.B.N. 84-499-7184-5

DEPÓSITO LEGAL: V. 1.135 - 1984

Printed in Spain by Artes Gráficas Soler, S.A., Valencia

for

GRANT & CUTLER LTD
11, BUCKINGHAM STREET, LONDON, W.C.2.

CONTENTS

ABBREVIATIONS

AAL	*Atti dell'Accademia dei Lincei*
Ae	*Aevum*
AIBL	*Académie des Inscriptions et Belles-Lettres. Comptes Rendus*
AION(SR)	*Annali dell'Istituto Universitario Orientale di Napoli: Sezione Romanica*
Arc	*Arcadia*
ASNS	*Archiv für das Studium der Neueren Sprachen und Literaturen*
BBB	*Bulletin du Bibliophile et du Bibliothécaire*
BFLACU	*Bulletin of the Faculty of Liberal Arts, Chukyo University*
BHR	*Bibliothèque d'Humanisme et Renaissance*
Bibliog. I	C.A. Mayer, *Bibliographie des œuvres de Clément Marot*, I: *Manuscrits*, Geneva: Droz, 1954 (F43)
Bibliog. II	C.A. Mayer, *Bibliographie des éditions de Clément Marot publiées au XVIᵉ siècle*, Paris: Nizet, 1975 (F49)
BSEL	*Bulletin de la Société des Études Littéraires, Scientifiques et Artistiques du Lot*
BSHP	*Bulletin de la Société de l'Histoire du Protestantisme Français*
BSLLW	*Bulletin de la Société de Langue et Littérature Wallonnes*
CAIEF	*Cahiers de l'Association Internationale des Études Françaises*
CAT	*Cahiers d'Analyse Textuelle*
CL	*Comparative Literature*
DisA	*Dissertation Abstracts (International)*
DLF	*Dictionnaire des lettres françaises*, publié sous la direction de Monseigneur Georges Grente (and others). *Le Seizième Siècle*, Paris: Fayard, 1951

ECla	*Les Études Classiques*
ELH	*English Literary History*
EsC	*L'Esprit Créateur*
EtLitt	*Études Littéraires*
Fa	*Fabula*
FM	*Le Français Moderne*
FR	*French Review*
Fra	*Francia*
FrF	*French Forum*
FS	*French Studies*
GRM	*Germanisch-Romanische Monatsschrift*
GSLI	*Giornale Storico della Letteratura Italiana*
HLQ	*Huntington Library Quarterly*
HR	*Humanisme et Renaissance*
IL	*L'Information Littéraire*
ISt	*Italian Studies*
It	*Italica*
KRQ	*Kentucky Romance Quarterly*
LevT	*Levende Talen*
MF	*Mercure de France*
MLJ	*Modern Language Journal*
MLN	*Modern Language Notes*
MLQ	*Modern Language Quarterly*
MLR	*Modern Language Review*
MP	*Modern Philology*
MRo	*Marche Romane*
N	*Neophilologus*
NL	*Nouvelles Littéraires*
NMi	*Neuphilologische Mitteilungen*
NS	*Die Neueren Sprachen*
OC	Clément Marot, *Œuvres complètes*. Édition critique par C.A. Mayer, 6 vols, London: Athlone Press, Univ. of London (I-V), Geneva: Slatkine (VI), 1958-80 (E37)

4

PMLA	*Publications of the Modern Language Association of America*
RBPH	*Revue Belge de Philologie et d'Histoire*
RCC	*Revue des Cours et Conférences*
RDM	*Revue des Deux Mondes*
REI	*Revue des Études Italiennes*
RenN	*Renaissance News*
RER	*Revue des Études Rabelaisiennes*
RevS	*Revue Savoisienne*
RF	*Romanische Forschungen*
RFE	*Revista de Filología Española*
RHLF	*Revue d'Histoire Littéraire de la France*
RHR	*ЯHR: Réforme, Humanisme, Renaissance*
RJ	*Romanistisches Jahrbuch*
RLC	*Revue de Littérature Comparée*
RLM	*Rivista di Letterature Moderne e Comparate*
RLR	*Revue des Langues Romanes*
RLV	*Revue des Langues Vivantes*
RoN	*Romance Notes*
RPh	*Romance Philology*
RQ	*Renaissance Quarterly*
RR	*Romanic Review*
RRen	*Revue de la Renaissance*
RSH	*Revue des Sciences Humaines*
RSPT	*Revue des Sciences Philosophiques et Théologiques*
RSS	*Revue du Seizième Siècle*
S	*Symposium*
Schutz	*A Critical Bibliography of French Literature*, II: *The Sixteenth Century*, ed. by Alexander H. Schutz, 1956 (see A6)
SFr	*Studi Francesi*
SP	*Studies in Philology*
SRen	*Studies in the Renaissance*
STFM	Société des Textes Français Modernes

THR	Travaux d'Humanisme et Renaissance
TLF	Textes Littéraires Français
TLLS	*Travaux de Linguistique et de Littérature, Strasbourg*
TNTL	*Tijdschrift voor Nederlandse Taal— en Letterkunde*
TSLL	*Texas Studies in Literature and Language*
VR	*Vox Romanica*
ZFSL	*Zeitschrift für Französische Sprache und Literatur*
ZRL	*Zagadnienia Rodzajów Literackich*
ZRP	*Zeitschrift für Romanische Philologie*
art.	article
BN	Bibliothèque Nationale (Paris)
CM	Clément Marot
col., cols	column(s)
ed., eds	edited, edition(s)
f. fr	Fonds Français (at Bibliothèque Nationale)
MS, MSS	manuscript(s)
tr.	translated, translation
UP (in particulars of publishers)	University Press

INTRODUCTION

'La bibliografia su Marot è vastissima', Enea Balmas observed in a study published in 1975 (HUb1). The purpose of the present volume is to take stock of this enormous amount of material — its volume has increased still further over the past few years — and to do so in the manner that is most likely to prove useful and convenient to the potential user. It is hoped that, in thus establishing a detailed record of publications dealing with Clément Marot and in providing brief explanatory and evaluative comments, this Bibliography will constitute a helpful reference tool for anyone wishing to study Marot's life, works, and ideas. Editions apart, it lists close to eight hundred and fifty items.

General arrangement. Obviously, the easiest solution, from the compiler's point of view, would be to present all these items in a single alphabetical list. The result, however, would surely be highly indigestible. Accordingly, the material has been divided into several sections. In seeking the most appropriate format, my aim has been to facilitate quick and easy access to as many different aspects of the subject as possible, while avoiding the disadvantages likely to arise from excessive fragmentation — notably inconsistency in the assignment of items to sections, and the need for a multiplicity of cross-references.

The Bibliography has been divided into the following areas: General Bibliographies; Iconography; Biographical and General Studies; The Quarrel with François Sagon; Principal Editions since 1600; Textual History (Manuscripts, Editions); Questions of Authenticity; Studies of Marot's Works; Language, Style, Versification; Ideas; Sources; Influence; Marot and Music; Marot in Fiction. Some of these sections have been further subdivided, where the nature of the material warrants it. One advantage of this arrangement is that the user can rapidly identify those aspects on which research has focused in any particular area. Another is that he is able to gain a clearer overview of certain debates in which scholars have engaged, for instance concerning the influence of Petrarchism, or Marot's place in the history of the French sonnet. Information on these two aspects, which would otherwise be buried in a mass of material relating to many different topics, can be readily found in the small subsections KA ('Petrarchism') and HS ('Sonnets').

In section H, which is devoted to studies of Marot's works, all items dealing with subjects related to more than one of the various subsections have been placed in HA. Elsewhere, however, classification of the material is less mechanical. The choice of section in the case of items concerned with several aspects is determined by the principal focus (which cannot always be identified with equal ease) of each publication. Usually cross-references have then been inserted in other relevant sections. The main exception to the latter practice occurs with the comprehensive studies in section C. No references to these will normally be found elsewhere, since it is felt that the user of the bibliography can be expected to deduce from the titles of the publications and from the heading of section C that such items will very probably deal with Marot's life as well as with his works and ideas.

Classification and titles of Marot's poems. C. A. Mayer's very good critical edition of Marot's works (E37), completed in 1980 (and hereafter designated by the letters *OC*, for *Œuvres complètes*), is likely to be the standard edition for an appreciable time. It has therefore been thought useful to give particulars of the volume and page(s) where poems which are cited in titles or comments can be found in *OC*. These particulars are regularly provided, except for some major poems whose location can be traced fairly easily. This information should save the user much time and effort, especially since the edition as a whole lacks unified indexes of titles and first lines. Moreover, the search for certain poems is rendered more difficult by the fact that Professor Mayer's system of classification differs in some respects from those normally used in nineteenth and twentieth-century editions; even his titles are not always the traditional ones.

For the sake of consistency and to facilitate consultation of *OC*, Professor Mayer's classification has been followed in this bibliography. (This should not be interpreted as necessarily implying agreement with his system in each case.) The following example illustrates the method which has been adopted. In his article 'Sur un parallèle traditionnel dans l'histoire de la poésie française', G. Vipper discusses Marot's 'elegy XXII'. In *OC*, this poem has been classified as a *complainte.* Accordingly, the article appears in the bibliography in subsection HG (*'Complaintes'*), and a cross-reference has been placed in subsection HK (*'Élégies'*). An exception has, however, been made in the case of the *blasons* which have been maintained as a distinct category (HC), in order to keep the discussion of the genre (and especially of the *blasons anatomiques*) separate from that of the epigrams, with which they appear in *OC*.

Furthermore, in the interest of uniformity, the titles or first lines of poems are cited in the comments as they appear in *OC*. In the titles of the publications themselves they are, of course, given in the form chosen by the author.

Items included. The aim has been to compile the maximum amount of information on studies of Marot's life, works, and ideas. In the first place, an effort has been made to offer as complete a list as possible of items entirely devoted to Marot. In addition, the bibliography includes items which, while concerned with a different or wider subject, nonetheless make significant reference to Marot. Obviously, the determination of what constitutes significance must perforce be, at least to some extent, a subjective one. Length is evidently an important factor. No useful purpose would surely be served in attempting to record every one of the numerous works published during the past centuries which contain a few brief remarks — often the same ones — about Marot. At the same time, extensive discussion is not an absolute necessity. Thus Boileau's celebrated short statement about Marot's 'élégant badinage' (HA9) appears to me significant, and even in more than one sense. It is significant directly inasmuch as it constitutes an illuminating appreciation by a major classical poet of one of the key elements of Marot's poetry, coupled with a clear expression of his characteristic distaste for what increasingly came to be known as the 'style marotique' (which offered features similar to those of the despised 'burlesque'). And the statement is also significant indirectly, because of its impact on later critical attitudes to Marot — mostly based, it is true, on an at least partial misunderstanding of Boileau's line.

Some selectivity has also been exercised in the presentation of material in certain specific areas, as will be further indicated in the notes below. One example occurs in the area of religious polemics which so frequently involved either scathing criticism or spirited defence of the Marot-Beza psalter. There seems little point in chronicling all the shots fired in this bitter war of words, especially since the arguments tend to become repetitious and often derive from the same main sources. Only the more important texts are therefore mentioned.

The bibliography also provides details of unpublished dissertations (the term 'unpublished' being taken to mean those not published in their entirety or near-entirety). It has not, as a rule, been possible to consult these dissertations. However, in the case of theses completed in North America during recent years, brief indications of the authors' aims and claims are supplied in the form of quotations from the summaries composed by them for *Dissertation Abstracts*.

Items excluded. It follows from the criterion of 'significant reference' formulated above that publications offering background information are not included unless they also deal in some depth with Marot. J. Mathorez's article 'Un Apologiste de l'alliance franco-turque au XVIe siècle: François Sagon (*BBB* (1913), 105-10) contains useful information about Marot's adversary and offers some insights into his ideas; Ph. Aug. Becker's study 'Die Versepistel vor Clément Marot' (in his *Aus Frankreichs Frührenaissance: Kritische Skizzen*, Leipzig, 1927, pp.47-84) presents a good analysis of the work of Marot's precursors in this genre and thereby helps us to appreciate better Marot's own achievements. But neither publication is directly concerned with Marot himself. They have, therefore, not been listed in the bibliography; otherwise, hundreds of similar background studies would have to be taken into account, and it would be very difficult to know where to stop. (In rare instances, exceptionally interesting publications of this kind, though not accorded separate entries, are mentioned in the notes. This happens, in fact, in the case of Becker's above-cited article — see HP1.)

Also excluded, as a general rule, are articles in histories of literature and encyclopaedias, and, in section I, dictionaries, grammars, and treatises on versification.

Lastly, a few words need to be said about offprints. It has not been an uncommon practice, especially in France, for authors to arrange for the preparation of separately-paginated offprints of their articles. The publishers of these offprints may or may not have been associated with the printing of the journal in which the article originally appeared. Occasionally, the offprint presents slight typographical changes, especially where the article extended over more than one issue of the periodical. Unless there are special reasons for citing them, such separately-paginated offprints are not listed in the bibliography. Two notable exceptions to this rule are Pierre Villey's important studies on the chronology of Marot's works, to which reference is frequently made in notes on other entries. The offprints of Villey's studies are likely to be more readily available to many users of this bibliography than the original articles, particularly since these offprints were reprinted by Slatkine in 1973. Articles and offprints are therefore listed separately (F64 and F65, HA102 and H103) and page references are given to both.

Presentation of the material. Except for section E, where editions are listed in chronological order, items are arranged in the alphabetical order of their authors' surnames. Anonymous works and edited volumes are placed in the alphabetical sequence in accordance with their titles, only significant words being considered for this purpose, i.e. no account is taken of articles, prepositions, or forenames (thus the anonymous article entitled 'Pierre Caroli . . . ' appears under the letter 'C', with a cross-reference under 'P').

The author's names — surname, forename(s), initial(s) — are always given as printed in the publication, except that where the surname was represented by the initial letter only, the rest of the surname has been added in brackets if known. Where more than one study is mentioned by the same author, the items are placed in the order of their publication. The establishment of this sequence is not affected by the various ways in which an author's forename(s) may appear in different publications (e.g. whether as 'Peter William Jones' or 'Peter Wm. Jones' or 'P. W. Jones' etc.).

The title of the book is followed in the entry by the date of publication and by the name of the publisher (whose forename or initial is also given in the case of works published before 1700). The printer's name is not usually included. Finally, the number of pages is stated for works consisting of not more than one volume. In the case of works which went through several editions, the one described in the bibliography is generally the first one. Occasionally there may be advantages in citing a later, corrected, augmented edition.

A further point of presentation arises in respect of significant references to Marot in books — and, more rarely, in articles — which have a different principal subject. Usually such references occupy all or the major part of a single chapter or section. Where the latter is furnished with its own title, that title forms the basis of the entry.

If the chapter does not possess a separate heading, or if discussion of Marot has been placed in a section which also deals extensively with other topics, the note 'On CM, see pp. ....' has been added. Lastly, when it happens that the principal study of Marot is located in one part of the book, while important references to him are found at various other points in the work, the fact is indicated by the phrase 'On CM, see esp. pp. ....'.

Many items are followed by details of reviews. It should be clearly understood that there was no intention of presenting an exhaustive coverage of critical reactions. Instead, the aim has been to offer a selection of the most interesting appraisals.

Use of the asterisk. Those items which I have not been able to examine myself are marked with an asterisk. Apart from the dissertations (see under *Items included* above), they are extremely few in number.

Note on section C. Several of the general studies in this section reflect the reputation enjoyed − or, as is more frequently the case, suffered − by Marot in the seventeenth and eighteenth centuries. The writer's assessment of Marot's character and qualities is often linked with severe criticism of his psalm translations and with a most uncharitable proclamation of his manifest unsuitability for such a task. These judgements clearly fall within the area of religious controversy to which reference was made earlier. Only a selection of the most interesting of these appraisals has been included.

Note on section E. The year 1600 has been chosen as the starting date for this section, since C. A. Mayer's *Bibliographie des éditions de Clément Marot publiées au XVIe siècle* (F49) covers earlier publications. In his bibliography, Professor Mayer lists editions of Marot's psalms only up to the year 1550, 'date à laquelle ils devinrent avec les *Bibles*, un moyen de propagande protestante'. For the same reason, separate editions of the psalms are not recorded in this section, except in the case of a modern critical edition or an important reprint (but the psalms are, of course, included in many editions of Marot's works). Several hundred editions of the Huguenot psalter appeared in the sixteenth century alone, and many more later. The benefits likely to be obtained from tracking them all down −even if that were possible − seem to me altogether negligible, and certainly out of all proportion to the effort which such an undertaking would entail.

The principal editions taken into account are primarily editions of the complete works, and of single works other than the psalms. No attention has been paid to the numerous anthologies containing a few poems by Marot.

Note to sections E and F. For the user's convenience, reference is made in the notes, where appropriate, to C. A. Mayer's bibliographies of manuscripts and editions containing works by Marot (F43, F49). A few such references will also be found in other sections.

Note on subsection HA. The vogue for the 'style marotique' in the seventeenth and eighteenth centuries must clearly be considered an example of Marot's influence on later poetry. The most appropriate location for any discussions of it might accordingly appear to be section L. However, such discussions are almost invariably linked to appraisals of Marot's own poems. For this reason, these items have been placed in section HA.

Note on subsection HUa. The study of the music of the Marot-Beza psalter is a highly complex subject, with a considerable bibliography of its own. Publications bearing on the music of the psalms have therefore been included only if they also examine literary or other aspects of the psalter.

Note on subsections HUb and KA. Marot's translations of Petrarch and the influence of Petrarchism on his original poems are treated in different sections, the former in HUb (i.e. in the part of the bibliography concerned with Marot's translations), the latter in KA (in the part dealing with his sources). This separation appears convenient as well as justified, whether or not one agrees with the standpoint taken by C. A Mayer, who, while ascribing Marot's translation of six sonnets by Petrarch to the period 1538-42, maintains nonetheless that his stay in Italy in 1535-36 had led him to abandon Petrarchism.

Note on section L. Here again, some selectivity has been exercised, for instance in presenting the works concerned with Marot's influence on English poets, particularly Spenser. No comprehensive study of Spenser can fail to mention that influence, and it would surely be tedious to list all examples. Several of the most important studies have been cited; even they are not free of a certain repetitiousness. Likewise, no claims to exhaustive coverage are made in respect of publications dealing with foreign imitations of the Marot-Beza psalter.

Note on section M. Items are limited to studies dealing with Marot's attitude to music, and with the setting to music of his poems but not of the psalms (see note on section HUa). No mention is made of histories or encyclopaedias of music, some of which may also offer comments on the subject.

Note on section N. The word 'fiction' has been chosen for the title of this section as a convenient umbrella term to cover novels or plays in which Marot appears as a character, works attesting to his emergence as a jester in popular literature, and even a modern poem written in his honour. Sixteenth-century epitaphs are not included, but mention is made of a publication referring to a contemporary *Déploration* lamenting his death.

Indexes. The Index of Persons includes poets and other authors, artists, musicians, and historical characters, as well as scholars. In the Index of references to works by Marot and to those which have been attributed to him, account is taken of articles and prepositions and letter-by-letter ordering has been used.

Marguerite de Navarre. For the sake of uniformity, Marguerite's name is always given in this form in the comments, irrespective of whether or not she was already Queen of Navarre at the period to which the remark refers.

Period covered. While no formal cut-off date has been imposed, the end of the year 1980 may, in a general way, be regarded as marking the limit of the period covered by this bibliography. There will, inevitably, be some unintentional omissions. But if some fish have escaped the net, I hope that not too many big ones have got away. I should, in any case, be grateful for information about items which, it is felt, ought to be added to the bibliography. They will be recorded in a future supplement.

*   *   *

In conclusion, I wish to express my warm appreciation for the considerable help I have received throughout the preparation of this bibliography from the ever-helpful staff of the Maxwell MacOdrum Library at Carleton University, and especially from the members of the Interlibrary Loan Section headed by Terry Clark. I am very much indebted to Peter Zohar for his help in checking both the typescript and the proofs. Pierre van Rutten also very kindly read the typescript. Albert Halsall generously shared in the proofreading. Last but certainly not least, I should like to record my sincere gratitude to the Social Sciences and Humanities Research Council of Canada for awarding me a grant towards the costs of research.

H. P. C.

Carleton University
Ottawa

A. BIBLIOGRAPHIES

A1   Aulotte, Robert, 'Quinze années d'études sur Clément Marot', *IL*, XXX (1978), 55-62.
Takes up where Saulnier (A8) left off. An objective, competent, very useful art.

A2   Cioranesco, Alexandre, 'Marot (Clément), 1496?-1544', in his *Bibliographie de la littérature française du seizième siècle.* Collaboration et préface de V.L. Saulnier, Paris: Klincksieck, 1959, pp. 465-72.
An exhaustive list.

A3   Giraud, Jeanne, 'Marot (Clément)', in her *Manuel de bibliographie littéraire pour les XVIe , XVIIe et XVIIIe siècles français: 1921-1935*, Publications de la Faculté des Lettres de l'Univ. de Lille, II, Paris: Vrin, 1939, pp. 40-41.

A4   Giraud, Jeanne, 'Marot (Clément)', in her *Manuel de bibliographie littéraire pour les XVIe, XVIIe et XVIIIe siècles français: 1936-1945*, Paris: Nizet, 1956, pp. 74-75.

A5   Giraud, Jeanne, 'Marot (Clément)', in her *Manuel de bibliographie littéraire pour les XVIe, XVIIe et XVIIIe siècles français: 1946-1955*, Paris: Nizet, 1970, pp. 148-49.

A6   Harvitt, Hélène, 'Clément Marot', in *A Critical Bibliography of French Literature*, General Editor: D.C. Cabeen, II: *The Sixteenth Century*, ed. by Alexander H. Schutz, Syracuse: Syracuse UP, 1956, pp. 66-71.
A selective bibliography, with concise, critical comments. A few other entries relating to CM are to be found elsewhere in the volume.

A7   Ito, Susumu, 'Clément Marot: Essai de bibliographie (1800-1980)', *BFLACU*, XXII (1981), 861-1000.
A most useful and sound bibliography, copiously and very informatively annotated. Specially valuable for details of publications in Japanese (the descriptions given of these in the present bibliography are based on the information supplied by Ito). Less comprehensive than the present

bibliography, both with regard to the period surveyed and the in-depth coverage (some five hundred items, as against eight hundred and fifty). Furthermore, numerous items listed by Ito but not seen by him are described here.

Mayer, C.A.: see F43, 49.

A8   Saulnier, V.L., 'État présent des études marotiques', *IL*, XV (1963), 93-108.
An excellent survey, divided into several sections. See B14.

A9   Saulnier, Verdun L., 'État présent des études marotiques', in *The Present State of French Studies: A Collection of Research Reviews*, ed. by Charles B. Osburn, Metuchen, N.J.: Scarecrow Press, 1971, pp. 166-98.
Reprint of A8. Osburn provides a supplementary bibliographical essay on p. 917.

A10   Weiss, N., 'Clément Marot, Ronsard, d'après quelques publications récentes', *BSHP*, LXXIV (1925), 360-71.
A selective, briefly annotated list of CM studies since the beginning of the century, followed by some notes on psalm translations and commentaries on the psalms published during the 1520s and early 1530s.

A11   Will, Samuel F., 'Marot, Clément', in his *A Bibliography of American Studies on the French Renaissance (1500-1600)*, Illinois Studies in Language and Literature, XXVI, 2, Urbana: Univ. of Illinois Press, 1940, pp. 25-27.

B. ICONOGRAPHY

B1   Aubert, Fernand, 'Sur trois achats du Musée historique de la Réformation', *Musées de Genève* (June 1951), p.l.
One of the acquisitions is a portrait in oils of CM. Aubert speculates that it may have been owned by Beza, since it resembles the type of portrait he used in his *Icones* (C14).

B2   Bentley-Cranch, D., 'A Portrait of Clément Marot by Corneille de Lyon', *BHR*, XXV (1963), 174-77.
Suggests that this portrait, apparently 'the only ... of Clément Marot painted during the poet's lifetime by a known painter', dates from CM's stay in Lyons on his return from his first exile, i.e. Dec. 1536-early 1537. The portrait was not known to Pannier (B9).

B3   Bentley-Cranch, D., 'Further Additions to the Iconography of Clément Marot', *BHR*, XXVI (1964), 419-23.
Describes a portrait of CM, not mentioned by Pannier (B9) or Calmon (B5), which was originally owned by the humanist Thomas Rhedinger (1540-76) and is now in the Museum Slaskie at Wroclaw, the former Breslau. No information is available concerning the painter or the date. Rhedinger also possessed a wax medallion of CM, as part of a medallion collection probably dating from the period 1560-74 (cf. B7).

Bèze, Théodore de: see C14, 15.

B4   Bouchot, Henri, *Les Portraits aux crayons des XVIe et XVIIe siècles conservés à la Bibliothèque Nationale (1525-1646): Notice, catalogue et appendice*, Paris: Oudin, 1884, 412 pp.

B5   Calmon, J., *Iconographie de Clément Marot*, 1948, 6 pp.
Typescript at BN, Département des Estampes, call-mark Na205(21). The most comprehensive list to date (but see B3). Very brief descriptions, no discussion.

B6   Clemen, Paul, and Eduard Firmenich-Richartz, *Meisterwerke westdeutscher Malerei und andere hervorragende Gemälde alter Meister aus Privatbesitz auf der kunsthistorischen Ausstellung zu Düsseldorf, 1904*, Munich: Bruckmann, 1905,

19

xxiii + 41 pp. + 90 plates.

No. 250 of the exhibits is described (p. 35) as 'Bildnis des Dichters Clément Marot (1495-1544)' by Titian, formerly in the collection of King William II of the Netherlands and now owned by the Prince of Wied. It is reproduced in plate 75. See B11.

B7   Courajod, Louis, 'La Collection de médaillons de cire du Musée des Antiquités Silésiennes à Breslau', *Gazette des Beaux-Arts*, 2nd ser., XXIX (1884), 236-41.
Describes twenty medallions dating from the reign of Charles IX and portraying mostly sixteenth-century royalty and courtiers, but including also heads of Luther, Melanchthon, and CM. (According to Dimier, B8, III, p. 268, the medallion of CM is identical with that at the Musée de Cluny.) On this collection, which is presumed to have been destroyed during World War II, see also B4, pp. 385-86, B8, III, pp. 264-69, and esp. B3, where information is given about the original owner.

B8   Dimier, Louis, *Histoire de la peinture de portrait en France au XVIe siècle, accompagnée d'un catalogue de tous les ouvrages subsistant en ce genre ...*, Paris & Brussels: Van Oest, 3 vols, 1924-26.

Firmenich-Richartz, Eduard: see B6.

B9   Pannier, Jacques, 'Les Portraits de Clément Marot: Notes iconographiques et historiques', *BHR*, IV (1944), 144-70.
The only extensive study to be published to date (but see B5). Much useful information, many interesting speculations concerning painters and dates. Evidently important gaps still remain to be filled in.

B10   Pariset, François Georges, 'Les Expositions du seizième siècle européen et le Clément Marot (?) de Moroni de la Société', *BSHP*, CXII (1966), 37-39.
The portrait, owned by the Société du Protestantisme Français, which supposedly represents CM (see B15) and has sometimes been attributed to Giovanni Moroni, Lorenzo Lotto or Dosso Dossi, is described by Pierre Rosenberg in the catalogue of the exhibition 'Le XVIe Siècle européen' (Paris, Petit Palais, 1965) as having indeed been painted by Moroni during the third quarter of the sixteenth century. Pariset contends, however, that the striking differences between the person shown in this portrait and the one depicted by Corneille de Lyon (see B2) make it unlikely that the sitters are the same. Pariset leaves open the question as to which one is likely to be CM.

B11   'Un Portrait de Marot', *BSHP*, LXXXII (1933), 513-14.
A portrait of CM attributed to Titian (reproduced in B6) has recently been sold in Germany for 105,000 marks.

B12   Puaux, Frank, 'Portraits protestants', *BSHP*, LIV (1905), 183-84.
A recent exhibition (in Paris) included a portrait of CM from the Tronchin collection in Geneva: 'A contempler cette figure en lame de couteau, dure, implacable, on se représente mal le poète de la Réforme ...'

B13   Romane-Musculus, P., ['Lettre'], *BSHP*, CXII (1966), 334.
Commenting on a remark in B10 about CM's portrait in Beza's *Icones* (see C14), Romane-Musculus states that it was engraved by Pierre Eskrisch from a painting owned by Beza which was subsequently in the Tronchin collection at Bessinge. Cf. B1, 12.

B14   Saulnier, V.L., in A8.
The art. has a section on portraits, and also reproduces five of them, including what Saulnier mistakenly believes to be a previously unknown one, in MS Arras 266 (it is already mentioned by Bouchot in B4, p. 297).

B15   Schickler, baron F. de, 'Rapport sur l'exercice 1891-92', *BSHP*, XLI (1892), 234-48.
Reports the acquisition by the Society of a portrait of CM 'attribué à Morone' (p. 243, see also p. 223). See B10.

C. BIOGRAPHICAL AND GENERAL STUDIES

C1   A[ignan Étienne], 'Sur l'exil de Clément Marot', *Minerve Française*, IV (Nov. 1818), 10-13.
Some very cursory remarks about CM's imprisonment in 1526 and about his first exile.

C2   *Annales poétiques; ou, Almanach des Muses, depuis l'origine de la poésie françoise*, II, Paris: Delalain, 1778.
On CM, see pp. 123-58 (essay) and pp. 159-324 (poems). On the whole, a sympathetic and, for the period, well balanced study of CM's life and works. The author accepts Lenglet-Dufresnoy's stories about CM's affairs with Diane de Poitiers and Marguerite de Navarre (see C96). Praises CM for his epigrams; considers him to have been, in the psalm translations, 'plus coupable envers le goût qu'envers la religion'.

Atance, Félix R.: see J3.

C3   Aubin, E., *Clément Marot: Sa vie, son caractère et ses œuvres. Entretien littéraire*, Cahors, 1866, 21 pp.

C4   B[aillet], A., 'Clément Marot', in his *Jugemens des sçavans sur les principaux ouvrages des auteurs*, Paris: Antoine Dezallier, 9 vols, 1685-86, IV, Pt. 3 (1686), 198-209.
A generally disparaging and hostile study, containing reflections such as the following: 'Marot ... joignit au malheur d'embrasser la nouvelle Reform des Protestans, celuy d'infecter la Cour de France par les ordures et les obscenitez de ses vers.' Quotes Maimbourg (C99) and Jurieu (C85).

C5   Bayle, Pierre, 'Marot (Clément)', in his *Dictionnaire historique et critique*. Nouvelle éd., augmentée de notes extraites de Chaufepié, Joly, La Monnoie, Leduchat, L.J. Leclerc, Prosper Marchand, etc., Paris: Desoer, 16 vols, 1820-24, X (1820), 312-36.
Gives good account of the highlights of CM's life. Bayle develops, justifies, or corrects some statements in appended notes which are of particular interest for their references to the views expressed by certain of his contemporaries. Says relatively little about CM's poems; but while acknowledging that 'il n'y a que trop de pièces obscènes parmi les œuvres', he also affirms

22

that 'non seulement ... la poésie française n'avait jamais paru avec les charmes et avec les beautés naturelles dont il l'orna, mais aussi ... dans toute la suite du XVIe siècle il ne parut rien qui approchât de l'heureux génie, et des agrémens naïfs, et du sel de ses ouvrages.'

C6   Beaulieu, Eustorg de, *Les Divers Rapportz*. Éd. critique, avec introduction et notes, par M.A. Pegg, TLF, CVII, Geneva: Droz, 1964, 422 pp.

C7   Becker, Ph. Aug., 'Marots Leben', *ZFSL*, XLI (1913), 186-232; XLII (1914), 87-139, 141-207.
This biography was superseded by C8, where Becker himself described this earlier study as 'rasch veraltet'.

C8   Becker, Ph. Aug., *Clément Marot: Sein Leben und seine Dich- tung*, Sächsische Forschungsinstitut in Leipzig, Forschungs- institut für Neuere Philologie, IV. Romanistische Abteilung, Heft I, Munich: Kellerer, 1926, 420 pp.
A splendidly detailed biography. Most of Becker's main data have stood the test of later research, but some points have been challenged (e.g. the identity of 'Monsieur Bouchart', by Mayer in C103). The life and the works are studied separately, but there is a certain overlapping, esp. since Becker treats the poems primarily as reflections of CM's feelings and experiences – an approach that is not without its dangers (see HA5, HK1).
Rev.: .1 Beves, Donald H., *MLR*, XXI (1926), 450-51.
      .2 Hämel, Adalbert, *NS*, XXXV (1927), 157-58.
      .3 Plattard, Jean, *Litteris*, IV (1927), 72-82. See also C114.

C9   Belloc, Hilaire, 'Clément Marot', in his *Avril; Being Essays on the Poetry of the French Renaissance*, London: Duckworth, 1904, pp. 75-113.
Brief essay, followed by poems. Belloc considers CM's fame excessive; attributes it to his having been the quintessential Frenchman in his character, his intellectual and social attitudes, and his 'complete sym- pathy with the atmosphere of the native tongue'.

C10   Bernard, Daniel, 'Clément Marot: Ses *Œuvres*, publiées par M. Charles d'Héricault, chez Garnier, éditeur', *Revue du Monde Catholique*, XX (1867-68), 761-82.
In fact, not a review of E12, but a highly biased portrait of CM, 'un vilain sire, un brouillon de la pire espèce, dont le génie est très discu- table, mais dont la mauvaise conduite ne peut être défendue' – and who, to crown a manifestly wicked life, 'finit par la pratique de cette

austérité protestante, si peu capable d'inspirer de beaux vers'.

C11 Bertoni, Giulio, 'Documenti sulla dimora di Clément Marot a Ferrara', in *Mélanges ... Jean Jacques Salverda de Grave*, Groningen: Wolters, 1933, pp. 9-11.

C12 Bertoni, Giulio, 'Clément Marot à Ferrare: Documents nouveaux', *REI*, I (1936), 188-93.

C13 [Bèze, Théodore de?], *Histoire ecclesiastique des eglises reformées au royaume de France*, Antwerp: Jean Rémy, 3 vols, 1580.
Attributes CM's departure from Geneva to his 'aiant esté tousjours nourry en une très mauvaise escole, et ne pouvant assubjectir sa vie à la reformation de l'Evangile' (I, p. 33). (Many modern scholars believe that the *Histoire* was prepared for publication by a friend of Beza's — perhaps Simon Goulart — from notes provided by him.)

C14 Bèze, Théodore de, 'Clemens Marotus, Cadurcensis, gallicus poeta', in his *Icones, id est verae imagines virorum doctrina simul et pietate illustrium ...*, [Geneva]: Jean de Laon, 1580.
CM's portrait is on fol.Yiiii. It is accompanied by the following remarks, of which especially those referring to CM's morals have been frequently quoted: 'Clemente Marotum citra ullam linguarum vel artium cognitionem, rara et excellente quadam ingenii felicitate Gallos omnes poëtas priores superantem, id circo placuit tantis viris adiungere, quod religionis causa bis exul in Psalterii triente gallicis rythmis exprimendo utilissimam, aeternaque memoria dignam operam Ecclesiis navarit, quanvis (ut qui in aula, pessima pietatis et honestatis magistra, vitam fere omnem consumpsisset) mores parum Christianos ne in extrema quidem aetate emendarit: Taurini, Pedemontani praefecti Regii favore tutus, circiter annum vitae sexagesimum mortuus.'

C15 Bèze, Théodore de, 'Clement Marot', in his *Les Vrais Pourtraits des hommes illustres en pieté et doctrine ... Traduicts du latin de Theodore de Besze [par Simon Goulart]*, Geneva: Jean de Laon, 1581, p. 162.
The text on CM: 'J'ai voulu adjouster aux illustres personnages susmentionnez cestui ci, lequel par une admirable felicité d'esprit, sans aucune cognoissance des langues, ni des sciences, surpassa tous les poëtes qui l'avoyent devancé: pource qu'estant sorti par deux fois hors du Royaume à cause de la religion, il fit un notable service aux églises, et dont il sera memoire à jamais, traduisant en vers françois un tiers des Pseaumes de David. Mais au reste, ayant passé presque toute sa vie à la

suite de Cour (où la pieté et l'honnesteté n'ont gueres d'audiance), il
ne se soucia pas beaucoup de reformer sa vie peu chrestienne, ains se
gouvernoit à sa maniere acoustumée, mesmes en sa vieillesse, et mourut
en l'aage de soixante ans à Turin, où il s'estoit retiré sous la faveur du
lieutenant du roy.' CM's portrait is on p. 161.

C16   Billy, André, 'On a oublié Clément Marot', *Le Figaro*, 21 Oct.
      1944, p. 2.
      The art., written on the occasion of the quatercentenary of CM's death,
      contains the following tribute: 'Nous avons vu des Français de la Résistance
      délivrer leurs camarades emmenés par la police de Vichy ou par la Gestapo,
      mais l'exploit de Clément Marot – un contre trois! – révèle un courage
      dont l'histoire offre peu d'exemples.'

C17   Blanc, Joseph, *Clément Marot: Simple esquisse*, Cahors, 1888,
      14 pp.
      On the occasion of the unveiling of CM's bust at Cahors.

C18   B[onnet], J., '*L'Epistre de M. Malingre envoyée à Clément
      Marot ..., avec la responce du dit Marot.* Nouvellement imprimé
      à Basle, par Jac. Estauge, ce 20 d'octobre, 1546', *BSHP*, XIX-XX
      (1870-71), 85-91.
      Occasioned by the publication of E13. On the basis of Malingre's poem,
      Bonnet dates CM's arrival in Geneva at 1542, instead of 1543 as previously
      believed. See C48, 80.

C19   Bonnet, Jules, 'Clément Marot à la cour de Ferrare, 1535-1536',
      BSHP, XXI (1872), 159-68.
      On the French ladies at Renée's court, esp. Mme de Soubise and her daugh-
      ters.

C20   Bonnet, Jules, 'Clément Marot à Venise, et son abjuration à
      Lyon, 1536', *BSHP*, XXXIV (1885), 289-303.
      Useful though not entirely reliable art. Unlike Douen (C49), Bonnet
      accepts as true the report of CM's abjuration.

C21   Bonnet, Jules, 'Les Premières Persécutions à la cour de Ferrare
      (1536)', *BSHP*, XXXIX (1890), 169-80, 289-302.
      Good, well-documented art. on the religious controversy centring on
      Renée in 1536. Various references to CM. Some erroneous statements
      are repeated from C20.

C22   Bonnet, Jules, 'Calvin à Ferrare, 1535-1536', *BSHP*, XLI (1892),
      171-91.

Affirms that Calvin was in Ferrara in 1536 and met CM, but that the latter was less affected by his proselytism than the Duchess and some other French persons in her retinue.

Boulenger, Jacques: see C93.

C23   Boysson, R. de, 'Un Humaniste toulousain: Jehan de Boysson (1505-1559)', *Bulletin de la Société Scientifique, Historique et Archéologique de la Corrèze*, XXXIII (1911), 303-30, 337-94, 489-553; XXXIV (1912), 83-120, 293-338.
On De Boyssoné's relations with CM, see esp. XXXIII, 352-53.

C24   Boyssoné, Jean de, ['Lettre à Jacques de Lect'], quoted from the MS at Toulouse, in E17, II, p. 20. n. 1.
This letter, written in 1547, contains the frequently cited statement 'Marotus latine nescivit', which has been variously interpreted by CM scholars.

C25   Boyssoné, Jean de, *Les 'Trois Centuries' de Maistre Jehan de Boyssoné, docteur régent à Tholoze*. Éd. critique publiée, avec une introduction historique et littéraire, par Henri Jacoubet, Bibliothèque Méridionale, 2nd ser., XX, Toulouse: Privat, 1923, 223 pp.
The introduction contains numerous references to CM. According to Jacoubet, 'Boyssoné' is the correct form and the one used by the poet's contemporaries.

C26   Boyssoné, Jean de, '*Les Poésies latines de Jehan de Boyssoné (Ms de Toulouse 835)*, résumées et annotées par Henri Jacoubet Annales de l'Univ. de Grenoble (Section Lettres-Droit), VI (192* 343-68; VII (1930), 95-146.
Two poems pay tribute to CM, a third refers to the quarrel with Sagon.

C27   Broc, [H.], vicomte de, 'Jean et Clément Marot', in his *Paysages poétiques et littéraires*, Paris: Plon, 1904, pp. 1-34.
On CM, see pp. 15-34. A factually unreliable biographical sketch, followed by some conventional observations on the poems.

Bucher, Germain Colin: see C39.

C28   Buttet, M.C. de, *Œuvres poétiques de M.C. de Buttet*, précédées d'une notice sur l'auteur et accompagnées de notes par le biblio phile Jacob [pseud. of Paul Lacroix], Cabinet du Bibliophile, XXVII-XXVIII, Paris: Librairie des Bibliophiles, 2 vols, 1880.

C29   Cadilhac, Paul Émile, 'Clément Marot de Cahors', in Cadilhac, Paul Émile and Robert Coiplet, *Demeures inspirées et sites romanesques*, Vol. III, Paris: Éds de l'Illustration (Baschet), 1958, pp. 1-8.
A well-illustrated biographical essay. One photograph shows the Impasse Hébrard at Cahors, in which street CM is stated to have been born (but cf. C30).

C30   Calmon, J., 'Jean Marot, père de Clément Marot, à Cahors (1470-1506)', *BSEL*, LXXXIII (1962), 112-18.
A series of speculative deductions, based on statements by earlier writers and on cadastral surveys of Cahors (see also Calmon, Jean, and René Prat, *Les Cadastres des XVIe et XVIIe siècles de la ville de Cahors (1500, 1606, 1650)*, Cahors, 1947, 372 pp.). Calmon surmises that Jean Marot lived with his first wife, a woman by the name of Rosières or Rouzières, in her parents' house in the Bote de Lalbenquat, now called Impasse Antoine Hébrard; and that, after her death in 1480, he married a woman named Gaubert. It is, however, not possible to determine where they resided.

C31   'Pierre Caroli, Clément Marot, Mathurin Cordier et quarante-six autres, ajournés par les gens du roi comme suspects d'hérésie, 1534 (1535)', *BSHP*, X (1861), 34-39.
The art. reproduces, with comments, a passage from C44, containing the list of persons sought by the authorities in the *affaire des placards*.

C32   Cartier, Alfred, and Adolphe Chenevière, 'Antoine du Moulin, valet de chambre de la reine de Navarre', *RHLF*, II (1895), 469-90; III (1896), 218-44.

Carvalho, Alfredo de: see HUb5.

Cary, Henry Francis: see HA12, 13.

C33   *Catalogue des actes de François Ier*, Paris: Imprimerie Nationale, 10 vols, 1887-1908.
For items concerning CM, see IV, p. 28; VI, p. 283; VIII, p. 33, 175, 757.

C34   Champion, Pierre, 'Clément Marot, poète de Paris', in his *Paris au temps de la Renaissance: Paganisme et Réforme. Fin du règne de François Ier. Henri II*, Paris: Calmann-Lévy, 1936, pp. 58-77.

C34bis Chassaigne, Marc, *Étienne Dolet*, Paris: Michel, 1930, 348 pp.

C35 Chenevière, Adolphe, *Bonaventure des Périers: Sa vie, ses poésies*, Paris: Plon, 1886, ii + 261 pp.

Chenevière, Adolphe: see also C32.

C36 Christie, Richard Copley, *Étienne Dolet, the Martyr of the Renaissance: A Biography*, London: Macmillan, 1880, xxii + 557 pp.

C37 Christie, Richard Copley, *Étienne Dolet, le martyr de la Renaissance: Sa vie et sa mort.* Ouvrage traduit de l'anglais sous la direction de l'auteur par Casimir Stryienski, Paris: Fischbacher, 1886, xxii + 557 pp.
Not simply a tr. of C36, but a revised version.

Chronique du roi François Ier: see C44.

C38 Cohen, Maurice, 'Note pour servir à la biographie posthume de Clément Marot', *BSEL*, VIII (1883), 300-03.
Cites two epitaphs of CM – one by Étienne Forcadel, the other anonymous – and a passage from Benoist Voron's *L'Enfer poétique* (N19).

C39 Colin, Germain, *Un Émule de Clément Marot: Les Poésies de Germain Colin Bucher angevin ...*, publiées pour la première fois, avec notice, notes, tables et glossaire, par M. Joseph Denais, Paris: Techener, 1890, 332 pp.
Separately-paginated offprint of C45. The introduction describes Colin's contacts with CM. See also D13.

C40 Colletet, G., 'Clément Marot', in *Notices biographiques sur les trois Marot par G. Colletet*. Précédemment transcrites d'après le manuscrit détruit dans l'incendie de la Bibliothèque du Louvre le 24 mai 1871 et publiées pour la première fois par Georges Guiffrey, Paris: Lemerre, 1871, pp. 17-56.
Though lavishly praising CM's literary achievements, Colletet gives the impression of being better acquainted with the accolades bestowed on CM by sixteenth-century writers than with the poems themselves. He certainly does not mine them very thoroughly for biographical data. Many factual errors.

C41 Collignon, Albert, 'Le Mécénat du Cardinal Jean de Lorraine (1498-1550)', *Annales de l'Est*, XXIV, 2 (1910), 175 pp.

On CM, see esp. pp. 92-94.

C42   *Correspondance des réformateurs dans les pays de langue fran-
çaise*, recueillie et publiée avec d'autres lettres relatives à la
Réforme et des notes historiques et biographiques par A.L.
Herminjard, Geneva: Georg, 9 vols, 1866-97.

C43   Coyssard, Michel, *Les Hymnes sacrez et odes spirituelles* ...,
Antwerp: Joachim Trognese, 1600, 168 pp.
The prefatory letter addressed to Jean Ursucci and signed 'Vostre serviteur' – presumably not Coyssard himself, since he is referred to in the
letter in the third person – pulls no punches: 'entre les ignorans qui
ont manié la harpe de David, a esté Clement Marot, Gascon de nation,
Calviniste de religion, bouffon de vacation, et de mœurs un vray borde-
lier. Qui se pensant un grand poëte, combien qu'il ne fut qu'un barbouil-
leur de papier, et aussi apte à faire des vers, qu'un asne à joüer du violon,
se voulut mesler de traduire ces psalmes en vers françois. Mais comment
il s'y porta, Dieu le sçait, et l'œuvre le monstre ...'

C44   *Cronique du roy Françoys, premier de ce nom*, publiée pour
la première fois d'après un manuscrit de la Bibliothèque Impé-
riale, avec une introduction et des notes, par Georges Guiffrey,
Paris: Vve J. Renouard, 1860, xvi + 493 pp.
Names CM among the persons sought by the authorities in the *affaire
des placards* (p. 130). Elsewhere reproduces several poems by CM, some
without mentioning his name. Cf. C31, 78, 84.

C45   Denais, Joseph, 'Un Émule de Clément Marot: Germain Colin
Bucher, poète angevin', *Mémoires de la Société d'Agriculture,
Sciences et Arts d'Angers*, 4th ser., III (1889), 63-394.
See C39.

C46   Dide, Auguste, 'Clément Marot', in his *Hérétiques et révolution-
naires*, Paris: Charavay, 1886, pp. 23-36.
Review-art. on C49. Praises the erudition of the study and the wealth
of important data, but is unconvinced by Douen's portrayal of CM as a
kind of evangelizing 'protestant libéral avant la lettre'.

C47   Diller, Georges, 'Puy-Herbault, Marot et Charles de Sainte-
Marthe', *HR*, V (1938), 143-47.
In his Latin dialogue *Theotimus* (written in 1544, though not published
until 1549), Gabriel du Puy-Herbault condemns CM's morals and Protestant tendencies, and stresses the pernicious influence of his extremely
popular amatory poetry. Suggests, however, that CM will soon see the

light, return to France, and devote himself to writing spiritual verse.

C48   Douen, O., 'A Monsieur Jules Bonnet ...', *BSHP*, XIX-XX (1870-71), 191-92.
In this letter prompted by C18, Douen surmises, on the evidence of CM's epistle to Pelisson, that CM remained in Geneva for only a few months. (Mayer, incidentally, strongly doubts the authenticity of this epistle – see *OC*, I, pp. 62-63, 64-65.) See also C80.

C49   Douen, O., *Clément Marot et le psautier huguenot: Étude historique, littéraire, musicale et bibliographique ...*, Paris: Imprimerie Nationale, 2 vols, 1878-79.
Offers a vast amount of information about translations, translators, editions, music, musicians; reproduces many of the musical settings. Much of this material remains valuable, even though some of Douen's theories (e.g. on the origins of the melodies) are no longer accepted. Douen proclaims the superiority of Protestant over Catholic music in the sixteenth century. His presentation of CM's life and works (I, pp. 36-262, 362-446, 462-533) is even more biased. It is constantly marred by overstatement and a naïve eagerness to find evidence of overt Protestantism in even the most unpropitious situations. CM is said to have displayed 'un peu de l'ardeur réformatrice du bouillant Farel', and he became 'l'un des premiers propagateurs de l'Évangile'. Indeed, 'sa constance invincible et les héroïques sacrifices que lui dicta son zèle pour la cause évangélique' entitle him to be regarded as a 'témoin (martyr)' at least as much as Calvin, who is here portrayed far less sympathetically. Douen readily accepts Morley's identification of 'Isabeau' with the Catholic Church (see C108), and he considers the report of CM's abjuration in Lyons an invention of Sagon's. The book constitutes a considerable scholarly achievement in many ways, but it is excessively polemical, unnecessarily long-winded, at times tediously detailed.
Rev.:   .1 Crawford, G.R.: see HUa10.
.2 Dide, Auguste: see C46.
.3 Dufour, Théophile, *Revue Critique d'Histoire et de Littérature*, new ser., XI (1881), 85-93, 103-14 (makes detailed criticisms, lists numerous errors).
.4 E[rnouf], B., *BBB* (1880), 415-18.
.5 Harvitt, Hélène, *Schutz*, no. 644.
.6 Lelièvre, Matth.: see C94.
.7 Weber, Édith, *BSHP*, CXIV (1968), 151-54.

C50   Doumergue, É., 'Paris protestant au XVIᵉ siècle, 1509-1572', *BSHP*, XLV (1896), 11-45, 57-71, 113-32.
On CM's house in the Rue du Clos Bruneau, see pp. 24-25. Cf. C64, 65.

C51   [Dreux du Radier, J.J.F.], 'Marot', in his *Récréations historiques, critiques, morales et d'érudition ...*, Paris: Robustel,
2 vols, 1767, II, pp. 160-69.
Rejects the idea that CM may have had an affair with Diane de Poitiers.
Suggests that 'Luna' stands for the Sorbonne (he had already advanced
the latter theory briefly in his *Mémoires historiques, critiques, et anecdotes de France*, Amsterdam: Neaulme, 4 vols, 1764, III, pp. 345-46).

Droz, E.: see E32.

C52   Espiner-Scott, Janet Girvan, *Documents concernant la vie et
les œuvres de Claude Fauchet: Documents. Inédits. Bibliothèque de Fauchet. Extraits de poèmes copiés d'après des
manuscrits perdus*, Paris: Droz, 1938, 291 pp.
Reproduces C54, pp. 165-67.

C53   Espiner-Scott, Janet Girvan, *Claude Fauchet: Sa vie, son œuvre*,
Paris: Droz, 1938, xxxviii + 450 pp.
Summary of C54, pp. 232-33.

Faguet, Émile: see HA29.

C54   Fauchet, Claude, 'De Clement Marot', in his *Veilles ou observations de plusieurs choses dinnes de memoire en la lecture d'aucuns
autheurs françois, par C.F. P[arisien], l'an 1555*, in MS BN f.fr.
24726, fols 37r°-38v°; reproduced in C52, pp. 165-67.
A sympathetic biography, based on data derived from CM's poems. Fauchet
may be the earliest commentator to interpret the first elegy as indicating
CM's presence and capture at Pavia. Brief but appreciative remarks about
the works, with particularly enthusiastic praise for the psalms: 'la fidelité
et heur de sa tra[ns]lation est telle qu'il ne s'est trouvé homme apres lui
aprochant de sa grace.' See C53.

Flögel, K.F.: see N6.

C55   Fontana, Bartolommeo, *Renata di Francia, duchessa di Ferrara.
Sui documenti dell'Archivio Estense, del Mediceo, del Gonzaga
e dell'Archivio secreto Vaticano*, Rome, 3 vols, 1889-99.
Gives much information about CM's stay at Ferrara and the religious
situation there, based on numerous contemporary documents. See esp.
'Clemente Marot', I, pp. 243-82.

C56   Fontana, B., 'Clemente Marot eretico in Ferrara', *Archivio della
Società Romana di Storia Patria*, XV (1892), 510-12.

With reference to CM's stay in Ferrara described in C55, Vol. I, publishes a document from the Inquisitor's investigation of heretical activities there, according to which CM 'apud omnes habet famam lutherani'. (The document is reprinted in C55, Vol. II. See also C105, pp. 321-22.)

C57 François, Alexis, *Le Magnifique Meigret, valet de François 1ᵉʳ, ami de Marot, sauveur de Genève: Une Figure du temps de Calvin*, Geneva: Georg, 1947, 181 pp.
In March 1532, Meigret was accused, with several others, including CM, of eating bacon during Lent (pp. 21-28). (On this incident, see also Mayer, J18, pp. 15-18, repeated in C105, pp. 103-10.)

C58 Françon, Marcel, 'Marot au Châtelet', *MLN*, LV (1940), 1-8.
Argues that CM was not being accused of eating bacon in 1526: the references to such an action in the ballad *Contre celle qui fut s'amye* and the first *coq-à-l'âne* merely echo a popular saying (cf. Haag C72 and Screech C128), while the similar reason given for the cat's predicament in the *Epistre à son amy Lyon* is simply 'un détail pittoresque'. In fact, CM was charged with heresy at the instigation of the ecclesiastical authorities, and not as a result of the denunciation by a mistress: 'Luna' in *L'Enfer* stands for the Catholic Church (cf. C59).

C59 Françon, Marcel, 'Un Symbole de l'église catholique: *Luna*', *PMLA*, LX (1945), 59-65.
Presents more extensively developed arguments in support of the thesis advanced in C58, that 'Luna' in *L'Enfer* (*OC*, II, pp. 53-73, line 22) alludes to the Catholic Church.

C60 Françon, Marcel, 'The Birth-Date of Clément Marot', *MLR*, LIII (1958), 83-85.
Argues, partly on the strength of Pannier's description of certain portraits of CM (B9), that he must have been about sixty at the time of his death, and therefore born ca 1484.

C61 Françon, Marcel, '*L'Enfer* de Clément Marot', *BHR*, XXIX (1967), 157-58.
Restates views and arguments already expounded in C58, 59.

C62 Françon, Marcel, 'Note sur Clément Marot et "l'affaire du lard mangé en Carême" ', *Fra*, no. 16 (1975), 49-52.
Essentially the same arguments as in C58, 59, 61. Françon dismisses Mayer's suggestion concerning the origin of the name 'Luna' (see C104) as improbable.

Françon, Marcel: see also HA32, 35.

C63   Frère, Henri, 'Notes sur Clément Marot', *Précis Analytique des Travaux de l'Académie des Sciences, Belles-Lettres et Arts de Rouen (1876-77)*, Rouen, 1877, pp. 190-216.
A sympathetic study which lays no claim to presenting new data.

C64   Fréville, E. de, 'La Maison de Clément Marot, à Paris, retrouvée au moyen des registres censiers', *Athenæum Français*, IV (1855), 420-21.
Quotes the following statement by Adolphe Berty (who, with Albert Lenoir, had been examining records of property rates) concerning CM's house in the Rue du Clos Bruneau: 'La maison donnée à Clément Marot par François Ier est représentée aujourd'hui par celle qui porte le n° 30, rue de Condé, et par une autre située derrière et ayant entrée rue de Tournon, n° 27; les deux terrains sur lesquels elles sont bâties étaient réunies au XVIe siècle.' (CM received the gift of the house in July 1539 – see Paris: Archives Nationales, Trésor des Chartes, JJ254, no. 301, fol. 57v°; C33, IV, p. 28, no. 11134. The document is reproduced in C105, pp. 448-49.)

C65   F[réville], E. de, 'La Maison de Clément Marot, à Paris, retrouvée au moyen des registres censiers', in his 'Notes sur les poètes Jean et Clément Marot, le père et le fils', *BSHP*, IV (1856), 249-57 (249-53).
Virtually identical with C64.

C66   Fromage, R., 'Clément Marot: Son premier emprisonnement. Identification d'Isabeau et d'Anne', *BSHP*, LIX (1910), 52-71, 122-29.
Rejects the identifications proposed by Lenglet-Dufresnoy (C96) and Douen (C49). His own candidates are: for 'Isabeau', 'Élisabeth Ruzé ..., la femme de Jean Ruzé, seigneur de Stains et de la Herpinière'; for 'Anne', whom CM 'paraît avoir aimée d'un pur amour', Anne de Beauregard. Cf. Lefranc, C91 and Philipot, C112.

Gaillard, G.H.: see HA37.

Gairdner, J.: see C145.

C67   Giono, Jean, *Le Désastre de Pavie, 24 février 1525*. Introduction par Gérald Walter. Trente Journées qui ont fait la France, XI, Paris: Gallimard, 1963, xxxvi + 364 pp.
Names 'le poète Clément Marot, blessé au bras' among the Frenchmen taken prisoner, but without citing any supporting evidence (p. 216).

C68   Giudici, Enzo, 'Clément Marot e il suo gruppo', in his *Spiritualismo e carnascialismo: Aspetti e problemi del cinquecento letterario francese*, I, Naples: Edizioni Scientifiche Italiane, 1968, pp. 445-535.

A competent account of CM's life and works, interspersed with the text of many poems – reproduced integrally, but usually without any critical comment – and with frequent, at times very lengthy, quotations from modern critics. CM is portrayed as 'il più moderno dei poeti antichi', receptive to new literary developments (which, to some extent, he incorporates in his works), but remaining essentially a medieval poet. Extensive notes (pp. 500-35) offering more assessments by modern scholars and a very useful bibliography.

C69   Goujet, Claude Pierre, 'Clément Marot', in his *Bibliothèque françoise; ou, Histoire de la littérature françoise*, Paris: Mariette, 18 vols, 1740-56, XI (1747), 37-86.

Well-balanced essay on CM's life and works. Considers Lenglet-Dufresnoy's conjectures about CM's love affairs with Diane de Poitiers and Marguerite de Navarre 'rien qu'une pure fiction'. Appreciative, though in varying degree, of the quality of most of CM's poems, but regards certain of them as obscene. Some remarks about eds, esp. E4.

C70   Greil, Louis, 'Compte rendu de l'excursion faite, le 21 juin 1888, par plusieurs membres de la Société des Études du Lot', *BSEL*, XIII (1888), 249-60.

Mentions two properties said to have belonged to CM's family, situated near Cézac, south of Cahors, one of them in the village of Saint-Clément. Cf. C88.

Guiffrey, Georges: see E17.

C71   Guy, Henry, *Histoire de la poésie française au XVIe siècle*, II: *Clément Marot et son école*, Bibliothèque Littéraire de la Renaissance, new ser., XII, Paris: Champion, 1926, 337 pp.

Well-researched study, more concerned with the character and ideas of the man than with the technique and achievement of the poet. Guy portrays CM as worldly, independent ('le cas sans exemple d'un courtisan qui appartient à l'opposition'), hostile to all constraint, impulsive, undisciplined ('il n'a ni l'esprit de suite ni le goût de suivre'), lacking in profound religious convictions ('ce qu'il approuve et goûte en la Réforme, c'est principalement le noir chagrin qu'elle cause à la Sorbonne'), but indomitable in spirit, facing adversity with a smile and an ironic quip, forever anticipating an improvement in his so frequently troubled existence; above

all, in spite of everything, deeply attached to his country. Conclusion: 'à certains égards, il incarne l'âme de chez nous.'
Rev.: .1 Dartigue, Ch., *BSHP*, LXXVI (1927), 287-89.
.2 Hämel, Adalbert, *NS*, XXXV (1927), 157-58.
.3 Plattard, Jean, *RSS*, XIII (1926), 295-98. See also C114.

Haag, Émile: see C72.

C72   Haag, Eugène and Émile, 'Marot (Clément)', in their *La France protestante; ou, Vie des protestants français qui se sont fait un nom dans l'histoire* ..., Paris: Bureaux de la Publication, Cherbuliez, 9 vols, VII (1857), pp. 266-82.
Circumstantial account of CM's life. No clear statement regarding his religious beliefs, but the authors seem, at all events, to play down his unorthodoxy, since they doubt the story of his abjuration, on the grounds that '[il] n'avait proprement aucune erreur formelle à abjurer; il n'avait jamais fait profession ouverte des doctrines de la Réforme ...'. Moreover, he is represented as innocent when arrested in 1526. In this connection, the authors do not take the accusation 'il a mangé le lard' levelled at CM literally, but in the sense of a traditional expression implying guilt − cf. C58, 128.

C73   Hamon, Auguste, *Un Grand Rhétoriqueur poitevin: Jean Bouchet, 1476-1557?*, Paris: Oudin, 1901, xxi + 430 pp.

C74   Hari, Robert, 'Les Placards de 1534', in *Aspects de la propagande religieuse. Études publiées par G. Berthoud (and others), THR, XXVIII, Geneva: Droz, 1957, pp. 79-142.
Repeats, but more confidently, Fromage's surmise (in E23) that CM's high place on the list of suspects in the *affaire des placards* (see C44, 84) was due to his having circulated his anti-papist poem *D'un monstre nouvellement baptizé* at Court shortly before (p. 106). (Hari is evidently unacquainted with Plattard's convincing rejection of CM's authorship in G9, 10.)

C75   Harrab, Thomas, *Tessaradelphus; or, The Foure Brothers.* Collected and Translated by Thomas Harrab, s.l., 1616.
Strongly criticizes CM's and Beza's psalm translations: 'rather paraphrases of their owne braine, then the text of Scripture'. As for CM, 'he was a wanton courtier, a poet, and a musition, altogether unlearned but in the mother tongue; a man in regard of his ignorance and lose life, most unfit to medle in such divine matters ...'

C76   Harvitt, Hélène J., 'Hugues Salel, Poet and Translator', *MP*, XVI (1918-19), 595-605.

C77   Hawkins, Richmond Laurin, *Maistre Charles Fontaine, Parisien*, Cambridge, Mass.: Harvard UP, 1916, vii + 281 pp.
Deals with Fontaine's relations with CM, his participation in the quarrel with Sagon, and his literary indebtedness to CM.

C78   'Les Hérétiques ajournés par les gens du roi avec Pierre Caroli, Clément Marot, Mathurin Cordier, etc., 1534-1535', *BSHP*, XI (1862), 253-58.
Reproduction of the list of suspects sought by the authorities in the *affaire des placards*, as transcribed in MS Soissons: Bibliothèque publique 189. This list differs slightly from that given in C44. Cf. also C31, 84.

C79   Héricault, Charles d', 'La Vie de Clément Marot', in E12, pp. i-cxvi.
The first important modern biography. Good description of court life and of the religious situation. A well-balanced account of CM's life (though, inevitably, now out of date in certain respects). Héricault is sceptical with regard to Lenglet-Dufresnoy's theory about CM's affair with Diane de Poitiers, firmly rejects the idea of his liaison with Marguerite de Navarre (C96). (Héricault is not the first critic to refute these conjectures — cf. Niceron, Goujet, Campenon — but his objections are based on far more telling arguments.) Scant discussion of CM's religious views. Little critical appraisal of his poems.

C80   Heyer, Théoph., 'Le Séjour de Clément Marot à Genève', *BSHP*, XIX-XX (1870-71), 285-87.
On Bonnet's (C18) and Douen's (C48) suggestions concerning the length and dates of CM's stay in Geneva. Heyer draws attention to the reference in the *Registres du Conseil* on 11 July 1543 to the permission granted to CM to publish an ed. of *L'Enfer* (i.e. *Bibliog. II*, no. 115).

Joukovsky, Françoise: see HP7.

C81   Jourda, Pierre, 'Un Disciple de Marot: Victor Brodeau', *RHLF*, XXVIII (1921), 30-59, 208-28.

C82   Jourda, Pierre, *Marguerite d'Angoulême, duchesse d'Alençon, reine de Navarre (1492-1549): Étude biographique et littéraire*, Bibliothèque Littéraire de la Renaissance, new ser., XIX-XX, Paris: Champion, 2 vols, 1930.
This outstanding, comprehensive study of Marguerite has countless references to CM.

C83   Jourda, Pierre, *Marot: L'Homme et l'œuvre*, Livre de l'Étudiant,

XXVI, Paris: Boivin, 1950, 167 pp.; nouvelle éd., revue et
mise à jour, Connaissance des Lettres, XXVI, Paris: Hatier,
1967, 191 pp.
Sound, competent introduction to CM. Summarizes the known data,
traces CM's development as a poet, reevaluates different aspects of his
works, judiciously assesses his religious views.
Rev.: .1 Becker, Georges, *IL*, III (1951), 27-28.
.2 Bourciez, J., *RLR*, LXX (1950), 317-18.
.3 Françon, Marcel, *MLQ*, XIII (1952), 314-15.
.4 Hanse, J., *RBPH*, XXX (1952), 564-65.
.5 Harvitt, Hélène, *FR*, XXIV (1950-51), 510-11.
.6 Macdonald, Iain, *FS*, V (1951), 167-69.
.7 Mayer, C.A., *BHR*, XII (1950), 390-92.
.8 Steele, A.J., *MLR*, XLVI (1951), 103-04.
.9 Will, Samuel F., *RR*, XLIII (1952), 126-27.

C84   *Le Journal d'un bourgeois de Paris sous le règne de François Ier
(1515-1536).* Nouvelle éd. publiée, avec une introduction et des
notes, par V.L. Bourrilly, Paris: Picard, 1910, xxv + 471 pp.
Mentions CM's name among those of 'Lutherans' summoned on 25
January 1535 to report to the authorities (p. 382). Cf. C31, 44, 78.

C85   [Jurieu, P.], 'Apologie pour Clement Marot ... De la version des
pseaumes. Ignorance du sieur Maimbourg sur la fidelité de la
version ...', in his *Histoire du calvinisme et celle du papisme
mises en parallele; ou, Apologie pour les reformateurs, pour
la Reformation, et pour les reformez ... contre un libelle inti-
tulé 'L'Histoire du Calvinisme' par Mr Maimbourg*, Rotterdam:
Reinier Leers, 2 vols, 1683, I, pp. 120-33.
In this reply to C99, Jurieu defends CM's psalm translations, but, regarding
CM himself, he does little more than plead mitigating circumstances for
a rather depraved life: 'C'estoit un esprit libre, et si vous voulés libertin,
qui s'estoit nourri de vanités dans une cour souverainement corrompuë.'
In any case, 'il n'est pas vray que Marot ait esté celebre parmi nous,
c'estoit un poëte, et un poëte de cour; et ce caractere est à peu prés
incompatible avec le grand merite.'

C86   Kalwies, Howard H., 'Clément Marot and Hugues Salel', *RoN*,
XIX (1978-79), 230-36.
Maintains that, although Salel closely imitated CM, accounts of an inti-
mate relationship between them are pure speculation.

*C87   Kane, June Ellen, 'Édition critique de l'œuvre du roi François Ier',

Ph. D. thesis, Univ. of Liverpool, 1976, 584 pp.

C88 Lacoste, Guillaume, 'Clément Marot', in his *Histoire générale de la province de Quercy*, publiée par les soins de L. Combarieu et F. Cangardel, Cahors: Girma, 4 vols, 1886, IV, pp. 78-85.
Jean Marot was taxed in the Pont-Vieux district of Cahors, 'de sorte que c'est dans ce quartier que devait être sa maison, qui, dans des actes postérieurs, est appelé "maison de Gaubert, dit Marot"'. Two properties, probably acquired by his father and mentioned by CM in his epistle *Au roy, pour avoir esté desrobé*, still retain their old names; they are located in the parish of Cessac. At Marot there is an old oak-tree, under which CM reportedly liked to sit. Cf. C30, 70.

C89 Lanson, G., 'Clément Marot', *Bibliothèque Universelle et Revue Suisse*, 3rd ser., XVI (1882), 302-29, 475-504.
A generally judicious analysis of CM's character, of the nature of his poetry (which is, however, only rarely examined in detail), and of his ideas. But Lanson is rather too ready to proclaim CM a convinced Protestant.

C90 Lanson, Gustave, 'Clément Marot', *Revue Universitaire*, XXII, Pt I (1912-13), 377-82.
Notes taken at a lecture on CM forming part of Lanson's Sorbonne course on 'Les Grands Maîtres et les grands courants de la littérature moderne'. The discussion is, of necessity, somewhat cursory.

C91 Lefranc, Abel, 'Le Roman d'amour de Clément Marot', *Revue Politique et Littéraire (Revue Bleue)*, LI, Pt 1 (1913), 455-59, 481-86, 521-24, 547-52.
Plausible identification, on the basis of the *huitain* 'J'ay une lettre entre toutes eslite' (*OC*, V, pp. 267-68), of 'Anne' with Anne d'Alençon, daughter of Charles d'Alençon, the illegitimate brother of Marguerite de Navarre's first husband (cf. C66, 112). Lefranc then interprets various poems as reflecting the course of CM's supposed love, described as a platonic one, for Anne d'Alençon. Lefranc's dating and interpretation of certain poems are not accepted by some more recent critics who accordingly reject his thesis of an Anne 'cycle', while retaining the overall identification of 'Anne' with Anne d'Alençon (see, for instance, Mayer in C105, pp. 79-80). Cf. HA39.

C92 Lefranc, Abel, 'Le Roman d'amour de Clément Marot', in his *Grands écrivains de la Renaissance*, Champion, 1914, pp. 1-61.
Reproduces C91.

C93   Lefranc, Abel, and Jacques Boulenger, *Comptes de Louise de Savoie (1515, 1522) et de Marguerite d'Angoulême (1512, 1517, 1524, 1529, 1539)*, Paris: Champion, 1905, viii + 122 pp.

C94   Lelièvre, Matth., 'Marot, poète de la Réforme française', *Revue Chrétienne*, XXVI (1879), 333-54.

Appreciative review-art. on C49, Vol. I, but with reservations about Douen's assessment of CM's character and his portrayal of CM as a more meritorious Protestant than Calvin.

C95   Lelièvre, Matthieu, 'Clément Marot, poète de la Réforme française', in his *Portraits et récits huguenots du XVIe siècle*, Toulouse: Société des Livres Religieux, 1895, pp. 245-82.

Reprint of C94, with some unimportant changes and a different introductory section adapted from the opening part of HUa19.

C96   [Lenglet-Dufresnoy, Nic.], 'Preface historique sur les œuvres de Clement Marot', in E4, I, pp. 1-116.

The preface, in the form of a discussion between three persons named Aristippe, Eugène, and Ménandre, deals with CM's life and his works. With the help of various appropriately interpreted passages in the poems, Lenglet-Dufresnoy constructs circumstantial histories of CM's supposed love for Diane de Poitiers (= 'Isabeau') and Marguerite de Navarre (= 'Anne'). On Diane: 'Il paroissoit bien que c'étoit plutôt la douceur d'une amitié tendre que le plaisir séducteur de l'amour, qui d'abord conduisoit Diane, puisqu'elle se refusa si constamment à un homme, dont elle goûtoit l'esprit ...' Eventually she avenged herself for the rondeau *De l'inconstance de Ysabeau* (cf. already C120). As for Marguerite, her love ripened slowly: 'Cette sœur devint donc son amie; et cette amie devint enfin sa maîtresse.' The precise nature of their relationship is left uncertain: 'On avoit eu même la témerité d'insinuer que les amans ne s'en tenoient pas aux sentiments du cœur.'

Lenglet-Dufresnoy's thesis that CM's poems contained cycles inspired by different mistresses was to be frequently accepted even by critics who rejected the identifications he proposed (e.g. Lefranc in C91). He was also responsible for creating the image of a sensuous Marguerite, freely indulging in the kind of amorous adventures she often describes in the *Heptaméron* (she is thus portrayed, for instance, in N18).

In the dedicatory letter to Comte Hoym, Lenglet-Dufresnoy calls CM 'le restaurateur de la poësie françoise, et celui qui sert encore aujourd'hui de modele pour badiner noblement et agreablement'. But he qualifies this judgement: 'si dans les temps heureux d'une sage conduite, sa poësie surpasse tout ce qui s'est fait avant et après lui, il est au dessous des plus mauvais poëtes, dès qu'il veut l'emporter par le dereglement de ses mœurs sur les plus determinez debauchez.'

Livingston, Charles H.: see L37.

C97 *Lettres de Marguerite d'Angoulême, sœur de François Ier, reine de Navarre*, publiées d'après les manuscrits de la Bibliothèque du Roi par F. Génin, Paris: Renouard, 1841, xvi + 485 pp.
Reproduces (p. 238) a letter from Marguerite to Anne de Montmorency, dated 25 March 1528 – not 1529, as tentatively proposed by Génin – in which she reminds him to enter CM's name on that year's roll of persons attached to the King's household. (It had been omitted in 1527 – see, among others, C105, pp. 134-40. The letter, transcribed from MS BN f.fr. 3026, fol. 18, is numbered 399 in Pierre Jourda's *Répertoire analytique et chronologique de la correspondance de Marguerite d'Angoulême, duchesse d'Alençon, reine de Navarre (1492-1549)*, Paris: Champion, 1930

C98 McFarlane, I.D., 'Jean Salmon Macrin (1490-1557)', *BHR*, XXI (1959), 55-84, 311-49; XXII (1960), 73-89.

C99 Maimbourg, Louis, *Histoire du Calvinisme par Monsieur Maimbourg*. Dernière éd., Paris: Sebastien Mabre-Cramoisy, 1682, 512 pp. + unnumbered pages at beginning and end.
On CM, see pp. 96-99. A text often quoted approvingly and as frequently attacked in later polemical literature. Very critical of CM's ideas and morals ('bon calviniste et méchant libertin') and also of the psalm translations ('il n'y a rien de moins conforme à son original que cette version') They contain countless errors and are characterized by their 'manière basse et infiniment éloignée de la majesté du style de ce grand prophète'. See C85, 122, HUa35.

C100 'La Maison de Clément Marot', *BSHP*, LXXXVIII (1939), 68.
On the recent demolition of the celebrated restaurant Foyot, at the corner of the Rue de Tournon and the Rue de Vaugirard, close to the site of CM's house (cf. C64, 65).

C101 Marye, Édouard, 'Destin de Marot', *NL*, 8 April 1939, p. 5.
Review-art. on C116.

C102 Mayer, C.A., 'Le Départ de Marot de Ferrare', *BHR*, XVIII (1956), 197-221.
Very good art., utilizing mainly documents published and discussed in C11, 12, 19, 55. Supersedes them all as the most authoritative interpretation of this material.

C103 Mayer, C.A., 'Clément Marot et le docteur Bouchart', *BHR*, XXI (1959), 98-102.
Suggests that the 'Monsieur Bouchart' responsible for CM's arrest in 1526 was not the theologian Nicolas Bouchart, as Becker thought (C8) and as CM himself may have believed, to judge by his epistle *A Monsieur Bouchart, docteur en théologie* (*OC*, I, pp. 124-27), but the lawyer Jean Bouchard.

C104 Mayer, C.A., 'Marot et "celle qui fut s'amye" ', *BHR*, XXVIII (1966), 369-76.
Maintains that the denunciation by a former mistress, which CM cites in several poems as the reason for his arrest in 1526, was a pure invention by CM who perhaps remembered that Villon had attributed his precipitate departure from Paris to an unhappy love affair, rather than to the true, more serious reason. Cf. KB34. CM may have taken the name 'Luna' from the mistress extolled in Cariteo's poems. See C62.

C105 Mayer, C.A., *Clément Marot*, Paris: Nizet, 1972, 566 pp.
The most informative and reliable biography so far. Incorporates almost unchanged the text of several important arts previously published by Mayer. Divides CM's life into eight sections, each of which offers ample biographical data (and where facts are lacking, very plausible suppositions) and discusses the literary output, with numerous and often extensive quotations from the works. Many interesting and frequently enlightening comments on the poems. However, the unrelenting denigration of the Rhétoriqueurs suggests a perhaps too ready acceptance of H. Guy's extremely destructive criticism in his *Histoire de la poésie française au XVIe siècle*, I: *L'École des Rhétoriqueurs*, Paris: Champion, 1910. On reactions to Mayer's thesis concerning the influence of Petrarchism on CM's earlier poetry, see section KA. This generally excellent book is likely to remain the authoritative biography of CM for many years.
Rev.: .1 Carrington, Samuel M., *FR*, XLVII (1973-74), 1176-77.
.2 Kalwies, Howard H., *EsC*, XV (1975), 394-95.
.3 Richter, M., *SFr*, XVII (1973), 336.

Mayer, C.A.: see also J18.

C106 Métivier, Jean de, *Chronique du Parlement de Bordeaux*, publiée par Arthur de Brezetz et Jules Delpit, Bordeaux: Vve Moquet, 2 vols, 1886.
There is a reference to CM's interrogation on 27 November 1534 in I, pp. 316-17. He is described as being twenty-eight years old.

C107 Molinier, H.J., *Mellin de Saint-Gelays (1490?-1558): Étude*

sur sa vie et sur ses œuvres, Paris: Picard, 1910, xxxii + 614 pp.
Many references to CM.

C108 Morley, Henry, 'Clement Marot', in his *Clement Marot and Other Studies*, London: Chapman & Hall, 2 vols, 1871, I, pp. 1-316; II, pp. 1-64.
Leisurely study, devoting much space to the historical background and the contemporary political and religious situation. Pays particular attention to poems 'which would appear to English readers nobly significant', but are likely to appeal less to French Catholic critics. Morley's aggressive Protestantism is also reflected in his identification of 'Isabeau' with the French Church which CM is said to have renounced because of its vice and inconstancy: 'Even the choice of her name points to the allegory, for that is a variation in form of Elizabeth, which means God is my oath, or a Worshipper of God' (pp. 174-75). Not surprisingly, this interpretation is hailed by Douen (C49, I, p. 65) as 'cette belle et importante découverte'.

C109 Mugnier, François, 'Le Séjour de Clément Marot en Savoie', *Mémoires et Documents publiés par la Société Savoisienne d'Histoire et d'Archéologie*, XXXIX (1900), lvii-lxiv.
Consists mostly of the reproduction of CM's epistle *A Monsieur Pelisson*. (Mayer doubts the authenticity of this poem, see *OC*, I, pp. 62-63, 64-65.)

C110 [Niceron, Jean Pierre], 'Clement Marot', in his *Mémoires pour servir à l'histoire des hommes illustres dans la république des lettres* ..., Paris: Briasson, 43 vols, 1729-45, XVI (1731), 108-48.
Careful, circumstantial account of CM's life. Rejects the suggestion that CM had affairs with Diane de Poitiers and Marguerite de Navarre (see C96; Niceron is writing very shortly after the publication of Lenglet-Dufresnoy's ed.). The second part is mainly bibliographical and includes a good list of the eds of the *Œuvres*. Little literary evaluation.

C111 Olivero, Adalberto, 'Una testimonianza trascurata sulla tomba di Clément Marot a Torino', *SFr*, VI (1962), 263-65.
According to the anonymous author – believed to be Nicolas Audebert – of the *Voyage d'Italie* in MS London: British Library Lansdowne 720, Lyon Jamet's epitaph on CM in the Metropolitan Basilica San Giovanni at Turin was effaced on the orders of the Archbishop and the Inquisition. The Duchess of Savoy (Marguerite de France, a niece of Marguerite de Navarre) had been opposed to its removal. Olivero suggests that it was

not obliterated until after the Duchess's death on 15 Sept. 1574, and thus only shortly before Audebert's visit in mid-October.

Pelan, Margaret: see KB34.

Pérouse, Gabriel: see HP.11.

Perrat, Charles: see HM15.

C112 Philipot, Emmanuel, 'Sur un amour de Clément Marot', *RHLF*, XIX (1912), 59-74.
Accepts Fromage's identifications of 'Isabeau' and 'Anne' (in C66). Even adds further poems to the Anne de Beauregard 'cycle', including 'J'ay une lettre entre toutes eslite' (*OC*, V, pp. 267-68), in which he correctly interprets the letter 'N' as designating the name 'Anne', while seeing in the mention of Alençon a reference to Anne's stay there at the time of the composition of the poem. (For a more convincing explanation, see Lefranc C91.)

'Pierre Caroli ...': see C31.

C113 Plan, Pierre Paul, 'Clément Marot à Genève', *Musées de Genève* (February 1948), 1.
An unreliable art., based mainly on poems published in E32 (whose authenticity is doubtful – see note to E32).

Plan, P.P.: see also E32.

C114 Plattard, Jean, 'Clément Marot', *Journal des Savants* (1927), 212-18.
Review-art. on C8 and C71.

C115 Plattard, Jean, 'Marot: Sa carrière poétique, son œuvre', *RCC*, XXXIX (1937-38), Pt I, 27-41, 129-41, 235-49, 345-59, 463-76, 632-43, 723-36; Pt II, 68-83, 177-91, 271-79, 372-84, 441-53, 553-61, 640-51, 728-34.
An eminently sound study which provides a good synthesis of earlier interpretations and a competent survey of the known data, as well as offering fresh insights into the poems. Demonstrates CM's lasting indebtedness to the medieval tradition, but also emphasizes the range and originality of his poetry and shows how his lyrical verse anticipates that of the Pléiade.

C116 Plattard, Jean, *Marot: Sa carrière poétique, son œuvre*, Bibliothèque de la *Revue des Cours et Conférences*, Paris: Boivin,

1938, 227 pp.
Text appears to be identical with that of C115.
Rev.: .1 Jourda, P., *RHLF*, XLV (1938), 527-28.
   .2 Marichal, Robert, *HR*, VI (1939), 382-85.
   .3 Marye, Édouard: see C101.
   .4 Rat, Maurice, *MF*, CCXCIII (1939), 383-86.

C117   Prescott, Anne Lake, 'The Reputation of Clément Marot in Renaissance England', *SRen*, XVIII (1971), 173-202.
The most comprehensive study of the subject so far published. Shows that CM was read, imitated and commented on in Renaissance England, but never famous. His image was two-fold: on the one hand, a talented and witty protégé of the great patron of learning, François I, and a poet who helped to civilize the French language; on the other, a rather foolish person, a court jester and a clown (cf. section N).

C118   Prescott, Anne Lake, 'Marot', in her *French Poets and the English Renaissance: Studies in Fame and Transformation*, New Haven: Yale UP, 1978, pp. 1-36.
Virtually identical in substance with C117.

C119   Raemond, Florimond de, *L'Histoire de la naissance, progrez et decadence de l'heresie de ce siècle*, Paris: Charles Chastellain, 2 vols, 1605.
On CM and his psalm translations, see 'Erreurs et faussetez commises en la version des pseaumes', II, fols 274r°-276v°, and 'De Clement Marot traducteur des psalmes, sa vie et sa mort', II, fols 277r°-279v°. Gives a very unfavourable account of CM's morals and his religious views. Concerning Vatable's help with the psalm translations, goes even further than Pasquier (HA67) in stating that Vatable translated the Hebrew text word for word for CM. Nonetheless criticizes CM's version at great length. Raemond's strictures are frequently quoted by later anti-Protestant writers.

C120   *Recueil des plus belles pieces des poëtes françois, tant anciens que modernes, depuis Villon jusqu'à M. de Benserade*, Paris: Claude Barbin, 5 vols, 1692. Also issued the same year by Barbin in Paris and Georges Gallet in Amsterdam with title *Recueil ... modernes avec l'histoire de leur vie par l'auteur des 'Mémoires' et 'Voyage d'Espagne'* [i.e. Marie d'Aulnoy].
The brief life of CM occupies three unnumbered pages in Vol. I in the first-named ed. (in the other, eight pages). It is of no special interest, except for the suggestion that 'Luna' may denote Diane de Poitiers.

The biographical sketch is followed by seventy poems by CM. (Lachèvre states in F32, III, p. 23, n. 2, that notwithstanding their attribution to Marie d'Aulnoy in the title of the second ed., the articles are generally believed to have been written by Barbin himself.)

Robillard de Beaurepaire, Eugène de: see HF3.

C121   Roche, Louis P., *Claude Chappuys (?-1575), poète de la cour de François Ier*, Poitiers, 1929, xvi + 194 pp.

C122   [Rocoles, Jean Baptiste], *L'Histoire veritable du Calvinisme; ou, Memoires historiques touchant la Reformation, opposés à 'L'Histoire du Calvinisme' de Mr Maimbourg*, Amsterdam, 1683, viii + 496 pp.
On CM, see pp. 152-64. Rocoles defends him, and his psalm translations, against Maimbourg's attacks in C99.

C123   Rodocanachi, E., *Une Protectrice de la Réforme en Italie et en France: Renée de France, duchesse de Ferrare*, Paris: Ollendorff, 1896, 573 pp.
Still of interest, though out of date in many ways, and in certain respects unreliable even at the time of publication – e.g. states that the tr. of the psalms was imposed on CM as a penance by the Inquisition.

C124   Rutson, E.M., 'The Life and Works of Jean Marot', B. Litt. thesis, Oxford Univ., 1961, 385 pp.

C125   Ruutz-Rees, Caroline, *Charles de Sainte-Marthe (1512-1555)*, New York: Columbia UP, 1910, xii + 664 pp.
Various references to Sainte-Marthe's contacts with CM and to the latter's influence on his poems.

C126   Ruutz-Rees, C., *Charles de Sainte-Marthe (1512-1555): Étude sur les premières années de la Renaissance française. Traduit par Marcel Bonnet*, Paris: Champion, [1919], xxiv + 387 pp. Tr. of C125.

C127   Saulnier, V.L., *Maurice Scève (ca 1500-1560)*, Paris: Klincksieck, 2 vols, 1948.

Saulnier, V.L.: see also HR11.

C128   Screech, M.A., ' "Il a mangé le lard" (What Marot Said and What Marot Meant)', *BHR*, XXVI (1964), 363-64.
Cites Cotgrave, among others, in support of the suggestion that CM was

merely using a common expression signifying that someone 'is guilty of a crime unspecified, especially theft'. Cf. Françon (C58, 62), and already Haag (C72).

C129 Seward, Desmond, 'Clément Marot, 1496-1544', *History Today*, XXIII (1973), 471-78.

C130 Shipley, Joseph T., 'First of the Moderns', *Poet-Lore*, XXXV (1924), 626-31.
Free English adaptation of a few short poems by CM, preceded by a brief introduction on him. The versions 'aim to convey the spirit of the courtly protestant, the dissolute dandy, Clément Marot'.

C131 Shishmareva, V., *Clément Marot*, Petrograd, 1915, 395 pp. (Text in Russian.)

C132 Sichel, Edith, 'Clément Marot', in her *Women and Men of the French Renaissance*, London: Constable, 1901, pp. 207-23.

C133 Smith, P.M., *Clément Marot, Poet of the French Renaissance*, London: Athlone Press, Univ. of London, 1970, vii + 320 pp.
Intended for students, hence essentially a synthesis of other scholars' discoveries; introduces no fresh biographical data, offers few profound original insights. Nonetheless a very well-done life-and-works study, competent and lucid, based on an excellent knowledge of the text. Many valuable analyses of poems; good discussions of such aspects as CM's borrowings and his use of archaisms. Useful descriptions of social conditions, of intellectual and religious trends. Smith clearly shares Mayer's views on many aspects (e.g. CM's religion, early Petrarchist influences). Rather overstates CM's achievements as a universal innovator, in consequence denies the Rhétoriqueurs any merit and takes a bite out of Ronsard's reputation. Altogether, though, a very informative and stimulating book.
Rev.: .1 Balmas, E., *RHLF*, LXXIII (1973), 883-84.
.2 Burgess, Robert M., *RQ*, XXV (1972), 91-93.
.3 Cave, T.C., *FS*, XXVII (1973), 53-55.
.4 Donaldson-Evans, Lance K., *FR*, XLV (1971-72), 751-52.
.5 Françon, M., *SFr*, XV (1971), 333-34.
.6 Giraud, Yves, *BHR*, XXXIV (1972), 187-88.
.7 Gray, Floyd, *MLQ*, XXXIII (1972), 186-88.
.8 Joukovsky, F., *RPh*, XXV (1971-72), 478-79.
.9 Quainton, Malcolm, *MLR*, LXVIII (1973), 169-70.
.10 Stone, Donald, *RR*, LXV (1974), 57-59.

Sonier, Joseph Ivan: see HA94.

C134 Theureau, Louis, *Étude sur la vie et les œuvres de Jean Marot*, Caen: Le Blanc-Hardel, 1873, 214 pp.

*C135 Tomlinson, Hilary Mary, 'La Poésie de Victor Brodeau: Édition critique', Ph. D. thesis, Univ. of Liverpool, 1976, 445 pp.

C136 Toulze, Sylvain, 'À la recherche de Clément Marot', *BSEL*, LXXXIII (1962), 89-109.
Text of a competent lecture presenting CM's life and poems to a non-specialist audience.

C137 Truffier, Jules, 'Villon et Marot', *Annales*, I (1907), 75-81.
A poetry reading, interspersed with a few remarks about the two poets.

C138 Usbek, 'Clément Marot: Inauguration de son monument à Cahors', *Revue de Bordeaux et du Sud-Ouest Littéraire, Historique et Artistique* (1892, Pt II), 91-96.
Quotes from speeches made at the unveiling of CM's bust.

C139 Van Brabant, Luc, *Louïze Labé et ses aventures amoureuses avec Clément Marot et le dauphin Henry*, Coxyde: Éditions de la Belle sans sy, 1966, 173 pp.
On the strength of some highly ingenious, not to say eccentric, ana-grammatic readings of certain poems by CM, concludes that (i) Louise Labé had a love affair with the future Henri II, but was fairly promptly abandoned by him; (ii) CM made amorous overtures to her which she rejected; and (iii) she was the 'Anne' of his poems. Cf. HA100, HH8.
Rev.: .1 Smet, Raphaël de, *Lettres Romanes*, XXII (1968), 174-79.
.2 Sozzi, L., *SFr*, XI (1967), 525-26.

C140 Vandam, Albert D., 'The Medal Reversed: Clément Marot', in his *Amours of Great Men*, London: Tinsley, 2 vols, 1878, I, pp. 311-65.
'Marot became a poet because he fell in love.' CM's poems are accordingly examined against the background of a series of supposed love affairs, including one with Marguerite de Navarre. The art. is as much fiction as fact.

C141 Varga, Bálint, *Marot Kelemen, első Francia protestáns zsoltá-rénekszerző: Élete és költészete* [*Clément Marot, the First French Protestant Author of Psalms: His Life and his Poetry*], Budapest: Sylvester, 1931, 64 pp.

C142 Vier, Jacques, 'Badinage ... et poésie: Clément Marot', *École*

(Classes du Second Cycle), XLV (1953-54), 420-22, 443.
A rapid biography, followed by a survey of the principal aspects of
CM's poems.

Villey, Pierre: see HA104.

C143   Vincent, Pierre, 'Sur le premier emprisonnement de Clément
Marot', *Annales de la Faculté des Lettres et Sciences Humaines
d'Aix*, XL (1966), 149-63.
CM may well have genuinely believed himself to be the victim of a
woman's denunciation, or he may have invented the story in order to
make his situation appear less perilous than it was. In either case, having
never fully appreciated the gravity of the religious controversy, he now
naïvely failed to realize that his imprisonment was merely an incident
in a momentous struggle, in which far more was at stake than his personal
fate.

C144   Vitet, L., 'Clément Marot', *RDM*, LXXVI (1868), 634-51.
Review-art. on E12.

C145   Wallop, John, 'English Report on the French Expedition', in
*A Collection of Documents Relating to Jacques Cartier and
the Sieur de Roberval*, ed. by H.P. Biggar, Publications of the
Public Archives of Canada, XIV, Ottawa, 1930, pp. 188-89.
Letter from Wallop, the British Ambassador in France to Henry VIII,
dated 26 Jan. 1541, reporting on preparations for an expedition to be
led by Cartier 'to seeke the trayde of spicerey by a shorter waye then
the portingallez doth use ... And the capitaine of the said [five or six
hundred] fotemen ys one Clement marotte: who heretofore fledde owte
of this Realme for the lutheryan secte.' The original document is in the
Public Record Office, London, in State Papers, Domestic, Henry VIII,
CLXIV, fol. 171^V. (A modern summary will be found in *Letters and
Papers, Foreign and Domestic, of the Reign of Henry VIII, Preserved
in the Public Record Office, the British Museum, and Elsewhere*,
arranged and catalogued by James Gairdner and R.H. Brodie, Vol. XVI,
London: Her Majesty's Stationery Office, 1898, p. 234.) Cartier sailed
for Canada on 23 May 1541 – without CM.

D. THE QUARREL WITH FRANÇOIS SAGON

D1   Ballu, C., 'Benoist de Cerisay', *RRen*, VII (1906), 224-27.
On 'Benedictus Serihoenus Salmuriensis' who supported CM in the
quarrel, and on his family.

D2   Bonnefon, Paul, 'Le Différend de Marot et de Sagon', *RHLF*,
I (1894), 103-38, 259-85.
Good account of the quarrel, with generous extracts from the poems.

Boyssoné, Jean de: see C26.

D3   Hawkins, R.L., 'The Books of Reference of an Adversary of
Marot', *RR*, VII (1916), 221-23.
The books are those which the author of the *Grande généalogie de
Frippelippes* ...claims to have consulted in order to learn something
about Frippelippes's ancestry.

D4   [Irail, Augustin Simon], 'Clément Marot, et deux poëtes dé-
criés, Sagon et La Huéterie', in his *Querelles littéraires; ou,
Memoires pour servir à l'histoire des révolutions de la République des Lettres, depuis Homere jusqu'à nos jours*, Paris:
Durand, 4 vols, 1761, I, pp. 105-13.

D5   Mayer, C.A., 'Clément Marot et le général de Caen', *BHR*, XX
(1958), 277-95.
On the marginal note against lines 43-46 in the first two eds of the
Épître de Frippelippes, which describes Sagon as 'le frère du général des
veaulx à Caen'. The 'general' in question is an anonymous poet who,
under the pseudonym 'le général Chambor' or 'le général de Caen', wrote
a violent reply to CM's *Epistre au roy, du temps de son exil à Ferrare*
in 1536 or 1537.

*D6   Murata, Yatsuka, 'Sur l'*Épître de Frippelippes*', in *Mélanges
offerts à Haruo Akiyama, professeur à l'Université Chuo, à
l'occasion commémorative de sa retraite*, Tokyo, 1980, pp. 19-
34. (Text in Japanese.)
An analysis of the *Épître* prompts the conclusion that CM proved himself the better poet in his quarrel with Sagon. (See note to A7.)

D7   Parmenter, C.E., 'The Authorship of *La Grande Généalogie de Frippelippes*', *MP*, XXIII (1925-26), 337-48.
At the end of the *Epistre* which precedes the *Grande généalogie ... composée par ung jeune poëte champestre*, the author states that his name can be found in that epistle. Parmenter surmises that the words 'mal au cul se cele' provide the solution, inasmuch as they form an anagram (perfect except for the third 'l') of the name 'Macé Vaucelles'. According to La Croix du Maine, Mathieu de Vaucelles, whose first name was originally Macé, wrote poems against CM under the pseudonym of 'poète champêtre'; but Parmenter points out that Macé and Mathieu were different persons.

D8   Plattard, Jean, 'Rabelais réputé poète par quelques écrivains de son temps', *RER*, X (1912), 291-304. See also in *RSS*, II (1914), 283-84.
The evidence includes CM's *Epître de Frippelippes*, line 6.

D9   *Querelle de Marot et Sagon*. Pièces réunies [par] Émile Picot, en collaboration avec Paul Lacombe. Introduction par Georges Dubosc, Rouen, 1920.
Reproduction in facsimile of twenty publications.

D10   Saulnier, V.L., 'Sur la querelle de Marot et de Sagon: Clément Marot "bourdican"', *FM*, XXIII (1955), 123-30.
The term *bourdiquen* (*bourdican*) applied to CM by the 'page de Sagon' (in *Pour les disciples de Marot: Le Page parle à eulx*) signifies 'lay brother', a simple servant not destined for holy orders, 'un frère de deuxième ordre' and, in a figurative sense, 'un poète, un savant, un clerc (ou tout ce qu'on voudra) de deuxième zone'. Saulnier cites three further uses of this rare term in another poem appertaining to the quarrel, *La Première Leçon des matines ordinaires du grand abbé des Conardz de Rouen* (see D11).

D11   Saulnier, V.L., 'Le Faux Dénouement de la querelle opposant Marot à Sagon', in *Mélanges ... Raymond Lebègue*, Paris: Nizet, 1969, pp. 33-44.
Prints the text of *La Première Leçon ...* (see D10) and discusses the pamphlets resulting from the intervention of the Conards in the quarrel.

D12   Voizard, E., *De disputatione inter Marotum et Sagontum*, Paris: Cerf, 1885, 62 pp.
A rather mediocre study of the quarrel.

D13   Weiss, N., 'Un Poète inconnu: Germain Colin et la Réforme

à Angers (1535-1545)', *BSHP*, XL (1891), 57-73.
Quotes from the epistle addressed by Colin jointly to Sagon and to CM, which, according to Weiss, smacks of early Protestantism: 'le langage d'un ... de ces hérétiques de la première heure qui rêvaient encore la réformation de l'église'. On Colin, see also C39.

E. PRINCIPAL EDITIONS SINCE 1600
(in chronological order)

E1   *Œuvres de Clement Marot de Cahors, revues, augmentées de plusieurs choses et disposées en beaucoup meilleur ordre que cy devant; plus quelques œuvres de Michel, filz du dict Marot,* Lyons: Pierre Rigaud, 1604.

Apparently identical with ed. Niort: Thomas Portau, 1596 (*Bibliog. II,* no. 232), on which see Villey, F64, VIII, 188-91 or F65, pp. 144-47. The 1596 ed., prepared by Dr François Mizières (see F39), contained no previously unpublished poems, but printed some omitted by recent editors. By grouping certain poems seemingly addressed to the same person (e.g. 'Ses Amours d'Anne', 'Ses Amours de Diane'), Mizières opened the way for Lenglet-Dufresnoy's fanciful identifications and datings (see E4, C96).

E2   *Les Œuvres de Clement Marot de Cahors en Quercy, valet de chambre du roy. Reveuës et corrigés [sic] de nouveau,* Rouen: Raphaël du Petit-Val, 1607.

E3   *Les Œuvres de Clement Marot de Cahors, valet de chambre du roy. Reveuës et augmentées de nouveau,* The Hague: Adrian Moetjens, 2 vols, 1700.

The works are preceded by an 'Abregé de la vie de Clement Marot', in which 'Luna' is tentatively identified with Diane de Poitiers. References to CM's licentious character and Calvinist leanings, but praise for his 'grace inimitable'. The ed. was reprinted more than once.

E4   *Œuvres de Clement Marot, valet-de-chambre de François I, roy de France. Revues sur plusieurs manuscrits, et sur plus de quarante editions; et augmentées tant de diverses poësies veritables, que de celles qu'on lui a faussement attribuées: avec les ouvrages de Jean Marot, son pere, ceux de Michel Marot, son fils, et les piéces du different de Clement avec François Sagon,* The Hague: P. Gosse & J. Neaulme, 4 vols, 1731. Also issued, with same date, in 6 vols of smaller format (12° instead of 4°).

Dedicatory letter to Comte Hoym (I, pp. iii-x) is signed 'Chevalier Gordon

de Percel', pseudonym of Nic. Lenglet-Dufresnoy. On the latter's 'Preface historique sur les œuvres de Clement Marot' (I, pp. 1-116), see C96. The 'Abregé de la vie de Clement Marot' (I, pp. 117-22) is identical with the 'Abregé' in E3. (The above volume and page references are to the 4-vol. ed.)
Lenglet-Dufresnoy indicates that he was guided by Portau's 1596 ed. (see E1), but has added poems from eds published by CM or his friends, from collections of poetry, and from MSS. An important ed., even though it includes various unauthentic poems, some fanciful dating, and an often faulty text (see .4 below and E6). Numerous notes, very useful in part, but extremely discursive, frequently irrelevant, and containing many errors. For details of the items included in this ed., see Villey, F64, VIII, 193-200 or F65, pp. 149-56.
Rev.: .1 Anon., *Journal des Sçavans* (1731), 605-09.
  .2 Auguis, Pierre René; see E6.
  .3 Desfontaines, P.F. Guyot: see HA23.
  .4 Goujet, Claude Pierre: see C69.
  .5 Lacroix, Paul, in E7, III, pp. 588-92. (Accepts Lenglet-Dufresnoy's theory about CM's love for Diane and Marguerite, but is highly critical of his style, and of the deficiencies in the notes and in the typographical presentation.)

E5   *Œuvres choisies de Clément Marot*, Paris: Imprimerie de P. Didot l'aîné, 1801.
    Contains unsigned 'Notice sur Clément Marot' (pp. 1-7) and 'Discours préliminaire' (pp. 9-32) [both by F.N.V. Campenon], on which see HA11. See also HA111.

E6   *Œuvres de Clément Marot. Nouvelle édition, revue sur toutes celles qui l'ont précédée, avec des notes historiques et un glossaire des vieux mots, par M. P[ier]re R[e]né Auguis*, Paris: Chantpie, 5 vols, 1823.
    Auguis claims to have found over fifty thousand major errors in Lenglet-Dufresnoy's ed. (E4), of which he offers an improved, somewhat shortened, version. It still leaves, however, much to be desired (see E7, III, pp. 593-99).

E7   *Œuvres complètes de Clément Marot. Nouvelle édition ... augmentée d'un Essai sur la vie et les ouvrages de Cl. Marot, de notes historiques et critiques, et d'un glossaire*, Paris: Rapilly, 3 vols, 1824.
    The ed. is by Paul Lacroix who signs the 'Essai' (I, pp. xvii-lxxvi) 'P.L.N. de St. H.' (= Paul Lacroix Niré de St. Hippolyte). Text taken partly from ed. Paris: Veuve Maurice, 1554 (not listed in *Bibliog. II*), partly from

various other eds. Some useful comments on previous eds (see E4.5 and E6).
Classification of poems is acc. to genres, then poems in each category are printed in chronological order; but some categories are subdivided: thus the *élégies amoureuses* form the first book of elegies ('on sait que Marot n'a aimé que Diane de Poitiers et Marguerite de Navarre'), while the second book contains the remaining elegies.

E8   *Œuvres choisies de Clément Marot. Accompagnées de notes historiques et littéraires par M. Després, ancien Conseiller de l'Université; et précédées d'un Essai sur Clément Marot, et sur les services qu'il a rendus à la langue, par M. Campenon, de l'Académie Française,* Paris: Janet & Cotelle, 1826.
On Campenon's 'Essai', see HA11.

E9   *La Farce de deux amoureux recreatis et joyeux,* in *Recueil de farces, moralités et sermons joyeux, publié d'après le manuscrit de la Bibliothèque royale, par Leroux de Lincy et Francisque Michel,* Paris: Techener, 4 vols, 1837, II, 23 pp. (Each item is separately paginated.)
No mention of author's name. A frequently incorrect transcription of MS BN f. fr. 24314 (for a reproduction in facsimile, see E41). See E16.

E10   Chavannes, Fréd., *Notice sur un manuscrit du XVIᵉ siècle, appartenant à la Bibliothèque Cantonale. Poésies inédites de Clément Marot, de Catherine de Médicis et de Théodore de Bèze,* Lausanne: Bridel, 1844, 72 pp.
On MS Lausanne: Bibliothèque cantonale et universitaire M1016, recently acquired by the library. Prints some of the previously unknown poems (certain of them are also reproduced in F52). Another is published by Fromage in E23, and still others by Droz and Plan in E32 where the scribe is identified as Gilbert Grenet. Chavannes's attribution to Catherine of the *Epistre de madame la daulphine escripvant à madame Marguerite* is rejected by Droz and Plan, whose tentative attribution to CM is echoed by Mayer (*OC*, I, pp. 61-62). For descriptions and discussions of the contents of this MS, see, in addition to the aforementioned studies, *Bibliog. I*, pp. 47-63 and also Mayer's introductions to various vols of the *OC*.

E11   *Deux farces inédites attribuées à la reine Marguerite de Navarre, sœur de François Iᵉʳ : 'La Fille abhorrant mariaige', 'La Vierge repentie', 1538, publiées avec une préface et des notes par Louis Lacour,* Paris: Aubry, 1856.

These are, in fact, translations – both probably by CM – of Erasmus's colloquies *Virgo misogamos* and *Virgo poenitens*. See also HUb2, 20, and esp. Mayer's remarks in *Bibliog. I*, p. 87, and *OC*, VI, pp. 41-44.

E12   *Œuvres de Clément Marot. Annotées, revues sur les éditions originales et précédées de la Vie de Clément Marot par Charles d'Héricault*, Paris: Garnier, 1867.
Text based on Dolet's 1538 ed. (*Bibliog. II*, no. 707), and on some other sixteenth-century eds. On the 'Vie', see C79.
Rev.:   .1 Bernard, Daniel: see C10.
        .2 Vitet, L.: see C144.

E13   *L'Epistre de M. Malingre, envoyée à Clément Marot: en laquelle est demandée la cause de son departement de France. Avec la responce dudit Marot, Basle, Jaq. Estauge, 1546*, Paris: Tross, 1868.
Reprint, by J. Enschedé of Haarlem, of *Bibliog. II*, no. 268. See C18.

E14   *Œuvres complètes de Clément Marot. Revues sur les éditions originales, avec préface, notes et glossaire, par M. Pierre Jannet*, Paris: Picard, (Vol. I), Marpon & Flammarion (Vols II-IV), 1868-72.
First three vols published by Jannet, the fourth by C. d'Héricault who contributes a 'Biographie de Clément Marot' and the glossary. Jannet reproduces the text of Constantin's 1544 ed. (*Bibliog. II*, no. 129) for all the poems appearing in it.

E15   *Œuvres de Clément Marot de Cahors, vallet de chambre du roy*, Lyons: Scheuring, 2 vols, 1869-70.
Reproduces Constantin's 1544 ed. (*Bibliog. II*, no. 129). Preface by A. Philibert-Soupé.

E16   *'La Farce de deux amoureux recreatis et joyeux' par Clément Marot*, in *Le Théâtre français avant la Renaissance, 1450-1550: Mystères, moralités et farces. Précédé d'une introduction et accompagné de notes ... par Édouard Fournier*, Paris: Laplace & Sanchez, [1872], pp. 307-13.
Identifies the text printed under this title by Le Roux de Lincy and Michel in E9 as the *Dialogue* published with CM's *Cantiques de la paix* (*Bibliog. II*, no. 90) and subsequent eds of the *Œuvres*. Fournier dates the *Cantiques* at 1542, after Dolet's ed. in that same year. Both Villey (F64, VIII, 89-90 or F65, pp. 91-92) and Mayer (*Bibliog. II*, no. 90) suggest 1541. In any case, Dolet's ed. (*Bibliog. II*, no. 105) contained

the *Dialogue.*

E17 *Les Œuvres de Clément Marot de Cahors en Quercy, valet de chambre du roy, augmentées d'un grand nombre de ses compositions nouvelles par ci-devant non imprimées. Le tout mieux ordonné comme l'on voirra ci-après et soigneusement reveu par Georges Guiffrey*, 5 vols, as follows: II, Paris: Imprimerie Claye (Quantin, successeur), 1875; III, Paris: Morgand & Fatout (Imprimerie Quantin), 1881; the remaining vols published posthumously: I. *Édition Georges Guiffrey mise au jour d'après les papiers posthumes de l'éditeur, avec des commentaires et des notes, par Robert Yve-Plessis*, Paris: Librairie de l'Art (Jean Schemit), 1912; IV, V. *Édition Georges Guiffrey mise au jour ...* [as above]... *par Jean Plattard*, Paris: Schemit, 1929, [1931].

Important ed., with innumerable, though not uniformly relevant and at times almost excessively copious, notes. But there is a lack of critical method: no reasons are offered for the choice of text for any particular poem, and the selection of variants appears haphazard. No notes or variants accompany the psalms in Vol. V. Guiffrey's 'C'est la Vie de Clément Marot' occupies the entire Vol. I; it is extensively researched, but not free of errors and rather diffuse (apparently only very minor changes were made in Guiffrey's text by Yve-Plessis). On this ed., see Villey, F64, VIII, 204-05 or F65, pp. 160-61 on Vol. II; F64, VIII, 206-07 or F65, pp. 162-63 on Vol. III.

Rev.: .1 Jourda, Pierre, *RSS*, XVII (1930), 160-64 (on Vol. IV); XVIII (1931), 357-58 (on Vol. V).

E18 *Œuvres complètes de Clément Marot. Revues sur les meilleures éditions, avec une notice et un glossaire, par B. Saint-Marc*, Paris: Garnier, 2 vols, 1879.

The 'Notice sur CM' (I, pp. v-xvi) is chiefly remarkable for its confident opening: 'Pour le biographe curieux qui tient à savoir à fond son Marot, il n'est peut-être plus de trouvaille, plus de regain à espérer ... Marot est connu presque tout entier.' See HP3.

E19 *'Dialogue nouveau, fort joyeulx', composé par Clement Marot*, in *Nouveau recueil de farces françaises des XVᵉ et XVIᵉ siècles, publié, d'après un volume unique appartenant à la Bibliothèque Royale de Copenhague, [par] Émile Picot et Christophe Nyrop*, Paris 1880, pp. xxxv-li, 71-95.

Text from a collection of nine French farces published in Lyons in 1619, entitled *Farce du cuvier* after the first farce. In the seventeenth-century ed the title read *Dialogue de deux amoureux*; the author's name was not mentioned.

E20 *Œuvres de C. Marot de Cahors, valet de chambre du roy. Édition revue sur celle de 1544. Notice par Benjamin Pifteau*, Paris: Delarue, 4 vols, [1884?].
Text based on Constantin's 1544 ed. (*Bibliog. II*, no. 129).

E21 *Œuvres choisies de Clément Marot. Accompagnées d'une étude sur la vie, les œuvres et la langue de ce poète, avec des variantes, des notes philologiques, littéraires et historiques, et un glossaire, par Eugène Voizard*, Paris: Garnier, [1888 or 1889?].
The preface is dated 26 Sept. 1888. The introduction offers a 'Biographie' (pp. xi-lii) and an essay on 'L'Œuvre de Clément Marot' (pp. liii-lxviii).

E22 Macon, Gustave, 'Poésies inédites de Clément Marot', *BBB* (1898), 157-70, 233-48.
Describes MS Chantilly: Musée Condé 748, the MS presented by CM to Anne de Montmorency in March 1538. Publishes several poems not previously printed (these are also listed in Villey, F64, VIII, 207-08 or F65, pp. 163-64). On this MS, see further Villey HA102, (1921), 50-61, 101-17, 171-75, or HA103, pp. 41-73, and *Bibliog. I*, pp. 10-18.

E23 Fromage, R., 'Poésies inédites de Clément Marot', *BSHP*, LVIII (1909), 44-50, 129-41, 225-42.
Prints a number of poems which he attributes to CM (see Villey, F64, VIII, 208-09 or F65, pp. 164-65). Their authenticity is questioned by Plattard (G9, 10), whose doubts are shared by Mayer (in *Bibliog. I* and the introductions to different vols in *OC*). See also note to E32.

E24 Becker, Ph. Aug., 'Clément Marot: Nachlese', *ASNS*, CXXXIII (1915), 142-47.
Reproduces, from MS Vienna: Nationalbibliothek 3525, the dizain 'Quant en mon nom assemblez vous serez' (*OC*, V, p. 313); and the *Epistre de complainte, à une qui a laissé son amy* which is printed at the end of the *Suite de l'Adolescence cl.* (*Bibliog. II*, no. 20, but not in no. 15) and might, Becker thinks, also be by CM. (In fact, Villey indicates in F64, VII, 96, n. 1 or F65, p. 51, n. 1, that the *Epistre* is by Jacques Colin.)

E25 *'Les Amoureux: Dialogue nouveau, fort joyeulx*, par Clément Marot', *Annales* (1920), 503-05.
Text of performance at the Comédie Française on 18 February 1915, by Berthe Bovy, Yvonne Lifraud and Marie Leconte, directed by Jules Truffier. This is a shortened and expurgated version, apparently prepared

with the help of Joseph Bédier (see HI1 where this bowdlerized text is reproduced).

E26   *Œuvres complètes de Clément Marot, revues sur les meilleures éditions, avec une notice et un glossaire, par Abel Grenier*, Paris: Garnier, 2 vols, [1920?].
The 'Notice sur Clément Marot' is in I, pp. v-li.

E27   Becker, Ph. Aug., 'Clément Marot und Lukian', *NMi*, XXIII (1922), 57-84.
CM's *Le Jugement de Minos* (*OC*, VI, pp. 79-92) closely imitates Jean Miélot's *Le Débat d'honneur entre trois chevaleureux princes* (1450, published in 1475), itself a free prose adaptation in French of Aurispa's Latin tr. (1425) of the twelfth of Lucian's *Dialogues of the Dead*. Becker prints CM's, Miélot's and Aurispa's versions. In *Le Chant de l'Amour fugitif* (*OC*, VI, pp. 108-12), CM's immediate source was probably the text printed in the Latin ed. of Lucian's works published in Venice in 1494, in which Moschus's idyll was wrongly attributed to Lucian. (Regarding CM's source, see also KB25, 26, 27.) See also HUb12.

E28   Becker, Philipp August, 'Clément Marot und Lukian', in his *Zur romanischen Literaturgeschichte: Ausgewählte Studien und Aufsätze*, Munich: Francke, 1967, pp. 580-603.
Reprint of E27.

E29   *Les Opuscules et petitz traictez de Clément Marot ... nouvellement imprimées à Lyon par Olivier Arnoullet*, Paris: Éditions des Bibliothèques Nationales de France, 1931.
Reproduction in facsimile of *Bibliog. II*, no. 6 (on this ed., see F55).

E30   *Calvin's First Psalter [1539]. Edited, with Critical Notes, and Modal Harmonies to the Melodies, by Sir Richard R. Terry*, London: Benn, 1932.
Very useful for the reproduction in facsimile of the psalter (*Bibliog. II*, no. 82), followed by its transcription into modern notation and type. In his introduction, Terry reprints Woodward's very faulty biographical sketch of CM (HUa42). On the melodies of this psalter, see also, among others, Yvonne Rokseth, 'Les Premiers Chants de l'église calviniste', *Revue de Musicologie*, XXXVI (1954), 7-20.

E31   Rau, Arthur, *L'Édition originale de la 'Deploration sur le trespa de feu messire Florimond Robertet' par Clément Marot. Avec u fac-similé intégral du seul exemplaire connu*, Paris: Rau, 1938.
Reproduction of ed. Lyons: Claude Nourry, s.d. (*Bibliog. II*, no. 5).

Rev.: .1 Lavaud, J., *HR*, V (1938), 489-91.

E32   Droz, E., and P.P. Plan, 'Les Dernières Années de Clément
Marot, d'après des poèmes inédits', *BHR*, IX (1947), 6-68.
Detailed description of MS Lausanne M1016 (see E10), whose scribe
is identified as Gilbert Grenet. Publication of the following seven poems —
which Droz and Plan attribute to CM — from the MS: (i) *Espitre de
madame la daulphine escripvant à madame Marguerite* (*OC*, I, pp. 269-
72), printed by Chavannes in E10, but attributed by him to Catherine
de' Medici; (ii) *Espitre de Marot* (*OC*, I, pp. 288-91), not printed by
Chavannes, but published by Fromage in E23; and these previously
unpublished poems: (iii) *Coq à l'asne de Marot à Me Guillaume le Coq*:
'Le coq, mon amy et mon frere'; (iv) *Autre epitre du coq à la coquette*:
'Ma sœur coquette, au bruict qui court'; (v) *Autre epistre de Clement
Marot*: 'Coquelicon, je te suplie'; (vi) *Autre epistre*: 'Amy, pour ung peu
t'esjoyr' (*OC*, II, pp. 168-74); (vii) *Aultre espitre de la poule à baudet*
'Tu m'as tant bien au long escript'. According to Droz and Plan, (ii), (iii),
(iv) and (v) were addressed to Dr Guillaume Le Coq, (vi) and (vii) to Lyon
Jamet. These various *épîtres* are said to be 'pleines de renseignements
sur la fuite [de CM] de France, le premier séjour en Savoie, le refuge
à Genève et le deuxième et dernier séjour en Savoie'. (N.B. In C105,
pp. 496-97, Mayer rejects the 'legend' of CM's stay in Savoy on the way
to Geneva.)
Potentially, an extremely valuable contribution to CM studies, which, it
is here claimed, throws much new light on his last years. However, the
authenticity of all the poems has been challenged by Mayer. In *Bibliog.
I*, pp. 47-63, he accepts the authenticity of (vi), considers that of (i),
(ii) and (vii) as 'probable', that of (iv) and (v) as 'doubtful', and rejects
(iii). But in *OC*, the status of (vi) has been reduced to 'd'authenticité
possible ou probable' (II, pp. 35-36, 39), (i) is regarded as 'd'authenticité
douteuse mais appartenant peut-être à Marot' (I, pp. 61-62, 64), (ii) 'ne
me [paraît] pas être de Marot' (I, pp. 63, 64), (vii) is rejected (II, pp. 38,
39), and (iv) and (v) are not even mentioned (nor is (iii), any further).
Incidentally, Droz and Plan identify the recipient of CM's epistle *A ung
sien amy* (I, pp. 272-76) as François de Bellegarde, though without
offering any conclusive arguments in support. (Mayer repeats this identification in *OC*, I, p. 272, and C105, pp. 505-07. See also various entries
in section HP.)

E33   Weinberg, Bernard, *Critical Prefaces of the French Renaissance*,
Evanston: Northwestern UP, 1950, xiv + 290 pp.
Prints CM's prefaces to *Œuvres de Francoys Villon* (1533) and to his tr.
of the first book of Ovid's *Metamorphoses* (1534); also what he calls the
'anomymous' preface to the *Roman de la Rose* (1526). (See HVa10 for

Weinberg's tentative attribution of the preface and the modernized text to Guillaume Michel.)

E34   Mayer, C.A., 'Une Épigramme inédite de Clément Marot', *BHR*, XVI (1954), 209-11.

Publishes *Response par Clément Marot à maistre Claude Galland (OC*, V, p. 299) which did not appear in CM's *Œuvres*, but in Galland's *Epistre à une noble dame religieuse* ... (1547). There it is followed by another *dizain*, 'Pensant en moy trouver l'or souverain' *(Audit Galland*, *OC*, V, p. 300) by an unidentified author who might well also be CM.

E35   *Guillaume de Lorris [et] Jean de Meung, 'Le Roman de la Rose',dans la version attribuée à Clément Marot, publié par Silvio F. Baridon*, Milan: Istituto Editoriale Cisalpino, 2 vols, 1954-57.

Text of ed. Paris: Galliot du Pré, 1529 *[1530]* (see *Bibliog. II*, no. 236), with variants from certain fifteenth-century versions. Preface contains a detailed discussion of the question of editorship (see HVa1).

E36   *'L'Adolescence clémentine' de Clément Marot. Texte établi et présenté par V.L. Saulnier*, Paris: Colin, [1958].

Text from ed. Lyons: Gryphius, 1538 *(Bibliog. II*, no. 71).
Rev.:   .1 Jourda, Pierre, *BHR*, XXI (1959), 535-36.
        .2 Sozzi, Lionello, *SFr*, II (1958), 448-50.

E37   *Clément Marot, Œuvres complètes. Édition critique par C.A. Mayer*, 6 vols, I: *Les Épîtres*, 1958, II: *Œuvres satiriques*, 1962, III: *Œuvres lyriques*, 1964, IV: *Œuvres diverses: Rondeaux, ballades, chants-royaux, épitaphes, étrennes, sonnets*, 1966, V: *Les Épigrammes*, 1970, all London: Athlone Press, Univ. of London; VI: *Les Traductions*, Geneva: Slatkine, 1980.

The first critical ed., and a generally outstanding one. An excellent text, meticulously established, with an impeccable critical apparatus. Extensive introductions, comprising useful literary studies and careful examinations of matters relating to authenticity and textual tradition. Glossaries, indexes of names and first lines. Superb typographical presentation throughout. The principles for establishing the text and classifying the poems are set out in the following articles: 'Le Texte de Marot' (F41), 'Les Œuvres de Clément Marot: L'Économie de l'édition critique' (HA57), 'Le Texte des *Psaumes* de Marot' (F47), 'Prolégomènes à l'édition critique des psaumes de Clément Marot' (F48). For certain criticism of this system – e.g. the separation of the *élégies déploratives* from the remaining elegies and their inclusion among the *complaintes*, or the definition of lyric poetry which determines the composition of Vol. III – see esp. HA33, HK12.

Rev.: .1 Burgess, Robert M., *RQ*, XXV (1972), 94 (on Vol. V).
.2 Carrington, Samuel M., *FR*, XLV (1971-72), 752-53 (V).
.3 Charpentier, Françoise, *RSH* (1967), 645-48 (I, II, III, IV); (1973), 166-67 (V).
.4 Françon, Marcel, *RenN*, XII (1959), 272-73 (I); *Lingue Straniere*, XII, 2 (1963), 34-36 (II); *SFr*, XV (1971), 334 (V). See also HA33 (III), HA34 (IV).
.5 Giraud, Yves, *BHR*, XXXIV (1972), 579-601 (V).
.6 Graham, Victor, *RR*, LVII (1966), 57-58 (III).
.7 Gray, Floyd, *S*, XIV (1960), 308-10 (I).
.8 Hall, Kathleen M., *MLR*, LXI (1966), 314-15 (III).
.9 Joukovsky, F., *RPh*, XXV (1971-72), 477-78 (V).
.10 Jourda, Pierre, *BHR*, XXI (1959), 535-37 (I).
.11 Lafeuille, Germaine, *RR*, LIX (1968), 218-19 (IV).
.12 Lawton, H.W., *FS*, XIII (1959), 351-52 (I); XVII (1963), 54-55 (II); XIX (1965), 53-54 (III); XXI (1967), 338-39 (IV); XXV (1971), 190-92 (V); XXXV (1981), 431 (VI).
.13 McFarlane, I.D., *MLR*, LXVIII (1973), 403-04 (V).
.14 Mehnert, Kurt Henning, *ASNS*, CCIX (1972-73), 205-09 (V).
.15 Nurse, Peter H., *MLR*, LV (1960), 117-19 (I).
.16 Richter, Bodo L.O., *FR*, XL (1966-67), 142-44 (III).
.17 Richter, Mario, *BHR*, XXIX (1967), 511-13 (IV).
.18 Stone, Donald, *RR*, LXV (1974), 57-59 (V).
.19 Voisine, Jacques, *RLC*, XLV (1971), 414-15 (V).
.20 Weber, H., *RHLF*, LXIII (1963), 465-66 (II); LXVI (1966), 498-99 (III); LXVIII (1968), 841-42 (IV). See also HA109 (I).
.21 Whitney, Mark S., *RenN*, XVI (1963), 206-07 (II).

E38 *'L'Enfer' de Clément Marot. Reproduction du texte de l'édition Jean de Tournes, Lyon, 1549. Avec introduction et notes [de] Marcel Françon*, Cambridge, Mass.: Schoenhof, 1960.
Reproduction in facsimile of ed. *Bibliog.* II, no. 169
Rev.: .1 Mayer, C.A., *FS*, XV (1961), 261-62.

E39 *'Le Sermon du bon pasteur'*, in G6, pp. 290-303.
Text from *Psalmes de David* ..., 1541 (*Bibliog. II*, no. 94), with variants from *Bergerie du bon pasteur et du mauvais* (*Bibliog. II*, no. 139) and MS BN f. fr. 12795.

E40 *Les Psaumes de Clément Marot. Édition critique du plus ancien texte (MS Paris BN fr. 2337) avec toutes les variantes des manuscrits et des plus anciennes éditions jusqu'à 1543, accompagnée*

du texte définitif de 1562 et précédée d'une étude par Samuel Jan Lenselink, Assen: Van Gorcum, 1969.
The introductory 'Étude sur les psaumes de Marot' (pp. 3-56) offers a brief biographical note (based on V.L. Saulnier's volume on Renaissance literature in the Que sais-je? series), a discussion of certain (but by no means all) MSS and of the early eds, and an examination of CM's sources which are said to be primarily Olivetan's French Bible and Bucer's Latin commentaries on the psalms, but to include also the Latin paraphrase by Campensis (Jan van Kampen), and, more surprisingly. a German psalm tr. by Matthaeus Greiter. Various interesting remarks, esp. about the MSS, but the overall argumentation is too sketchy, the investigation too incomplete, to warrant the confidently affirmed conclusions. Nor is any justification offered for choosing the 1562 ed. by F. Jaquy of the CM-Beza psalms as the definitive printed text for the critical ed. For a detailed analysis of some of the more obvious deficiencies of Lenselink's book, see esp. .1 and .5 below.
Rev.: .1 Albaric, M.: see HUa1.
.2 Goosse, Marie Thérèse, *RBPH*, XLIX (1971), 245-47.
.3 Jonker, G.D., *LevT* (1969), 805-06.
.4 Lebègue, Raymond, *RLC*, XLIV (1970), 551-52.
.5 Mayer, Claude Albert: see F47.
.6 Pineaux, Jacques, *RHLF*, LXXI (1971), 68-69.
.7 Thiry, Cl., *RLV*, XXXVII (1971), 184-85.
.8 Weber, Édith, *BSHP*, CXVII (1971), 342-43.

E41 *'Farce de deulx amoureux recreatis et joyeux'*, in *Manuscrit La Vallière: Fac-similé intégral du manuscrit 24314 de la Bibliothèque Nationale de Paris, avec une introduction de Werner Helmich*, Geneva: Slatkine Reprints, 1972.
The *farce* is transcribed, without the author's name, on fols 183v^o -190r^o of the MS. The latter, executed by an unidentified scribe, has been dated at ca 1575.

E42 *Clément Marot, Œuvres poétiques. Choix, établissement du texte, chronologie, introduction, glossaire, notes et archives de l'œuvre par Yves Giraud*, Paris: Garnier-Flammarion, 1973.
For some corrections, see HA97.
Rev.: .1 Joukovsky, Fr., *IL*, XXVI (1974), 121.
.2 Kalwies, Howard H., *FR*, XLVIII (1974-75), 621-22.
.3 P[y], A., *BHR*, XXXVI (1974), 423.

E43 *Clément Marot, 'L'Enfer, les coq-à-l'âne, les élégies'. Édition critique par C.A. Mayer*, Paris: Champion, 1977.

In addition to *L'Enfer*, the four *coq-à-l'âne* and the twenty-four *élégies amoureuses*, which are reproduced from *OC*, II and III and form the main body of this volume, ten poems are printed in the appendices, on the grounds that 'plusieurs poèmes de Marot ont été faussement classés comme épîtres, d'autres comme élégies. Ces poèmes doivent donc figurer à part.' These include the three *élégies déploratives* classified by Mayer as *complaintes* (cf. note to E37), the *Epistre de Maguelonne* ..., the *Épître de Frippelippes*, and *Aux dames de Paris qui ne vouloient prendre les precedentes excuses en payement*.
Rev.: .1 Françon, M., *Fra*, no. 17 (1980), 7-8.

E44   *Clément Marot, Les Épîtres. Édition critique par C.A. Mayer*, Paris: Nizet, 1977.

Apart from a different preface, this appears to be a reprint of *OC*, I.

F. TEXTUAL HISTORY
(MANUSCRIPTS, EDITIONS)

F1   *Arrêts du Conseil de Genève sur le fait de l'imprimerie et de la librairie, de 1541 à 1550*, recueillis et annotés par Alfred Cartier, Geneva: Georg, 1893, 206 pp.

F2   Babelon, Jean, *La Bibliothèque française de Fernand Colomb*, *Revue des Bibliothèques*, Supplément X, Paris: Champion, 1913, xliii + 340 pp.
No. 128 in this catalogue of French books in the Biblioteca Colombina, Seville, is the undated first ed. of CM's tr. of psalm VI (*Bibliog. II*, no. 8). See Harrisse, F23. Babelon explains that Harrisse misread Colón's date '1535' as '1525'.

F3   Baudrier, [Henri], *Bibliographie lyonnaise*, Lyons: Brun, 12 vols, 1895-1921.

F4   Becker, Ph. Aug., 'Das Druckprivileg für Marots Werke von 1538', *ZFSL*, XLII (1914), 'Referate und Rezensionen', 224-29.
Reproduces undated *Declaration sur l'impression des œuvres de Marot* from MS BN f. fr. 18111. Argues that CM obtained this privilege for the publication of his *Œuvres* in 1538 (Mayer takes same view in C105, p. 427 ff.). Suggests that Gryphius's ed. (*Bibliog. II*, no. 71) appeared before Dolet's (no. 70). (Mayer places it a few days after Dolet's — C105, p. 425.)

F5   Becker, Ph. Aug., 'Une Édition des psaumes de Marot imprimée par E. Dolet', *BSHP*, LXXVIII (1929), 471-72.
The ed. described by Pannier in F53 must have been published in 1542, before Dolet's arrest in July. Its text is derived from 1541 Antwerp ed. (*Bibliog. II*, no. 94). See also Chassaigne F10 and Villey F70.

Becker, Ph. Aug.: see also HUa3.

F6   Brun, Robert, *Le Livre illustré en France au XVIe siècle*, Paris: Alcan, 1930, 334 pp.
On CM, see pp. 255-56.

F7   Brun, Robert, *Le Livre illustré de la Renaissance: Étude suivie du catalogue des principaux livres à figures du XVIe siècle,* Paris: Picard, 1969, 322 pp.
Revised ed. of F6. On CM, see pp. 245-46.

F8   Brunet, Jacques Charles, 'Marot (Clément)', in his *Manuel du libraire et de l'amateur de livres,* 5e éd., Paris: Firmin-Didot, 6 vols, 1860-65, III (1862), cols 1446-65.
See also F13.

Brunet, G.: see F13.

F9   Cartier, Alfred, *Bibliographie des éditions des De Tournes, imprimeurs lyonnais.* Mise en ordre, avec une introduction et des appendices, par Marius Audin, et une notice biographique par E. Vial, Paris: Éditions des Bibliothèques Nationales de France, 2 vols, 1937-38.

Catach, Nina: see G1.

F10   Chassaigne, M., 'Encore le psautier édité par Dolet', *BSHP,* LXXIX (1930), 302.
Agrees with Becker's conclusions in F5. Cf. also Villey F70.

F11   Clive, H.P., 'The Psalm Translations in Bibliothèque Nationale Manuscript fr. 2336', *BHR,* XXVII (1965), 80-95.
The erroneous statement in the BN catalogue of MSS that the psalms are incomplete and in arbitrary order results from the folios being bound in wrong sequence. The art. indicates the correct one. The MS contains twenty-one psalms by CM.

F12   Collignon, Albert, 'La Bibliothèque du duc Antoine: Recherches bibliographiques suivies de l'inventaire annoté', *Mémoires de l'Académie de Stanislas, 1906-1907,* 6th ser., IV (1907), 1-135.
Includes description (pp. 26-28) of MS of CM's tr. of book I of Ovid's *Metamorphoses,* presented by him to Duc Antoine de Lorraine in 1531. (The current whereabouts of this MS are unknown. MS BN nouv. acq. 12037 may be a faulty copy of it, or of the MS described by Gaudu in F19 – see *OC,* VI, pp. 11-12.)

F13   Deschamps, P., and G. Brunet, 'Marot (Clément)', in *Manuel du libraire et de l'amateur de livres: Supplément,* Paris: Firmin-Didot, 2 vols, 1878-80, I, cols 956-67.
Supplement to F8.

F14 Droz, E., 'Antoine Vincent: La Propagande protestante par le psautier', in *Aspects de la propagande religieuse. Études publiées par G. Berthoud (and others)*, THR, XXVIII, Geneva: Droz, 1957, pp. 276-93.

The *editio princeps* of the complete CM-Beza psalter was published by Jean de Tournes in Lyons at the beginning of 1562. It was immediately followed by numerous other eds printed for Antoine Vincent on presses in Lyons, Paris and several provincial cities, as well as in Geneva.

F15 Droz, E., 'La Marque aux trois colonnes couronnées: b) *Les Œuvres de Clément Marot*, Paris, Claude Micard, 1er mai 1577 [Genève, François Estienne?]', in her 'Fausses adresses typographiques', *BHR*, XXIII (1961), 138-52, 379-93, 572-91 (583-88).

Detailed description of this ed. (*Bibliog. II*, no. 222).

F16 Duplessis, Georges, *Essai bibliographique sur les différentes éditions des œuvres d'Ovide ornées de planches, publiées aux XVe et XVIe siècles*, Paris: Vve L. Techener, 1889, 55 pp.

Lists several eds of CM's partial tr. of the *Metamorphoses*, issued separately or as part of his *Œuvres*.

F17 Du Verdier, Antoine, 'Clement Marot', in *La Bibliothèque d'Antoine du Verdier, seigneur de Vauprivas*, Lyons, 1585, pp. 220-31.

List of works preceded by praise of CM, 'de son temps poëte des princes et prince des poëtes de son aage' (a phrase repeated by many later writers). '[Il] a si doucement escrit, et si gracieusement entassé les mots de sa composition yssante ou de son propre esprit, ou de l'esprit d'autruy, que jamais on ne verra son nom estaint, ne ses escrits abolis.'

F18 Escoffier, Maurice, *Autour d'une supercherie de libraire: Clément Marot, Étienne Dolet, Heluyn Dulin*, Trévoux, [1965].

The 1544 ed. of CM's *Œuvres* by Constantin (*Bibliog. II*, no. 129) was in reality a publishing fraud perpetrated by Hélouin du Lin, an agent of Cardinal du Bellay. (Du Lin is also known to have helped finance Dolet's printing-works.)

F19 Gaudu, F., 'Un Manuscrit de la traduction du premier livre des *Métamorphoses* par Marot', *RSS*, XI (1924), 258-69.

This MS, owned by Henri Parguez, dates from the end of the sixteenth century, but offers an earlier text than the first known ed., published in 1534 (*Bibliog. II*, no. 21). It could be a copy of the MS presented

by CM to the Duc de Lorraine in 1531 (see F12). (The present whereabouts of the MS which was in Parquez's possession in 1924 are not
known. MS BN nouv. acq. 12037 may offer a faulty version of it –
see *OC*, VI, pp. 11-12. See also F60.)

Gérold, Th.: see HUa14.

F20   Graesse, Jean George Théodore, 'Marot, Clément', in his
*Trésor de livres rares et précieux; ou, Nouveau dictionnaire
bibliographique ...*, Dresden: Kuntze, 7 vols, 1859-69, IV
(1863), 409-14.

F21   Gutknecht, Dieter, *Untersuchungen zur Melodik des Hugenotten-
psalters*, Kölner Beiträge zur Musikforschung, LXVII, Regensburg:
Bosse, 1972, vii + 207 pp.
Has a long section on the early psalter eds. Good bibliography on the CM-
Beza psalter.

F22   Hämel, Adalbert, 'Clément Marot und François Juste', *ZFSL*,
L (1927), 131-34.
The Bayerische Staatsbibliothek, Munich, possesses (i) a hitherto unknown,
unauthorized ed. by Juste of the *Adolescence cl.*, dated 12 July 1533
(*Bibliog. II*, no. 14bis), which also already contains additional poems by
CM subsequently reprinted in Juste's ed. of 12 Dec. 1534 (*Bibliog. II*, no.
24); (ii) an ed. of Jean Lemaire's *Épîtres de l'amant vert* in a revision attributed on the title page to CM, published by Juste in 1537 (*Bibliog. II*, no.
248). This ed. was presumably used by Pierre de Tours as the basis for the
further ed. in 1552 (*Bibliog. II*, no. 276) which Villey describes in F64,
VIII, 172-73 or F65, pp. 128-29. (Unlike Villey, Hämel all but rules out
any possibility of CM's collaboration in the 1537 ed.) On (i) and (ii), see
also F68 and F69. Cf. F46.

F23   Harrisse, Henry, 'La Colombine et Clément Marot', *Livre*, VII
(1886), 65-74. A 2nd, expanded, ed. was published under the
same title in Paris, 1886, 38 pp.
Describes and discusses an undated separate ed. of CM's tr. of psalm VI,
preserved in the Biblioteca Colombina Seville (*Bibliog. II*, no. 8), which
offers an earlier text than the version printed with Marguerite de Navarre's
Miroir de l'âme pécheresse in 1533 (*Bibliog. II*, no. 240). Puzzles over
date '1525' given by Colón for the purchase, surmises that it is a mistake
for '1535' (in fact, Harrisse misread the latter date – see F2). The 2nd
ed. of Harrisse's study, after reproducing the contents of the first virtually
unchanged, gives details of a copy of CM's *Opuscules* (*Bibliog. II*, no. 6)
which used to be, but is apparently no longer, in the Colombina. See also
F24.

F24   Harrisse, Henry, *Excerpta Colombiniana: Bibliographie de quatre cents pièces gothiques françaises, italiennes et latines du commencement du XVIe siècle, non décrites jusqu'ici ...*, Paris: Welter, 1887, lxxv + 315 pp.
No. 145 is CM's *Opuscules*, no. 193 his tr. of psalm VI (see F23). The descriptions are followed by the remarks – in the case of the psalm, in a slightly condensed version – printed in the 2nd ed. of F23.

F25   Jacob, P.L. (Bibliophile) [pseud. of Paul Lacroix], 'Recherches sur les éditions de François Juste, libraire et imprimeur, à Lyon', in his *Recherches bibliographiques sur des livres rares et curieux*, Paris: Rouveyre, 1880, pp. 66-80.
The list of forty-seven eds bearing Juste's name or address contains several of CM's works. (More are mentioned in *Bibliog. II.*)

F26   Jacob, P.L. (Bibliophile), [pseud. of Paul Lacroix], '*Les Blasons anatomiques du corps féminin*', in his *Recherches* [as FD25], pp. 144-59.
Briefly reviews the vogue enjoyed by the *blasons* and discusses different eds. Notes that the existence of the 1536 Lyons ed. by Juste (*Bibliog. II*, no. 247), of which no copies are known, is confirmed by Draudius in his *Bibliotheca classica* (1625).

F27   Johns, Francis A., 'Clément Marot's *Pseaumes octantetrois ...*, 1551: Report of a Surviving Copy', *BHR*, XXXI (1969), 351-54.
Describes the copy recently acquired by Rutgers University. The only previously known one was destroyed in Dresden.

F28   Jourda, Pierre, 'Tableau chronologique des publications de Marguerite de Navarre', *RSS*, XII (1925), 209-55.

F29   Karl, Louis, 'Une Découverte bibliographique, à propos de la chronologie marotique', *RSS*, X (1923), 107-10.
The Bayerische Staatsbibliothek, Munich, possesses an ed. dated 1543 of the *Recueil de vraye poesie françoyse* (which contains poems by CM), i.e. a year earlier than the ed. of Dec. 1544 described by Villey in F64, VIII,157-60 or F65, pp. 113-16. (Mayer lists the 1544 ed. – *Bibliog. II*, no. 264 – but not the 1543 one.)

F30   Karl, Louis, 'Une Édition posthume des *Œuvres* de Marot', *RSS*, XI (1924), 270-72.
The Archbishop's library at Calocza, Hungary, has an ed. of CM's *Œuvres*

published by Oudin Petit in 1551, which is not mentioned by Villey in F64, 65. (The ed., but not this copy, is listed in *Bibliog. II*, no. 187.)

F31 Labarthe, Olivier, 'Jean Gérard, l'imprimeur des *Cinquante pseaumes* de Marot', *BHR*, XXXV (1973), 547-61.
Disagrees with Mayer's view (F48) that this 1543 psalm ed. (*Bibliog. II*, nos 116, 117) cannot be attributed to Gérard. Argues that a close comparison with the typographical material used by Gérard in several books during this period — the art. reproduces several pages in facsimile — shows conclusively that the psalm ed. was indeed printed by his press. Since CM was then in Geneva, he could well have supervised its production. (Mayer maintains his position and rejects the ed. as unauthoritative in *OC*, VI, pp. 46-49, with no reference to this art.) Cf. F36.

F32 Lachèvre, Frédéric, *Bibliographie des recueils collectifs de poésies publiés de 1597 à 1700 ...*, Paris: Leclerc, 5 vols, 1901-22.

F33 Lachèvre, Frédéric, *Bibliographie des recueils collectifs de poésie du XVIe siècle (du 'Jardin de plaisance', 1502, aux 'Recueils' de Toussaint du Bray, 1609)*, Paris: Champion, 1922, 613 pp.

F34 La Croix du Maine, 'Clement Marot', in *Premier volume de la bibliothèque du sieur de La Croix du Maine*, Paris:Abel l'Angelier, 1584, p. 65.
Very few details of CM's works. States that the psalm translations were based on a French prose version prepared for CM by Mellin de Saint-Gelais. CM 'estoit estimé le premier de son siecle, et peut-estre de ceux qui viendront apres luy.'

F35 La Fons-Mélicocq, de, 'Un Exemplaire des *Œuvres* de Clément Marot annoté par Jamet', *Bulletin du Bouquiniste* (1864), 319-22.
Gives some extracts, mostly of a bibliographical nature, from notes made by the eighteenth-century book collector François Louis Jamet in a copy of Portau's 1596 ed. of CM's works (on this ed., see E1).

F36 Lebègue, Raymond, 'Pour une édition critique des *Psaumes* de Marot', *RR*, L (1959), 95-98.
Stresses the need for a critical ed. Lists MSS and early eds. Considers that the *Cinquante psaumes* of 1543 offer the definitive text. (Mayer rejects this ed. as unauthoritative — see F48 and *OC*, VI, pp. 46-49; but cf. F31.)

F37   Le Petit, Jules, *Bibliographie des principales éditions originales d'écrivains français du XVe au XVIIIe siècle*, Paris: Quantin, 1888, vii + 583 pp.

F38   ['Literarische Mitteilung'], *Literaturblatt für Germanische und Romanische Philologie*, XLVII (1926), 78.
Adalbert Hämel has discovered, in Spain, a MS once owned by Charles V, which contains CM's tr. of book II of the *Metamorphoses*. See also F40.

Macon, Gustave: see E22.

F39   Maillard, P^r, 'François Mizière, médecin du Poitou, et l'édition des *Œuvres* de Cl. Marot publiée par lui à Niort, en 1596', *BSHP*, III (1855), 6-7.
Gives text of letter from Dr Sauzé concerning this ed. (*Bibliog. II*, no. 232; see also note to E1).

F40   'Un Manuscrit de Marot', *RSS*, XIII (1926), 306.
The author believes that the MS of CM's tr. of book II of the *Metamorphoses*, said to have been discovered by Hämel (F38), may be the MS 'fasc. IV. 6' of the Escorial Library. (In his *Catálogo de los manuscritos franceses y provenzales de la Biblioteca de El Escorial*, Madrid, 1933, p. 13, Arturo García de La Fuente gives a fairly detailed description of MS f. IV. 6 which does indeed give the text of CM's tr. of book II of the *Metamorphoses*. The MS appears to have been owned by Charles V before coming into the possession of Philip II, who eventually presented it to the Escorial – see Rudolf Beer, *Die Handschriftenschenkung Philipp II. an den Escorial vom Jahre 1576 nach einem bisher unveröffentlichen Inventar des Madrider Palastarchivs*, Jahrbücher der Kunsthistorischen Sammlungen des Allerhöchsten Kaiserhauses, XXIII, 6, Vienna: Tempsky, 1903, p. cxx, no. 218. – Mayer makes no mention of this MS or of the two notes F38 and F40, either in *Bibliog. I* or in his introduction to *OC*, VI, where he states (p. 63) that the only known version of CM's tr. of book II is that published in Dolet's 1543 ed. of the *Œuvres* [i.e. *Bibliog. II*, no. 118]; see also *OC*, VI, pp. 39, 52.)

F41   Mayer, C.A., 'Le Texte de Marot', *BHR*, XIV (1952), 314-28; XV (1953), 71-91.
Important art., explaining and justifying the method adopted by Mayer in the establishment of the text of *OC* (E37). Concludes that Dolet's 1538 ed. of the *Œuvres* (*Bibliog. II*, no. 70) should form the basis of the critical ed. However, because of certain manifest shortcomings of Dolet's ed., the actual text must be a hybrid one, drawing also on other

authoritative versions. (On Dolet's 1538 ed., see also F64, VII, 217-34 or F65, pp. 64-81, and HA102, (1923), 49-51 or HA103, pp. 166-68.) Cf. F71.

F42   Mayer, C.A., 'Une Édition inconnue de Clément Marot', *BBB* (1953), 151-66.
Description of the *Petit traicté* (*Bibliog. II*, no. 6 bis), which Mayer dates at between February and June 1532.

F43   Mayer, C.A., *Bibliographie des œuvres de Clément Marot*, I: *Manuscrits*, II: *Éditions*, THR, X, XIII, Geneva: Droz, 2 vols, 1954.
Excellent reference works, very informative, clearly presented, very well indexed. Vol. 1 – designated '*Bibliog. I*' in the present *Bibliography* – offers a detailed examination of the three signed MSS (Chantilly: Musée Condé 748; Paris: BN Rothschild 2964; Lausanne: Bibliothèque cantonale et universitaire M1016), followed by a discussion of CM's poems in certain anonymous MSS. The vol., while still useful, now requires revision, among other reasons because of Mayer's discovery of a further important MS (see F45) and the publication of material (e.g. by Meylan in HH5, cf. *OC*, II, p. 38, n. 3) which may prompt a reassessment of the question of authenticity with regard to some poems (see note to E32 concerning Mayer's different appraisal in *Bibliog. I* and *OC* of the authenticity of certain poems in the Lausanne MS). In his introduction of F49, Mayer himself writes of Vol. I: 'il me semble dépassé et je ne crois pas qu'il puisse y avoir de l'intérêt à le rééditer.'
Vol. II is presented as a complement to Villey's *Tableau chronologique* (F64, 65). It lists eds before 1600, except for CM's psalms, where it stops in 1550, 'date à laquelle [les psaumes] devinrent, avec les *Bibles*, un moyen de propagande protestante'. Further information on works by CM in collections of poems can be found in Lachèvre's *Bibliographie* (F33); see also his F32 on the seventeenth-century collections. For a reprint of F43, Vol. II, see F49.
Rev.: .1 Becker, Georges, *IL*, VII (1955), 73.
     .2 Lawton, H.W., *BHR*, XVII (1955), 337-39.
     .3 Silver, Isidore, *RR*, XLVI (1955), 291-92.
     .4 Steele, A.J., *MLR*, LI (1956), 140.
     .5 Taylor, Robert E., *RenN*, IX (1956), 97-98.

F44   Mayer, C.A., 'Encore une édition inconnue de Clément Marot', *BHR*, XXVII (1965), 669-71.
Describes an ed. of *L'Histoire de Leander et de Hero* (Paris: Charles l'Angelier, 1542) preserved in the Royal Library, Windsor (*Bibliog. II*, 'Addenda', no. 107 bis).

F45   Mayer, C.A., 'Un Manuscrit important pour le texte de Marot',
        BHR, XXVIII (1966), 419-26.
        Description of the little-known MS BN nouv. acq. 477 – not mentioned
        in *Bibliog. I* – which contains numerous poems by CM and throws new
        light esp. on his elegies, as well as on the dates of certain poems.

F46   Mayer, C.A., '*La Tierce Epistre de l'amant verd* de Jean Lemaire
        de Belges', in *De Jean Lemaire de Belges à Jean Giraudoux:
        Mélanges ... Pierre Jourda*, Paris: Nizet, 1970, pp. 27-36.
        Agrees with Hämel (F22) that CM's name must have been invoked by
        Juste without justification in his ed. of the *Épîtres de l'amant vert*.
        Moreover, doubts that the *Tierce epistre* included in the volume is by
        Lemaire. Cf. F68.

F47   Mayer, Claude Albert, 'Le Texte des *Psaumes* de Marot', *SFr*,
        XV (1971), 1-28.
        Lists, for each of CM's psalms, all eds up to and including 1543, as well
        as MS versions. The most authoritative texts are those of the *Trente
        psaumes (Bibliog. II*, no. 101) and *Vingt psaumes* (in no. 119) published
        by Roffet in 1541 and 1543 respectively. Mayer very severely criticizes
        Lenselink's ed. E40 on several important counts.

F48   Mayer, C.A., 'Prolégomènes à l'édition critique des psaumes
        de Clément Marot', *BHR*, XXXV (1973), 55-71.
        Reaches same conclusions as in F47 – based here on closer analysis and
        more elaborate arguments – regarding the authoritativeness of Roffet's
        1541 and 1543 eds. After detailed examination of *Cinquante pseaumes*
        of 1543 (*Bibliog. II*, nos 116, 117), Mayer rules out the possibility of
        this ed. having been printed in Geneva and, accordingly, of CM's colla-
        boration in it. (For a different view, see F31.)

F49   Mayer, C.A., *Bibliographie des éditions de Clément Marot
        publiées au XVIe siècle*, Paris: Nizet, 1975, 107 pp.
        Reprint of F43, Vol. II, with a brief introduction and some addenda.
        Designated '*Bibliog II*' in the present *Bibliography*.

        Mayer, C.A.: see also HS16.

F50   Mortimer, Ruth, *Harvard College Library, Department of
        Printing and Graphic Arts: Catalogue of Books and Manuscripts
        I: French 16th Century Books*, Cambridge, Mass.: Harvard UP,
        2 vols, 1964.
        On CM, see II, pp. 464-65.

Natori, Seiichi: see HA65.

F51   O[livier], J., 'Une Découverte littéraire', *Revue de Paris*, XXVIII (1844), 276-82.
Describes MS Lausanne M1016 (see E10), containing various poems by CM. Reproduces text of *Espitre de madame la daulphine escripvant à madame Marguerite* which may have been composed by CM but, he believes, was more probably written by Catherine de' Medici herself (on this attribution, see notes to E10 and E32). See also F52.

F52   [Olivier, J], 'Vers inédits de Clément Marot. Épître en vers attribuée à Catherine de Médicis', *Revue Suisse*, VII (1844), 228-44.
Extensive summary of Chavannes's conclusions concerning the authorship of the contents of MS Lausanne M1016. Reproduces many of the poems. See F51 and esp. E10; also E32.

F53   Pannier, Jacques, 'Une Première Édition (?) des psaumes de Marot imprimée par Ét. Dolet', *BSHP*, LXXVIII (1929), 238-40.
Description of ed. Vatican Library Racc. Gen. Biblia VI. I Riserva Speciale, published by Dolet, lacking title page (*Bibliog. II*, no. 112). For a more probable dating than Pannier seems to envisage, see Becker (F5) and Villey (F70).

F54   Picot, Émile, *Catalogue des livres composant la bibliothèque de feu M. le baron James de Rothschild*, Paris: Morgand, 5 vols, 1884-1920.

Pidoux, Pierre: see HUa30.

F55   Rahir, Édouard, 'La Première Édition des œuvres de Clément Marot', in *Mélanges ... Émile Picot*, Paris: Rahir, 2 vols, 1913, II, pp. 635-45.
On *Opuscules et petitz traictez ...* (*Bibliog. II*, no. 6).

F56   Rawles, Stephen, 'An Un-recorded Edition of the Works of Clément Marot printed by Denis Janot', *BHR*, XXXVIII (1976), 485-88.
Describes ed. of CM's *Œuvres* printed by Janot in 1544, of which a copy is in the library of the École des Beaux Arts, Paris (shelf-mark: Masson 292). Also gives title of 1545 ed. of *Cinquante pseaumes de David* printed by Janot's widow, Jeanne de Marnef, and almost certainly intended to be a companion to the above ed. Neither ed. is listed in

Bibliog. II.

F57 Renouard, Philippe, *Imprimeurs et libraires parisiens du XVIe siècle. Ouvrage publié d'après les manuscrits de Philippe Renouard*, Paris: Service des Travaux Historiques de la Ville de Paris ..., 1964-

F58 Saulnier, V.L., 'Poésies de Saint-Gelais, Marot et autres Marotiques, d'après un manuscrit non signalé', in *Mélanges ... Daniel Mornet*, Paris: Nizet, 1951, pp. 11-19.
The *Recueil de vers françois*, at the end of MS BN latin 4813, contains four poems by CM imitated from Martial (*A Ysabeau, De la tristesse de s'amye, De Pauline, D'une vieille – OC*, V, pp. 231, 222-23, 234, 232-33)

F59 Saulnier, V.L., 'Dans le cercle des palinods rouennais: Richard de La Porte, Adrien de Saint-Gelais, Nicolas Boyssel et quelque autres auteurs de la Renaissance, d'après un manuscrit non étu *BBB* (1952), 143-58, 182-96, 239-51.
The 'La Porte' MS, now in private possession, contains CM's *Exploration de Jacques de Beaune* ... (i.e. *La Complaincte du riche infortuné messire Jaques de Beaune, seigneur de Samblançay, OC*, III, pp. 134-39).

F60 Saulnier, V.L., 'Glanes bibliographiques sur Marot, Ronsard et Montaigne, à propos d'une vente récente', *Het Boek*, 3rd ser., XXXIII (1958-59), 9-15.
Dr Lucien Grau's library, sold at public auction in 1956-57, contained a MS of CM's tr. of book I of the *Metamorphoses*, which had previously belonged to H. Parguez (see F19). As for MS BN nouv. acq. 12037, which Mayer identified as the 'Parguez' MS (*Bibliog. I*, p. 91, see also *Bibliog. II* p. 95), this is merely a modern copy. Cf. *OC*, VI, pp. 11-12.

Sauzé, D^r : see F39.

F61 Tannery, Jean, 'Des Livres perdus et retrouvés', *BBB* (1939), 53-66.
Describes CM's *Œuvres*, Paris: A. & C. les Angelier, 1541, (*Bibliog. II*, no. 95) from copy in his possession.

F62 Tchemerzine, Avenir, 'Clément Marot', in his *Bibliographie d'éditions originales et rares d'auteurs français des XVe, XVIe, XVIIe et XVIIIe siècles, contenant environ 6.000 fac-similés de titres et de gravures*, Paris: 10 vols, 1927-34, VII (1933), pp. 473-80; VIII (1933), 3-90.

F63 Veyrin-Forrer, Jeanne, 'Antoine Augereau, graveur de lettres et imprimeur parisien (vers 1485?-1534)', *Paris et Île-de-France: Mémoires publiés par la Fédération des Sociétés Historiques et Archéologiques de Paris et de l'Île-de-France*, VIII (1956), 103-56.
Authoritative study. On CM, see pp. 117-30 concerning Marguerite de Navarre's *Miroir de l'âme pécheresse* and the *Briefve doctrine pour deuement escripre selon la proprieté du langaige françoys*. Veyrin-Forrer believes that CM may have collaborated in the latter and advances some persuasive arguments in support of this view (cf. G1, G12).

F64 Villey, P., 'Tableau chronologique des publications de Marot', *RSS*, VII (1920), 46-97, 206-34; VIII (1921), 80-110, 157-211.
Carefully-established catalogue of first appearances of CM's different works, with detailed description and discussion of the eds and other publications in which they were printed. An excellent reference work, and an invaluable companion to Mayer's bibliography (F43, Vol. II; F49). See also note to HA102 and F66-69.

F65 Villey, Pierre, *Tableau chronologique des publications de Marot*, Paris: Champion, 1921, 167 pp.
Separately-paginated offprint of F64.

F66 Villey, P., 'Addition au *Tableau chronologique des publications de Marot* (1920)', *RSS*, IX (1922), 220.
See F64, 65.

F67 V[illey], P., 'Errata au *Tableau chronologique des publications de Marot*', *RSS*, XI (1924), 257-58.
See F64, 65.

F68 Villey, P., 'A propos d'une édition de Marot', *RSS*, XV (1928), 156-60.
On the ed. of the *Adolescence cl.* discovered by Hämel in Munich (see F22, also F69) and on its implications for the dating of CM's poems and the history of their publication. As for the reference to CM's editorship in the 1537 ed. of the *Épîtres de l'amant vert* (see F22, also F46), Villey, unlike Hämel, appears ready to accept it as correct.

F69 Villey, P., 'Pour la bibliographie de Marot', *RSS*, XV (1928), 388-89.
Summary of Hämel's art. F22. See also F68.

F70 Villey, P., 'Encore une édition inconnue de Marot', *RSS*, XVI

(1929), 331-34.
Reaches, independently of Becker (F5), the conclusion that the psalm
ed. described by Pannier in F53 was published in 1542. Cf. also F10.

F71   Villey, P., 'Introduction à l'explication des pièces de Marot
(portées au programme de l'Agrégation des jeunes filles)',
RCC, XXXIII, Pt 2 (1931-32), 111-20, 229-47.
Interesting mainly for the second, longer section (the first traces the
development of CM's poetry). There Villey refines his earlier guidelines
(see HA102) for preparing a critical ed., as follows: (i) the text of Dolet's
1538 ed. (*Bibliog. II*, no. 70) is authoritative for all poems printed in it;
(ii) for poems written before 1538 but not included in Dolet's ed., consult
MS Chantilly: Musée Condé 748 (see E22); (iii) for pre-1538 poems not
appearing either in the ed. or in the MS, each case should be considered
separately, in accordance with certain principles proposed by Villey. (For
Mayer's discussion of Villey's suggestions and his own conclusions, see F41

Villey, Pierre: see also HA102,103.

F72   W[eiss], N., 'Pierre Alexandre. Sa veuve', *BSHP*, LXI (1912),
421-22.
A few biographical particulars about Alexandre, who was the theologian
responsible for having 'Veu, recongneu et corrigé' the text of one of the
two psalm eds of 1541 (*Bibliog. II*, no. 93). The details are taken mainly
from Rodolphe Reuss, *Notes pour servir à l'histoire de l'église française
de Strasbourg, 1538-1794*, Strasbourg: Treuttel & Würtz, 1880, and
Baron F. de Schickler, *Les Églises du refuge en Angleterre*, Paris:
Fischbacher, 3 vols, 1892, where further information can be found.
(On Alexandre, see also Oswald Michotte, *Un Réformateur, Pierre
Alexandre*, Nessonvaux, 1913, and Philippe Denis, 'Pierre Alexandre
et la discipline ecclésiastique', *BHR*, XXXIX (1977), 551-55.)

G. QUESTIONS OF AUTHENTICITY*

Becker, Ph. Aug.: see E24.

Berdan, John M.: see KA2.

G1   Catach, Nina, *L'Orthographe française à l'époque de la Renaissance (auteurs, imprimeurs, ateliers d'imprimerie)*, Publications Romanes et Françaises, CI, Geneva: Droz, 1968, xxxiii + 495 pp.
Highly interesting study of the spelling, punctuation, and type of sixteenth-century books, including CM's works. Catach believes – like Riemens (G12) and, though more tentatively, Veyrin-Forrer (F63) – that CM had a hand in the *Briefve doctrine pour deuement escripre selon la proprieté du langaige françoys*. (For Mayer's contrary view, see *Bibliog. II*, no. 257, and G1, p. 53, n. 5.) Catach even extends CM's collaboration to 'les poèmes qui entourent la *B.D.*' (pp. 54-55), which would evidently include the *Epistre familiere de prier Dieu* and the *Aultre epistre familiere d'aymer chrestiennement* which immediately preceded the *B.D.* in the text. (Mayer, in C105, p. 240, n. 257, rejects out of hand the attribution of the first epistle to CM – he does not mention the other at all – but he mistakenly ascribes the original attribution, not to Catach, but to Riemens. The latter, in fact, named Florimond Robertet as the author of both epistles. See also *Bibliog. II*, no. 241.)

G2   Chavannes, Fréd., 'Une Lacune à remplir dans les éditions modernes des *Œuvres* de Clément Marot', *BSHP*, IV (1856), 319.
Reproduces a *dizain* appearing in early eds of CM but omitted in more recent ones, which attributes *Le Baladin* to him. (The *dizain* is printed in *OC*, III, p. 56.)

Droz, E.: see E32.

G3   Françon, Marcel, 'Sur Pétrarque et la littérature française', *RoN*, VII (1965-66), 190-92.
Contests the attribution by Mayer and Bentley-Cranch of the rondeau 'S'il est ainsi que ce corps t'abandonne' to Jean Marot (KA14; see also

---

*On the editorship of the *Roman de la Rose* (1526), see section HVa.

L59). Prefers the classification 'authenticité douteuse', but leans towards accepting CM's authorship.

Fromage, R.: see E23.

Hämel, Adalbert: see F22.

G4   Johns, Francis A., 'Clément Marot, M.C. and the *Quatre epistres chrestiennes*', *BHR*, XXXVII (1975), 445-46.
Confirms the correctness of Mayer's assumption (*OC*, V, p. 65) that the poem 'Que gaignes tu, dy moy, chrestien' should not be attributed to CM. The author is Mathurin Cordier, as Pidoux has already indicated in HUa30 II, p. 32.

G5   Kalwies, Howard H., 'Marot's *De la ville de Lyon*: The Problem of Authenticity', *BHR*, XXXVI (1974), 321-24.
Argues strongly in favour of CM's authorship of this epigram (*OC*, V, p. 251), notwithstanding the fact that it first appeared, not in Constantin's 1544 ed. of CM's *Œuvres*, as stated by Mayer (ibid.), but in Salel's *Œuvres* in 1539.

Labarthe, Olivier: see F31.

G6   Mayer, C.A., '*Le Sermon du bon pasteur*: Un Problème d'attribu tion', *BHR*, XXVII (1965), 286-303.
While acknowledging that its authorship cannot be determined with certain argues that the *Sermon* was probably the work of Almanque Papillon rathe than of CM. Prints critical ed. of the *Sermon* (see E39).

Mayer, C.A.: see also E34, F46, HH2, HS14, HS16, KA14.

Olivier, J.: see F51, 52.

G7   Pegg, Michael A., 'A Poem Wrongly Attributed to Clément Marot', *MLR*, LII (1957), 566-68.
The *Dieu gard de l'autheur à la ville et aux citoyens de Genève* which Droz and Plan tentatively attribute to CM (E32, p. 63) is in reality by Eustorg de Beaulieu and was published in his *Chrestienne resjouyssance* in 1546.

G8   Pelletier, A., 'Sur une épître attribuée à Marot', *N*, XXXIX (1955), 81-95.
Reaches the conclusion, independently of Mayer (*Bibliog. I*, pp. 53-56) and on different grounds, that CM is not the author of the *Coq à l'asne ... à Me Guillaume le Coq* ('Le Coq, mon amy et mon frère') which is

attributed to him in MS Lausanne M1016 and also by Droz and Plan (E32).

Plan, P.P.: see E32.

G9   Plattard, Jean, 'De l'authenticité de quelques "poésies inédites de Clément Marot"', *BSHP*, LXI (1912), 278-80.
Indicates that two of the poems attributed by Fromage to CM in E23 are by different authors, rejects the authenticity of a third, and shares Chavannes's doubts (in E10) concerning CM's authorship of 'Je pense bien que tu t'esbayras'. (This last poem is printed under the title '*Espitre de Marot*' in *OC*, I, pp. 288-91, but Mayer also regards its authenticity as suspect.)

G10   Plattard, Jean, 'De l'authenticité de quelques "poésies inédites de Clément Marot"', *RER*, X (1912), 68-71.
Same text as G9, except for slight changes at the beginning.

G11   Plattard, J., 'Deux epîtres inédites attribuées à Clément Marot', *RSS*, XVIII (1931), 217-22.
Doubts the authenticity of two epistles (here reprinted) – one addressed to François I ('Cuydant avoir receu, Sire, la somme'), the other to Anne de Montmorency ('Ce roy qui doit mieux estre que Pompée') – which appear, without the author's name, in MS BN f. fr. 12795, but are attributed by Guiffrey to CM in his ed. E17, V, pp. 345-50 (Plattard's doubts are also expressed there in a footnote on p. 345). (Mayer excludes both poems from *OC* as unauthentic – see *Bibliog. I*, p. 87.)

G12   Riemens, K.J., '*La Briefve Doctrine pour bien & deuëment escripre selon la proprieté du langaige françois*. (L'Édition d'Anvers. L'Auteur. Une Traduction néerlandaise)', *RSS*, XVII (1930), 146-57.
Maintains that CM contributed some passages to the *B.D.*, but hesitates to attribute the entire work to him; instead, credits Antoine Augereau with the lion's share. (The *B.D.* was published anonymously in 1533, but CM was named as the author in the 1540 ed. (*Bibliog. II*, no. 257). For Veyrin-Forrer's and Catach's support for Riemens's view, and Mayer's rejection of it, see F63 and G1.)

G13   Saulnier, Verdun L., 'Maurice Scève et l'épitaphe de Laure', *RLC*, XXIV (1950), 65-78.
Rejects attribution of the *huitain* 'En petit lieu compris vous povez veoir' to either François I or CM. The frequent attribution to François is based on a remark in Jean de Tournes's preface to his 1545 ed. of Petrarch; that to CM on the publication of the poem in Constantin's 1544 ed. of his *Œuvres* (*Bibliog. II*, no. 129): the remark may well have been misinterpreted,

the ed. is known to be an unreliable one. Saulnier tentatively ascribes the *huitain* to Scève. (Mayer unquestioningly accepts François's authorship in *OC*, V, p. 170, n. 3, without any discussion and without reference to this art.)

Saulnier, V.L.: see also HA85, HR11.

Screech, M.A.: see J28.

G14   Sturel, René, 'Poésies inédites de Marguerite de Navarre', *RSS*, II (1914), 149-68.
Speculates about the authorship of the rondeau *Du Vendredi sainct*, attributed to Marguerite in Thiboust's *Farrago*, but printed in the 1544 ed. of CM's *Œuvres*. (Sturel is evidently unaware that the poem (*OC*, IV, p. 97) had already appeared in the *Adolescence cl.*)

Vaganay, Hugues: see KB42.

Van Brabant, Luc: see HA100.

Veyrin-Forrer, Jeanne: see F63.

Villey, Pierre: see F68.

H. STUDIES OF MAROT'S WORKS

General studies (including all publications concerning more than one
of categories HB to HV)

*HA1   Akiyama, Haruo, 'Clément Marot et son exil en Italie', *Bulletin
d'Études Françaises de l'Université Chuo*, VII (1975), 1-39.
(Text in Japanese.)
Analysis of the poems written by CM during his exile. (See note to A7.)

HA2   Bailbé, Jacques, 'Le Thème de la vieille femme dans la poésie
satirique du seizième et du début du dix-septième siècles', *BHR*,
XXVI (1964), 98-119.

HA3   Bailey, John C., 'Marot', in his *The Claims of French Poetry:
Nine Studies in the Greater French Poets*, London: Constable,
1907, pp. 47-78
A highly favourable assessment. While not ignoring the serious side of CM's
poetry, with its 'definitely Protestant note', Bailey praises above all CM's
'incomparable ease' and 'irresistible charm'.

HA4   Balzac, Jean Louis Guez de, *Les Entretiens (1657)*. Éd. critique,
avec introduction, notes et documents inédits, établie par B.
Beugnot, STFM, Paris: Didier, 2 vols, 1972.
See 'Entretien XXXVIII: Du Style burlesque', II, pp. 497-504. Here, as
in many similar discussions in the classical period, the term 'burlesque'
embraces the 'style marotique', as well as the burlesque proper. Balzac's
objection to the 'style marotique' emerges clearly from the following
sentence: 'Est-il impossible de donner un spectacle aux sujets de Louis
quatorziesme, à moins que de remuër un fantosme, qui represente le regne
de François premier, à moins que d'evoquer l'âme de Clement Marot, et
de desenterrer une langue morte?' Later, Balzac criticizes CM's 'inconditos
sonos, frigidas argutias, et obsoletam barbari saeculi dicacitatem'.

HA5   Becker, Philipp August, *Clément Marots Liebeslyrik*, Kais.
Akademie der Wissenschaften in Wien, Philosophisch-Historische
Klasse, Sitzungsberichte, CLXXXIV, 5, Vienna: Hölder, 1917,
179 pp.

Arranges CM's amatory poems, irrespective of genre, into their supposed chronological order, with a view to tracing the course of his different sentimental attachments. The interest of such an undertaking is obvious, as is the risk of thereby forcing poems into imaginary patterns (cf. HK1). The anthology of CM's love poems occupies pp. 67-179.

HA6   Bellenger, Yvonne, 'Quelques poèmes autobiographiques au XVIe siècle: fiction et vérité', *SFr*, XXII (1978), 217-30.
For CM, the use of autobiographical details serves the purpose of *captatio benevolentiae*. The Pléiade poets, on the other hand, achieve this object by other means and reserve the personal tone for their more intimate compositions.

HA7   Bellenger, Yvonne, *Le Jour dans la poésie française au temps de la Renaissance*, Études Littéraires Françaises, II, Tübingen: Narr, 1979, 255 pp.
On CM, see esp. pp. 185-88.

HA8   Besant, Walter, 'La Famille Marot', in his *Studies in Early French Poetry*, London: Macmillan, 1868, pp. 248-87.

HA9   Boileau, Nicolas, *Œuvres diverses du sieur D[espréaux]*, *avec le 'Traité du sublime ou du merveilleux dans le discours'*, *traduit du grec de Longin*, Paris: Denys Thierry, 1574, 178 + 102 pp.
Lines 96-97 of the *chant premier* of *L'Art poëtique* read: 'Imitons de Marot l'élégant badinage, / Et laissons le Burlesque aux plaisans du Pont-Neuf.' The first of these lines is nearly always quoted out of context and its meaning consequently distorted. Contrary to common belief, Boileau is not singling out the only aspect of CM's poetry he deems successful and arrogantly dismissing the rest. He is unfavourably comparing the affectation, artificiality and 'bassesse' of the so-called 'style marotique' (a term often used almost synonymously with 'burlesque' − cf. HA4) with the natural grace and the wit of the Renaissance model. On Boileau, see also HA36.

HA10   Brockmeier, Peter, *Darstellungen der französischen Literaturgeschichte von Claude Fauchet bis Laharpe*, Deutsche Akademie der Wissenschaften zu Berlin, Schriftenreihe der Arbeitsgruppe zur Geschichte der deutschen und französischen Aufklärung, XVII, Berlin: Akademie Verlag, 1963, x + 287 pp.

HA11   Campenon, [F.N.V.], 'Sur Clément Marot, et sur les services qu'il a rendus à la langue', in E8, pp. v-xxviii.

Combines, in a revised version, the two studies published anonymously
in E5 and reprinted, at least in part, in different eds during the inter-
vening period. 'Le mérite de Marot c'est d'avoir le premier débrouillé
notre poésie naissante ... C'étoit beaucoup d'avoir montré aux écrivains
qui auroient été tentés de le suivre, que la grace du françois réside dans
une tournure facile, vive, serrée, et sur-tout claire et directe. Ce mérite
seul ne suffiroit pas à tous nos styles: il suffisoit, il suffira toujours aux
genres où excella Marot. Lui-même s'égare dans les sujets nobles ou
sérieux.'

HA12   Cary, Henry Francis, 'The Early French Poets: Cl. Marot',
       London Magazine, IV (1821), 587-93.
       Art. intended to introduce CM to English readers. A major part is
       devoted to a description of *Le Temple de Cupido* in which Cary discerns
       a strong resemblance to the style of Chaucer: CM 'has the same liveli-
       ness of fancy; the same rapidity and distinctness of pencil; the same arch-
       ness; the same disposition to satire; but he has all these generally in a
       less degree.'

HA13   Cary, Henry Francis, 'Clement Marot', in *The Early French
       Poets: A Series of Notices and Translations, by the late Rev.
       Henry Francis Cary* ..., London: Bohn, 1846, pp. 1-17.
       Reprint of HA12.

HA14   Chamard, Henri, 'Sur une page obscure de la *Deffence*', *RHLF*,
       IV (1897), 239-45.
       Argues that a passage in the *Deffence*, II. ii (lines 29-31 in Chamard's
       own later ed. for STFM, Paris: Didier, 1948), as well as certain state-
       ments elsewhere in Du Bellay's pamphlet, constitute fairly transparent
       attacks on CM. Cf. HA78.

HA15   Chamard, Henri, 'L'Invention de l'*ode* et le différend de Ronsard
       et de Du Bellay: Contribution à l'histoire de la Pléiade', *RHLF*,
       VI (1899), 21-54.
       Sixteenth-century disagreements as to who created the French ode (whether
       CM, Saint-Gelais, etc., or the Pléiade, esp. Ronsard) stem from different
       conceptions of the genre: 'un chant lyrique quelconque en mètres libres
       et variés' (according to Sebillet, Aneau), as against a definition based on
       classical models.

HA16   Chamard, Henri, *Histoire de la Pléiade*, Paris: Didier, 4 vols,
       1939-40.
       Numerous references to CM's works. See esp. 'Les Précurseurs de la
       Pléiade' I, pp. 138-43. Chamard shows that CM's achievements were

greater than the Pléiade acknowledged and that they encompassed types of poetry which it was to champion and develop.

HA17 Chamard, Henri, 'Lyrisme', in *DLF*, pp. 463-68.

HA18 Cohen, Gustave, 'L'Annonciateur de la Pléiade: Clément Marot', *Année Propédeutique*, I-II (1952), 12-24.

HA19 Cohen, Gustave, 'Clément Marot et le théâtre', *MRo*, II (1952), 14-19.
Text of a lecture. Cohen cites poems by CM referring to the contemporary theatre, e.g. the ballad *Des Enfans sans soucy* (*OC*, IV, pp. 139-40) and the epitaph *De Jehan Serre* (*OC*, IV, pp. 202-05). Inevitably a thin harvest

HA20 Cohen, Gustave, 'Clément Marot et le théâtre', in his *Études d'histoire du théâtre en France au moyen-âge et à la Renaissance*, Paris: Gallimard, 1956, pp. 346-53.
Reprint of HA19.

HA21 Conley, Tom, 'Verbal Shape in the Poetry of Villon and Marot', *Visible Language*, IX, 2 (1975), 101-22.
An unconvincing attempt to relate the text of certain poems to their visual form. Various factual errors and frequent misunderstandings of fifteenth and sixteenth-century French.

Cordonnier, Hyacinthe: see HA84.

HA22 Cremonesi, Carla, 'Clément Marot (1496-1544)', in her *Corso di letteratura francese: La poesia lirica francese tra Villon e Malherbe (Università degli Studi di Milano, Anno accademico 1960-61)*, Milan: La Goliardica, 1961, pp. 115-41.
A good general study.

HA23 Desfontaines, P.F. Guyot, 'Dix-neuvième lettre' and 'Vingt-unième lettre', *Le Nouvelliste du Parnasse; ou, Reflexions sur les ouvrages nouveaux*, see II (1731), 49-64, 97-108.
Review-art. on E4. Many caustic remarks about the style, prolixity and frequent irrelevance of Lenglet-Dufresnoy's observations. But Desfontaines welcomes the ed. of the text itself, because 'Marot ... merite, plus qu'aucun poëte ancien, d'être aujourd'hui lû et entendu de tous ceux qui ont quelque goût pour la poësie.'

HA24 *Les Deux Cents Plus Beaux Poèmes de la langue française (XIIIe au XIXe siècles) choisis par les auditeurs de la Radio-Télévision*

Française, présentés par Philippe Soupault et Jean Chouquet, Paris: Laffont, 1955, 436 pp.

Results of a survey conducted in June 1955, during which listeners were invited to indicate their preferences among five hundred selected poems. The 4200 replies received established CM in sixteenth place out of seventy in the poets' popularity table, just behind Boileau and directly ahead of Rimbaud – but a very long way behind the winner, Ronsard.

HA25 Doucet, J., 'Clément Marot (1497-1544), *ÉCla*, IX (1940), 419-37.

Competent, though not very searching, study of the rondeau *A ses amys apres sa delivrance* (*OC*, IV, pp. 133-34), the chanson 'Changeons propos, c'est trop chanté d'amours' (*OC*, III, pp. 200-01), and the epistle *Au roy, pour avoir esté desrobé*.

HA26 Dussault, [J.J.F.], '*Œuvres choisies* de Clément Marot', in *Annales littéraires; ou, Choix chronologique des principaux articles de littérature insérés par M. Dussault dans le 'Journal des Débats', depuis 1800 jusqu'à 1817 inclusivement*, recueillis et publiés par 'L'Auteur des *Mémoires historiques sur Louis XVII*' [i.e. Jean Eckart], Paris: Maradan, Eckart & Lenormant, 4 vols, 1818, I, pp. 198-204.

See HA111, of which this is a reprint. The corresponding Gregorian Calendar date is here erroneously given as 23 Sept. 1801.

HA27 [Duval, François], 'De l'usage où l'on est aujourd'hui d'écrire dans le style de Marot', in his *Nouveau choix de piéces de poësie*, Nancy, Paris: Witte, 2 vols, 1715, I, pp. xxxviii-xxxix.

'On trouvera en ce recueil beaucoup de piéces dans le goût de Marot. Elles ont fort la vogue. Notre façon d'imiter cet auteur, consiste dans un mélange de son tour, de quelques-uns de ses termes, et des expressions d'aujourd'hui.'

Du Verdier, Antoine: see F17.

HA28 Elsen, Claude, 'Clément Marot', in Arthur Adamov and others, *Tableau de la littérature française de Rutebeuf à Descartes*, Paris: Gallimard, 1962, pp. 199-203.

Considers CM 'l'un des ancêtres de la poésie la plus "pure" ... poète "professionnel" dont le dessein n'est rien moins que d'exprimer l'ineffable, de célébrer le mystère (joyeux ou tragique) de l'extase poétique, de communier ou de communiquer avec l'invisible ou le surréel ...'.

HA29 Faguet, Émile, 'Clément Marot', in his *Seizième siècle: Études*

littéraires, Paris: Lecène & Oudin, 1894, pp. 35-75.
A sound, well-balanced study, except for the absence of any literary appraisal of the psalm translations. Stresses that CM imparted a new vigour and brilliance to the French poetic language ('la précision, le tour net, le relief ferme ...') and that he was, with Ronsard and Malherbe, one of three architects of French classical poetry.

HA30 [Formey, Jean H.S.], *Conseils pour former une bibliothèque peu nombreuse, mais choisie*, 3ᵉ éd., corrigée et augmentée, Berlin: Haude & Spener, 1755, 122 pp.
'Les deux auteurs de ce tems-là, qui ont conservé le plus de reputation, sont les *Satyres* de Regnier, et les *Œuvres* de Clement Marot', (p. 50).

HA31 François, L., 'Sur Clément Marot', *Arts et Idées*, II, 12 (1937), 33-35.
A letter protesting against the excessive importance accorded by literary historians to this 'vil courtisan et poète mineur ... qui commença sa carrière par un plagiat du *Roman de la Rose* et composa une œuvre sans sincérité, sans harmonie et sans profondeur'. The editor observes soothingly 'Que notre correspondant se console. Marot est aimé par ceux qui lui ressemblent.'

HA32 Françon, Marcel, 'A propos de *L'Enfer*; Essai de mise au point', *Lingue Straniere*, XI, 3 (1962), 16-18.
Believes that only *L'Enfer* and the epistle *A Monsieur Bouchart* may refer to CM's imprisonment in 1526, and that the rondeaux *De l'inconstance de Ysabeau* and *A ses amys apres sa delivrance*, the ballad *Contre celle qui fut s'amye*, and the *Epistre à son amy Lyon* may none of them have been written until after CM had been accused in 1532 of eating bacon in Lent. See also HA35.

HA33 Françon, Marcel, 'Lyrisme et technique poétique', in his 'Deux notes d'un seiziémiste', *FS*, XXII (1968), 99-106 (100-06).
Maintains that the term 'lyrique', when applied to poems in the sixteenth century, characterized not the subject, but the technique employed. It designated a poem capable of being set to music, and thus usually implied uniform versification in all stanzas. Accordingly, Françon contests Mayer's application of the term in *OC*, III to poems not in that category, and criticizes his classification of CM's works.

HA34 Françon, Marcel, 'Clément Marot et les genres à forme fixe', *SFr*, XII (1968), 279-81.
Contains various critical remarks about *OC*, IV.

HA35 Françon, Marcel, 'A propos de *L'Enfer* de Clément Marot', *RQ*, XXII (1969), 229-33.
Summary of position taken up in HA32.

HA36 Françon, Marcel, 'Boileau, critique de Clément Marot', *RoN*, XIV (1972-73), 317-18.
On Boileau's erroneous statement that CM wrote triolets, and on how he may have come to make it.

Françon, Marcel: see also C58.

HA37 Gaillard, [G.H.], *Histoire de François premier, roi de France, dit le grand roi et le pere des lettres*, 2ᵉ éd., revue, corrigée et augmentée, Paris: Saillant & Nyon, 8 vols, 1769.
On CM's poetry, see VIII, pp. 24-36; on his life, VIII, pp. 68-78. 'Marot fut, avant [La Fontaine], non pas le plus naïf de tous nos poëtes, car ils n'étoient tous que trop naïfs avant Marot, qui souvent l'est trop lui-même, mais celui qui sut le mieux être naïf avec décence; voilà ... le changement qu'il fit dans la langue; c'est moins un changement qu'un perfectionnement.'

HA38 Gendre, André, *Ronsard, poète de la conquête amoureuse*, Neuchâtel: La Baconnière, 1970, 572 pp.

HA39 Giraud, Yves, 'Clément Marot et les Amours d'Anne: *Membra disjecta* d'un *canzoniere*', *AION (SR)*, XIV (1972), 337-61.
Cautiously reconstructs – after Lefranc (C91) and Becker (HA5) but using a different classification of the material – the poetic history of CM's attachment to Anne d'Alençon: 'passion, ou ... divertissement ... badinage? Le vrai est à mi-chemin, sans nul doute, mais plutôt du côté de la passion.'

HA40 Griffin, Robert, *Clément Marot and the Inflections of Poetic Voice*, Berkeley: Univ. of California Press, 1974, 322 pp.
Aims to correct the type of criticism which fuses – and confuses – CM's poetic persona with his historical one. Sets out 'to isolate the role of the poet in his poetry'. Part I ('Form') examines CM's adaptations of medieval themes and forms, his stylistic techniques and his versification. Part II ('Reform') studies CM's reactions to contemporary religious trends and stresses the difficulty of determining his precise standpoint. Part III ('Formlessness') seeks to establish 'his uniquely personal contribution to literary speech', focusing on, among other things, the role of irony and satire in his works.
A very interesting study, though more satisfying in part than as a whole.

Among its undoubted merits: many suggestive, often illuminating, observations; various good, detailed analyses of individual poems. But the presentation is rather formless, the style at times turgid. The uniformly ferocious denigration of the Rhétoriqueurs makes one wonder about the validity of certain other critical judgements, esp. those bearing on late medieval influences on CM. On the whole, though, a thoroughly stimulating book.

Rev.: .1 Donaldson-Evans, Lance K., *FrF*, I (1976), 185-86.
.2 Kalwies, Howard H., *BHR*, XXXVII (1975), 482-84.
.3 Lloyd-Jones, K., *EsC*, XVIII, 1 (1978), 92-93.
.4 Rigolot, François, *FR*, XLIX (1975-76), 609-10.
.5 Weinberg, Florence M., *RR*, LXXI (1980), 200-01.
.6 Williams, Annwyl, *Lettera*, no. 14 (1977), 122-33.

HA41 Henriot, Émile, 'Marot amoureux', in his *Poètes français, de Turold à André Chénier*, Lyons: Lardanchet, [1944], pp. 46-51.
Reprint of an agreeably-written art. on CM's poems inspired by 'Anne'. The publication in which it originally appeared in 1935 is not identified.

HA42 Hervier, Marcel, 'Clément Marot (1497-1544)', in his *Les Écrivains français jugés par leurs contemporains*, I: *Seizième siècle, dix-septième siècle*, Paris: Mellottée, s.d., pp. 1-12.
Quotes remarks by Du Bellay, Pasquier, Scévole de Sainte-Marthe, and others.

HA43 Heylbut, Rose, *English Opinions of French Poetry, 1660-1750*, New York: Columbia UP, 1923, xi + 103 pp.
Cites a few references to CM.

*HA44 Ito, Susumu, 'Clément Marot et la brunette: Un Problème d'histoire littéraire', *BFLACU*, XX (1979), 673-714. (Text in Japanese.)
CM's choice of the brunette in preference to the traditional blonde had three literary causes: colour symbolism; the celebrated statement 'Nigra sum sed formosa' in the Song of Songs; and Anti-Petrarchism (or the influence of popular literature, esp. songs). (See note to A7.) Cf. J8.

*HA45 James, Margaret Anne, 'La Nature dans la poésie de Clément Marot', Ph. D. thesis, Univ. of Liverpool, 1968, 455 pp.

*HA46 Jordan, Nicole Amon, 'Des Couleurs et des signes: Essai sur la symbolique des couleurs chez quelques auteurs du moyen âge et de la Renaissance', Ph. D. thesis, Univ. of California at

Berkeley, 1975, 206 pp. *DisA*, XXXVII (1976-77), 361A.
Studies the development of colour symbolism in the early periods. 'The second chapter focuses on three poets of the medieval tradition: Guillaume de Machaut, Charles d'Orléans, and Clément Marot. With the help of representative texts we describe how each one has created a mood by pursuing a particular color while remaining faithful to the tradition they represent.'

HA47 Katz, Richard A., 'The Lyricism of Clément Marot', in *From Marot to Montaigne: Essays on French Renaissance Literature*, ed. by Raymond C. La Charité, *KRQ*, XIX (1972), Suppl. I, 21-35.
Distinguishes two aspects in CM's lyric poetry: on the one hand, as exemplified by his earlier compositions, a 'poetry deriving its essential characteristics from a fairly limited body of accepted modes, disciplined by the exigencies of music and manifesting its originality ... only through stylistic variation'; on the other hand, more evident in his later verse, 'poetry as unique subjective utterance, the rhythms of which are dictated by the poet's sentience'.

HA48 Kinch, Charles E., *La Poésie satirique de Clément Marot*, Paris: Boivin, [1940], ix + 286 pp.
Argues that CM, though often successful as a satirist, was not a great one. Separate chapters are devoted to *L'Enfer* and each of the different genres containing satirical elements. The commentaries are mostly descriptive rather than analytical, and there is no discussion of the language, style, rhetorical devices, etc.

La Croix du Maine: see F34.

HA49 La Harpe, J.F., *Lycée; ou, Cours de littérature ancienne et moderne*, Paris, 14 vols, 1818.
On CM, see IV, pp. 90-105. 'Le nom de Marot est la première époque vraiment remarquable dans l'histoire de notre poésie, bien plus par le talent qui brille dans ses ouvrages et qui lui est particulier, que par les progrès qu'il fit faire à notre versification, qui furent très lents et peu sensibles depuis lui jusqu'à Malherbe.' Suggests replacing 'l'élégant badinage' by 'le charmant badinage' in Boileau's famous line (HA9). As for CM's psalms, '[ils] ne sont bons qu'à être chantés dans les églises protestantes.'

HA50 [La Porte, Joseph de], *Nouvelle bibliothèque d'un homme de goût; ou, Tableau de la littérature ancienne et moderne, étrangère et nationale ...*, Paris, 4 vols, 1777.
On CM, see II, pp. 235-36, 247-48. CM 'a sur-tout réussi dans le genre épigrammatique ... Les juges les plus sévères seront forcés de convenir

qu'il avoit beaucoup d'agrément et de fécondité dans l'imagination. S'il avoit vécu de nos jours, le goût la lui auroit réglée.'

HA51 La Sorinière, M. de, 'Réflexions sur l'abus et le mauvais usage que l'on fait du style marotique ...', *MF*, XLII (1742), 1356-61.

Leblanc, P.: see J12.

Lefranc, Abel: see C91,92.

HA52 Lenient, C., 'Marot et l'école gauloise', *Revue des Cours Littéraires de la France et de l'Étranger*, VI (1868-69), 802-09.

HA53 Lenient, C., *La Satire en France; ou, La Littérature militante au XVIe siècle*, 3e éd. revue et corrigée, Paris: Hachette, 2 vols, 1886.
On CM, see I, pp. 25-40. Amusingly, though rather fancifully, depicts CM as a harum-scarum, 'véritable enfant terrible, dont les coups de tête et les malices désespéraient ses protecteurs comme ses ennemis ... Vive et capricieuse abeille égarée sans lest au milieu de la tourmente du seizième siècle.' A bee, moreover, which constantly used its sting to spread mild satirical venom throughout the poems. In *L'Enfer*, the dose is evidently stronger. As for the coq-à-l'âne, it was tailor-made for CM: 'Ces sauts perpétuels ... ces mille étincelles qui brillent et jaillissent deça, delà, comme autant de feux follets, ce gaspillage puéril des qualités les plus précieuses, sont l'image fidèle de la vie et du talent de Marot.'

Lerber, Walther de: see L35.

HA54 Lloyd-Jones, Kenneth, 'Une "Supercherie" de Marot', *SFr*, XXII (1978), 369-73.
Believes that the ballad *A ma dame la duchesse d'Alençon* ... (*OC*, IV, pp. 145-47) may have been written in the same year, 1528, as the original version of the poem, addressed to the Comte d'Étampes. As for the epistle *Au révérendissime Cardinal de Lorraine* (*OC*, I, pp. 144–47), likewise written in 1528, it appears to be modelled on the *Epistre du despourveu* of 1519, in form as well as content.

Lutkus, Anne Dougherty: see J15.

HA55 Mallet, E., *Principes pour la lecture des poëtes*, Paris: Durand, 2 vols, 1745.
On CM and the 'style marotique', see I, pp. 50-58. 'Ses ouvrages sont entre les mains de tout le monde, et quoique tous ne soient pas de la

même force, on y reconnoit néanmoins par tout un air de liberté, un génie aisé qui les tire du pair ...'

*HA56 Mayer, C.A., 'Satire in French Literature from 1525 to 1560, with Particular Reference to the Sources and the Technique', Ph. D. thesis, Univ. of London, 1949, 604 pp.

HA57 Mayer, C.A., 'Les Œuvres de Clément Marot: L'Économie de l'édition critique', *BHR*, XXIX (1967), 357-72.
On the problems of classification facing an editor of CM's works. An essential art. for understanding the reasons for the system adopted by Mayer in *OC*, which, he claims, broadly conforms to CM's intentions.

HA58 Mayer, C.A., 'Clément Marot and Literary History', in *Studies in French Literature Presented to H.W. Lawton ...*, ed. by J.C. Ireson, I.D. McFarlane, and Garnet Rees, Manchester: Manchester UP, 1968, pp. 247-60.
Contends that in CM's case, later value judgements have been based entirely on mistaken literary history. Points out, as other modern critics have done, the falseness of various traditional judgements. In this connection quotes Boileau (but out of context — see HA9).

HA59 Mayer, C.A., 'Clément Marot et ses protecteurs', in *Culture et pouvoir au temps de l'humanisme et de la Renaissance: Actes du Congrès Marguerite de Savoie, Annecy, Chambéry, Turin, 29 avril-4 mai 1974*, publiés par Louis Terreaux, Geneva: Slatkine, 1978, pp. 259-70.
CM was not just a court poet, nor can his literary innovations or intellectual attitudes simply be attributed to trends prevailing at court. His finest achievements are manifestly due to his own genius.

Mayer, C.A.: see also F41, 45.

HA60 Mensch, Jos., *Das Tier in der Dichtung Marots*, Münchener Beiträge zur Romanischen und Englischen Philologie, XXXVI, Leipzig: Deichert (Böhme), 1906, 100 pp.
Examines the introduction of animals into the poems, either for external reasons (as part of the setting) or internal ones (to enhance the tone). In the second and more interesting section, studies CM's use of animals for purposes of comparison and allegory.

Mills-Pont, Jeanne Dorothée: see M3.

Muller, A.: see J21.

HA61 Naïs, Hélène, *Les Animaux dans la poésie française de la Renaissance*, Paris: Didier, 1961, 718 pp.

*HA62 Natori, Seiichi, 'Sur le classement des pièces funéraires de Clément Marot', *Bulletin de la Société Japonaise de Littérature Française*, 1956, 2-8. (Text in Japanese.)
On CM's likely reasons for dividing these poems into four categories and on the characteristic features of each group: 'L'épitaphe nous montre le poète burlesque ou satirique, le cimetière le poète banal, la complainte le poète rhétoriqueur, enfin l'élégie le poète lyrique' (from Ito's summary see note to A7).

*HA63 Natori, Seiichi, 'François Ier et Clément Marot', *Journal of Social Sciences and Humanities* (Tokyo Municipal University), XXIV (1961), 19-39. (Text in Japanese.)
Examines the poems written by CM during his first exile. Both before and after the *affaire des placards*, CM portrayed François as the ideal sovereign. (See note to A7.)

*HA64 Natori, Seiichi, 'Clément Marot et "faute de pécune"', *Littérature Française de la Renaissance*, I (1963), 25-40. (Text in Japanese.)
The poems written by CM in 1527-28 with the aim of securing the post of *valet de chambre* show certain medieval influences, but at the same time prove his superiority over the Rhétoriqueurs. (See note to A7.)

*HA65 Natori, Seiichi, 'Sur les thèmes des pièces exclues de la première édition de l'*Adolescence clémentine*', *Littérature Française de la Renaissance*, III (1967), 21-62. (Text in Japanese.)
Argues that CM excluded those poems which were likely to displease readers at Court and might therefore have endangered his position. (See note to A7.)

HA66 Noo, Hendrik de, *Thomas Sebillet et son 'Art poétique françoys' rapproché de la 'Deffence et illustration de langue françoyse' de Joachim Du Bellay*, Utrecht: Beijers, 1927, xi + 162 pp.

HA67 Pasquier, Étienne, *Les Œuvres d'Estienne Pasquier, contenant ses 'Recherches de la France'* ..., Amsterdam: Compagnie des Libraires Associez, 2 vols, 1723.
The following passages seem to have been the direct source for later commentators' belief that (i) CM was helped by Vatable in his psalm translations, and (ii) CM was responsible for the 1526 ed. of the *Roman de la Rose*.

In *Les Recherches de la France*, VII.v: 'quant à Clement Marot, ses œuvres furent recueillies favorablement de chacun. Il avoit une veine grandement fluide, un vers non affecté, un sens fort bon ... Bref, jamais livre ne fut tant vendu que le sien, je n'en excepteray un tout seul, de ceux qui ont eu la vogue depuis luy ... Mais entre ses inventions je trouve le livre de ses épigrammes trés plaisant. Et entre ses traductions il se rendit admirable en celle des cinquante pseaumes de David, aidé de Vatable, professeur du roy ès lettres hébraïques ...' (I, col. 700).

In *Les Recherches de la France*, VII.iii (on the *Roman de la Rose* and its two authors): 'Clément Marot les voulut faire parler le langage de nostre temps, afin d'inviter les esprits flouëts à la lecture de ce roman' (I, col. 690). In *Les Recherches de la France*, VIII.iii: 'Voyez les anciennes coppies de leur [Guillaume de Lorris's and Jean de Meung's] roman et les parangonnez au langage que Clement Marot leur donna du temps du Roy François premier, vous en direz tout autant [that it is a translation]. Vray que par une grande prudence il y voulut laisser quelques vieilles traces en la fin de plusieurs vers, pour ne sortir du tout des termes de la venerable ancienneté' (I, col. 762). In *Les Recherches de la France*, VIII.iii: 'Chacun se fait accroire que la langue vulgaire de son temps est la plus parfaite et chacun est en cecy trompé.' Pasquier then rejects the argument that 'Lorry [Guillaume de Lorris] mesmes, et Clopinel [Jean de Meung] fussent aussi au tombeau: si Marot ne les en eust garentis par le langage de nostre temps qu'il leur donna' (I, col. 765). *Les Lettres*, II.vi: *A Monsieur Cujas ...* Stressing the merits of reading foreign texts in the original rather than in translation, and earlier French texts in the original rather than in a modernized version, Pasquier writes: 'il n'y a homme docte entre nous qui ... n'embrasse le *Roman de la Rose*, lequel à la mienne volonté, que par une bigarrure de langage vieux et nouveau, Clément Marot n'eust voulu habiller à la moderne françoise' (II, col. 38).

For an annotated ed. of this letter, see *Estienne Pasquier: Choix de lettres sur la littérature, la langue et la traduction*, publiées et annotées par D. Thickett, TLF, LXX, Geneva: Droz, 1956, pp. 124-30. Thickett dates the letter at May to Nov. 1576.

HA68   Patterson, Warner Forrest, *Three Centuries of French Poetic Theory: A Critical History of the Chief Arts of Poetry in France (1328-1630)*, Univ. of Michigan Publications, Language and Literature, XIV-XV, Ann Arbor: Univ. of Michigan Press, 2 vols, 1935.

On CM, see esp. 'The School of Marot', I, pp. 233-90. Primarily a detailed examination of Sebillet's *Art poétique françois*. In this connection, various aspects of CM's works are appraised, at a fairly superficial level.

HA69   Pauphilet, Albert, *Clément Marot*, Cours de Sorbonne, Certificat

d'Études Supérieures de Littérature Française, Paris: Centre
de Documentation Universitaire, 1936, 2 vols.
Succinct comments on a number of CM's poems.

HA70 Plattard, Jean, *Clément Marot (1518)*, Cours de Sorbonne,
Agrégation et Certificat d'Études Supérieures de Littérature
Française, Paris: Centre de Documentation Universitaire, 2
vols, 1938.
Detailed analysis of the *Epistre du despourveu*, *L'Enfer*, the epistle *Au
roy, pour le deslivrer de prison*, the *Epistre au roy, du temps de son
exil à Ferrare*, *Le Dieu gard à la court de France*, and the *Eglogue au
roy, soubz les noms de Pan et Robin*.

Prescott, Anne Lake: see C117, 118.

HA71 Prévot, Georges, 'Clément Marot est-il normand?', *Grande
Revue*, CXII (1923), 293-306.
Neither the content and language of CM's poetry, nor his temperament,
justify one in counting him among the poets of Normandy rather than
of Quercy, as Ch. Th. Féret did in his anthology of Norman poetry (1920
Above all, though, CM belongs to the French tradition.

HA72 Richter, Mario, 'Considerazioni e proposte per una storia della
poesia lirica francese nel secolo XVI', *Ae*, XLIV (1970), 72-11!
On CM, see pp. 76-80.

HA73 Richter, Mario, 'Introduzione', in his *La poesia lirica in Francia
nel secolo XVI*, Milan: Istituto Editoriale Cisalpino, 1971, pp.
7-51.
Reprint of HA72. On CM, see pp. 10-14.

HA74 Riniker, Rudolf, *Die Preziosität der französischen Renaissance-
poesie (nach den Dichtungen von Cl. Marot, Sainct-Gelais,
Ronsard, Belleau, Magny und Desportes)*, Zurich, 1898, 127 pp
Cursory, but quite interesting, card-index type study which focuses prima
on metaphors, and on Renaissance interpretations and uses of classical my
logy. Many references to CM.

HA75 Robert, Jules, 'Les Plagiaires (Seizième siècle): Clément Marot',
France Littéraire, XXXVII (1840), 65-73.
Equates imitation with plagiarism and largely ignores poetic recreation:
'*Je suis fou de mon Marot* quand il est lui-même original, naïf ... Je préfè
une faible épigramme de lui à une excellente renouvelée de Martial.' It
is ironic that Robert's idea of the perfect Marot should be the *Dialogue*

de deux amoureux which may not be by CM (cf. *OC*, III, pp. 50-51).

HA76 Rouillard, Clarence Dana, *The Turk in French History, Thought, and Literature (1520-1660)*, Paris: Boivin, 1940, 700 pp.
On CM, see pp. 602-03.

HA77 Roustan, M., *La Littérature française par la dissertation: 605 sujets proposés ...*, Paris: Delaplane, 4 vols, s.d.
On CM, see IV, pp. 58-63.

HA78 Roy, E., 'Charles Fontaine et ses amis: Sur une page obscure de la *Deffence*', *RHLF*, IV (1897), 412-22.
Agrees with Chamard (HA12) that CM is the first of the unnamed poets criticized by Du Bellay at the beginning of the *Deffence*, II.ii.

HA79 S[abatier] de Castres, 'Marot (Clément)', in his *Les Trois Siecles de la littérature françoise; ou, Tableau de l'esprit de nos écrivains, depuis François I jusqu'à nos jours*, 5e éd., corrigée et augmentée considérablement, The Hague: Gosse Junior, 4 vols, 1778, III, p. 237.
'Le plus ancien des poëtes françois, dont la lecture soit capable de procurer encore quelque plaisir ... Ses poésies sont legeres, agréables, délicates, et surtout d'une finesse qui plaît infiniment aux personnes de goût.' On CM's psalm translations: 'Le peuple protestant a pu chanter quelques tems ces cantiques bizarrement travestis, mais le bon sens a toujours rejetté des productions, où le naïf s'efforce en vain d'atteindre au sublime qui n'a rien de commun avec lui.'

HA80 Sainéan, L., 'Un Chapitre d'histoire littéraire', in his 'Mélanges du XVIe siècle', *RSS*, II (1914), 331-66 (350-60).
Cites, among the 'rudiments' of literary history published in the sixteenth century, certain passages from the *Galliade* of Guy Le Fèvre de la Boderie and Du Bartas's *Seconde semaine*, which contain highly appreciative references to CM's poetry.

HA81 Sainte-Beuve, C.A., *Tableau historique et critique de la poésie française et du théâtre français au seizième siècle*, Paris: Sautelet, 1828, 396 pp.
On CM, see pp. 19-39. Notwithstanding certain classical influences, CM remains essentially the disciple of his French predecessors: 'il représente la vieille poésie française dans sa plus grande pureté'. He was not a poet of genius: 'Une causerie facile, semée par intervalles de mots vifs et fins, est presque le seul mérite qui le distingue ... .' Sainte-Beuve confines himself almost entirely to CM's lighter verse.

HA82 Sainte-Marthe, Scévole de, 'Clemens Marotus', in his *Gallorum doctrina illustrium, qui nostra patrumque memoria floruerunt, elogia. Recens aucta ...*, Poitiers: J. Blanchet, 1602, pp. 23-24.
Tribute includes the following: 'Hoc certe Galliae praestitisti, quod cum illius temporis scriptores sermone uterentur tam impuro, ut nec intelligi possent, primus in meliorem apte et dilucide loquendi viam ingressus es.'

HA83 Sainte-Marthe, Scévole de, 'Clement Marot', in *Eloges des hommes illustres, qui depuis un siecle ont fleury en France dans la profession des lettres. Composez en latin par Scevole de Saint-Marthe, et mis en françois par G. Colletet*, Paris: Antoine de Sommaville, Augustin Courbe, François Langlois, 1644, pp. 65-6₆
See HA82.

HA84 Saint-Hyacinthe, Thémiseul de [pseud. of Hyacinthe Cordonnier *Le Chef-d'œuvre d'un inconnu. Poëme heureusement découvert et mis au jour, avec des remarques savantes et recherchées, par M. le Docteur Chrisostome Matanasius* [i.e. Saint-Hyacinthe], The Hague: La Compagnie, 1732.
Prints various quotations from Renaissance poets, esp. CM.

HA85 Saulnier, V.L., 'Charles Quint traversant la France: ce qu'en dirent les poètes français', in *Les Fêtes de la Renaissance*, II: *Fêtes et cérémonies au temps de Charles Quint. IIe Congrès de l'Association Internationale des Historiens de la Renaissance (2e section), Bruxelles, Anvers, Gand, Liège, 2-7 septembre 1957.* Études ... réunies et présentées par Jean Jacquot, Paris: Centre Nationale de la Recherche Scientifique, 1960, pp. 214-16.
On poems by CM, see pp. 214-16. However, of the five poems listed by Saulnier, only *Clement Marot sur la venue de l'empereur en France* (here titled *Sur l'entrée de l'empereur à Paris*) is regarded by Mayer as undoubtedly authentic (*OC*, III, pp. 302-04). The authenticity of *A l'empereur* Mayer regards as 'probable or very probable' (V, pp. 61, 74, 270), that of *Marot à l'empereur* as doubtful (III, pp. 47-49, 59, 366-67); he rejects *L'Adieu de France à l'empereur* as unauthentic (IV, pp. 41, 50), and attributes *France à l'empereur à son arrivée* to Salel (III, p. 49).

HA86 Schérer, Edmond, 'Clément Marot', in his *Études sur la littérature contemporaine*, Paris: Lévy, 10 vols, 1863-95, VIII (1885), pp. 1-18.
Points out that there is a serious note to CM's poetry, quite apart from

the psalm translations. But considers that the vast majority of his poems are devoid of literary value, and interesting solely as historical or linguistic documents: 'On le connaît suffisamment quand on a lu l'épître à son ami Lion Jamet et ses requêtes à François Ier ... .'

HA87 Schutz, A.H., *Vernacular Books in Parisian Private Libraries of the Sixteenth Century According to the Notarial Inventories*, Univ. of North Carolina Studies in the Romance Languages and Literatures, XXV, Chapel Hill: Univ. of North Carolina Press, 1955, 88 pp.
On CM, see p. 56.

HA88 Scudéry, M[r] de [i.e. Madeleine de], *Clélie, histoire romaine*, Pt IV, 2, Paris: Augustin Courbé, 1660.
Contains this 'prophetic' tribute to CM: 'Il y aura tousjours du bon sens dans sa plus folle raillerie, et des choses plaisantes dans ses plus graves discours ... Ce poète aura l'avantage d'estre imité par tous les poëtes qui voudront estre plaisants, et d'estre pourtant tousjours inimitable.'

HA89 [Scudéry, Madeleine de], *Conversations sur divers sujets*, Paris: Claude Barbin, 2 vols, 1684.
The *Histoire du comte d'Albe* (II, pp. 595-999) contains a section entitled in the table of contents – but not in the text itself – 'De la poësie françoise, jusques à Henry huitiéme [sic]'. This section offers a passage on CM (pp. 779-80) very similar to the one cited in HA88. (For a modern ed. of this section, see *Madeleine de Scudéry, 'De la poësie françoise jusques à Henry Quatrième'*. Éd. ornée d'un portrait frontispice, avec une introduction et des notes par G. Michaut, Petite Bibliothèque Surannée, Paris: Sansot, 1907, 111 pp.)

HA90 [Sebillet, Thomas], *Art poétique françois. Pour l'instruction des jeunes studieus, et encor peu avancez en la poésie françoise*, Paris: Arnoul l'Angelier, or Gilles Corrozet, 1548.
Though by no means a hidebound traditionalist, Sebillet stresses the importance of the lessons to be learnt from earlier French writers. Very numerous references to CM, who is frequently cited as the model to follow; many quotations from his poems. The Pléiade's opposition to various ideas expressed by Sebillet did not prevent the success of the *Art poétique* which was reprinted six times during the next thirty years. For a modern ed., see *Thomas Sebillet, Art poétique françoys*. Éd. critique, avec une introduction et des notes, publiée par Félix Gaiffe, STFM, Paris: Cornély, 1910, xxvi + 226 pp.

HA91 Sepet, Marius, *Les Maîtres de la poésie française*, Tours: Mame,

1898, 360 pp.
On CM, see pp. 129-35.

Silver, Isidore: see M6, 7.

HA92 Sleidanus, Johannes, *De statu religionis et reipublicae, Carolo Quinto, Caesare, commentarii*, [Strasbourg: W. Rihel's Heirs, 1555].
On CM, see fol. 237r°-v°. Sleidanus warmly praises CM's poetry, and esp. the psalms 'qui ... non sine summi ingenii admiratione leguntur, nihil enim est illius oratione suavius, nihil purius, nihil illustrius, nihil magis proprium et concinnum.' (The encomium is reproduced in full in HA95 by Telle, who mistakenly states that it was not added until a later ed.)

HA93 Sleidanus, Johannes (Sleidan, Jean), *Histoire de l'estat de la religion et republique, sous Charles V* [tr. by Robert Le Prevost], [Geneva]: Jean Crespin, 1557.
The passage on CM (see HA92) is on fol. 239r°. It is reproduced in HA95.

*HA94 Sonier, Joseph Ivan, 'Clément Marot courtisan-poète: Étude de sa poésie personnelle', Ph. D. thesis, Univ. of Illinois at Urbana-Champaign, 1972, 150 pp. *DisA*, XXXIII (1972-73), 331A.
'This study ... establishes the symbiotic relationship between the poet's life and his work ... An analysis of his poems shows how, very early, he was able to create a literary poetic persona by the use of converging linguistic factors which constitute the famous 'style marotique' ... and through the establishment of the poetic persona, the poem becomes the medium for the special relationship that existed between the courtier-poet and the king.'

Spiker, Claud Carl: see J29.

HA95 Telle, Émile V., 'L'Éloge de Clément Marot par Sleidan', *SFr*, XII (1968), 469-71.
See HA92, 93. Telle reproduces the complete text of the encomium in Latin and in Le Prévost's tr.

HA96 Théret, Auguste, 'François Habert', in his *Littérature du Berry. Poésie: Les XVI, XVII et XVIIImes siècles ...* Paris, 1898, pp. 7-147.
On Habert's admiration for CM and on his literary indebtedness to the

latter, see 'Habert et Marot', pp. 10-21.

HA97 Thierry, André, 'Errata de l'édition Garnier-Flammarion des *Œuvres poétiques* de Marot', *RHR*, no. 6 (1977), 17.
A short list of corrections to E42.

HA98 Thiry, Claude J., 'Sur la date de deux œuvres de Clément Marot', *MRo*, XVI (1966), 111-16.
CM's celebrated discussion with Lemaire de Belges about the 'couppes femenines' could have taken place only in late 1511, or in the spring of 1512, or in early 1514. According to the preface of the *Adolescence cl.*, CM had translated Virgil's first eclogue before their meeting; the tr. must therefore have been completed at the latest by 1514. It was probably finished already by May 1512, since the second of the three possible dates for the meeting is the most likely. (But this last assumption — which could nonetheless be correct — is here based partly on the perhaps too confident assertion that the *Jugement de Minos* and *Temple de Cupido* 'ont pu être datés avec certitude de 1514'.) Thiry suggests further that, judged on purely literary considerations, the *Dialogue de deux amoureux* is more likely to have been written shortly before its publication in 1541 than in CM's youth. (Unlike Mayer — see *OC*, III, pp. 50-51 — Thiry does not question the authenticity of the *Dialogue*.)

HA99 Thiry, Claude J., 'La Jeunesse littéraire de Clément Marot', *RLV*, XXXIV (1968), 436-60, 567-78.
CM's gradual progress towards greater originality should not be thought to imply his rejection of late medieval rhetoric. The mediocrity of his earlier works is due to his uninspired and inexpert efforts to imitate the Rhétoriqueurs by concentrating entirely on external features of their poetry. Between 1519 and 1526-27, however, he achieves an increasingly well-balanced synthesis of traditional rhetoric and Renaissance humanism. A thoughtful, enlightening study.

HA100 Van Brabant, Luc, *Présence de Louïze Labé au cœur de l'œuvre de Clément Marot*, Coxyde: Éditions de la Belle sans sy, 1969, 261 pp.
Develops the thesis of C139 in eight studies which offer further striking examples of Van Brabant's highly imaginative decoding of CM's poems through anagrammatic and homophonic readings. The first essay is a reprint of HH8. The others: (ii) 'De l'authenticité de l'épître de Clément Marot au seigneur du Pavillon les Lorris et de l'itinéraire de sa fuite après l'affaire des Placards': argues, mainly against Mayer (*OC*, I, pp. 57-60), for accepting the authenticity of this epistle (I, pp. 283-86); (iii) 'Des rimes équivoquées dans les coq-à-l'âne de Clément Marot'; (iv) 'Clément

Marot et dame Anne Philethime: *Épttre de Frippelippes*': Anne 'qui aime le thym' = Louise Labé; (v) 'Clément Marot et la belle sans si: Épître *A la royne de Navarre*': in this poem (*OC*, I, pp. 243-51) the expression 'la belle sans si' = 'Labé sans sille', where *sille* means either 'sail of a ship' or 'mockery', hence two possible interpretations: either 'Labé sans voile, c'est à dire dévoilée' or 'c'est sans aucune idée de moquerie ... que [CM] met la beauté, la noblesse de cœur, l'intelligence et l'esprit de Louïze au-dessus de tout' (in either case, CM is making it clear that he is referring to Louise Labé); (vi) 'La Secrète Vengeance de Clément Marot dans l'*Epistre de madame la daulphine escripvant à madame Marguerite*': CM, in this poem, informs Catherine of her husband's affair with Louise; (vii) 'Le Message secret de Clément Marot dans l'*Epistre au roy, du temps de son exil à Ferrare*'; (viii) 'Louïze Labé et les élégies *Seiziesme* et *Dixseptiesme* de Clément Marot': an analysis of the astrological aspects of these poems (in *OC*, III, elegies XV and XVI) which, it is claimed, throws new light on CM's relationship with Louise Labé.
Rev.: .1 Giraud, Yves, *BHR*, XXXII (1970), 220-22.

HA101   Van Roosbroeck, Gustave L., 'Un Débat sur Marot au XVIIIe siècle', *RSS*, IX (1922), 281-85.
Prints the Marquis de la Fare's reply (from MS BN f. fr. 15029) to Anthony Hamilton's attack on the 'style marotique', to which the Abbé Chaulieu likewise responded.

HA102   Villey, Pierre, 'Recherches sur la chronologie des œuvres de Marot', *BBB* (1920), 185-209, 238-49; (1921), 49-61, 101-17, 171-88, 226-52, 273-87; (1922), 263-71, 311-17, 372-88, 423-32; (1923), 48-54.
An admirable study, erudite, meticulous, well-documented. Villey corrects numerous errors in dating made by earlier commentators, demonstrates the unsoundness of certain theses (e.g. Fromage's assumption in C66 of the existence of an 'Isabeau' cycle), points out the inconclusiveness of the evidence for CM's presence at Pavia. In an appendix Villey proposes principles for the establishment of a critical ed. (see also F71). In this connection, he shows that Dolet's 1542 ed. (*Bibliog. II*, no. 105) and Constantin's 1544 ed. (no. 129) do not merit the importance which they have traditionally been accorded.
This study and F64 complement each other. Together they form a monumental contribution to Marot scholarship, laying the foundation for all subsequent bibliographical research, profoundly influencing literary studies, and providing much essential material for a critical ed. (Even though Mayer's views on textual authority differ somewhat

from Villey's, his debt to the latter is obvious and is generously acknowledged by him.)

HA103 Villey, Pierre, *Recherches sur la chronologie des œuvres de Marot*, Paris: Leclerc, 1921, 176 pp. Separately-paginated offprint of HA102.
Rev.: .1 Plattard, Jean, *RSS*, XI (1924), 105-06.

HA104 Villey, Pierre, 'Clément Marot', in his *Les Grands Écrivains du XVIᵉ siècle*, I: *Marot et Rabelais*, Bibliothèque Littéraire de la Renaissance, new ser., XI, Paris: Champion, 1923, pp. 1-153.
Less concerned than Becker (C8) and Guy (C71) with biographical details; concentrates on CM's evolution as a poet. Uses the results of his extensive chronological research (see F64, 65 and HA102, 103) to trace the development of CM's poetry, under the influence of the court, of the humanist movement, and, to a lesser extent, of Italianism. A valuable study: objective, scholarly, illuminating. An appendix offers a 'Table chronologique des œuvres de Marot, classées selon l'ordre alphabétique des incipit', pp. 339-84. This is followed by the 'Chronologie de Marot', pp. 385-97, and a useful 'Note bibliographique sur Marot', pp. 404-23.
Rev.: .1 Plattard, Jean, *RSS*, XI (1924), 106-07.

Villey, Pierre: see also F68, 71.

HA105 Voigt, Julius, 'Marot', in his *Das Naturgefühl in der Literatur der französischen Renaissance*, Berliner Beiträge zur Germanischen und Romanischen Philologie, XV, Romanische Abteilung, VIII, Berlin: Ebering, 1898, pp. 8-10.
Considers that the only example of sincere feeling for nature occurs in the *Eglogue au roy, soubz les noms de Pan et Robin*. (Voigt is evidently unaware of CM's indebtedness to Lemaire de Belges in this poem – see KB4, 7.)

HA106 Voltaire, *Œuvres complètes*. Nouvelle éd. ... conforme pour le texte à l'édition de Beuchot [1829-40], Paris: Garnier, 52 vols, 1877-85.
On CM, see esp. the following passages:
General reflections. 'Marot, qui n'a qu'un style, et qui chante du même ton les psaumes de David et les merveilles d'Alix, n'a plus que huit ou dix feuillets [in the library of the temple]' (*Le Temple du goût*, VIII, p. 577). 'Marot, qui avait forgé le langage de Montaigne,

n'a presque jamais été connu hors de sa patrie: il a été goûté parmi
nous pour quelques contes naïfs, pour quelques épigrammes licen-
cieuses, dont le succès est presque toujours dans le sujet; mais c'est
par ce petit mérite même que la langue fut longtemps avilie ... Il
n'y a de véritablement bons ouvrages que ceux qui passent chez les
nations étrangères, qu'on y apprend, qu'on y traduit; et chez quel
peuple a-t-on jamais traduit Marot?'(*Discours de M. de Voltaire à
l'Académie Française*, XXIII, pp. 210-11).'On admire Marot, Amyot,
Rabelais, comme on loue des enfants quand ils disent par hasard
quelque chose de bon. On les approuve parce qu'on méprise leur
siècle, et les enfants parce qu'on n'attend rien de leur âge' (*Supplément aux Œuvres en prose*, XXXII, p. 556).

On the epigrams. 'Marot en a fait quelques-unes, où l'on retrouve
toute l'aménité de la Grèce.' Then quotes approvingly 'Plus ne suis
ce que j'ay esté' (*OC*, V, p. 280). But on the poem 'Ton vieux couteau,
Pierre Marrel, rouille' (*OC*, V, p. 289): 'Est-ce un courtisan qui est
l'auteur d'une telle épigramme? est-ce un matelot ivre dans un cabaret?
Marot, malheureusement, n'en a que trop fait dans ce genre' ('Épigramme', in *Dictionnaire philosophique*, XVIII, pp. 560, 562). On *Du
Lieutenant criminel de Paris et de Samblançay* (*OC*, V, p. 129):
'Voilà, de toutes les épigrammes dans le goût noble, celle à qui je
donnerais la préférence' ('Épigramme', in *Connaissance des beautés
et des défauts de la poésie et de l'éloquence dans la langue française*,
XXIII, p. 376).

On the psalm translations. 'A mesure que le bon goût se perfection-
nait, les psaumes de Marot et de Bèze ne pouvaient plus insensible-
ment inspirer que du dégoût. Ces psaumes, qui avaient charmé la cour
de François II [*sic*], n'étaient plus faits que pour la populace sous
Louis XIV' (*Siècle de Louis XIV*, XV, p. 22).

On the 'style marotique'. 'Il [Voltaire himself] prouvait que le style
qu'on appelle de Marot ne doit être admis que dans une épigramme
et dans un conte, comme les figures de Callot ne doivent paraître que
dans des grotesques. Mais quand il faut mettre la raison en vers, peindre,
émouvoir, écrire élégamment, alors ce mélange monstrueux de la langue
qu'on parlait il y a deux cents ans, et de la langue de nos jours, paraît
l'abus le plus condamnable qui se soit glissé dans la poésie. Marot parlait
sa langue; il faut que nous parlions la nôtre' (*Conseils à un journaliste*,
XXII, 254). 'Vingt bons vers en quinze jours sont malaisés à faire ...
Et voilà pourquoi tout le monde s'est jeté dans ce misérable style
marotique, dans ce style bigarré et grimaçant, où l'on allie monstrueuse-
ment le trivial et le sublime, le sérieux et le comique, le langage de
Rabelais, celui de Villon, et celui de nos jours' ('A M. Helvétius', 1738,
in *Correspondance*, XXXV, p. 60).

*HA107   Watanabe, Kazuo, 'L'Ennemi d'hier est devenu l'allié
          d'aujourd'hui', in *The Works of Kazuo Watanabe*, vol.
          XIII, Pt 1, Tokyo: Chikumashobo, 1977, pp. 545-76.
          (Text in Japanese.)
          Written in 1971. Examines the poems composed by CM on the
          occasion of Charles V's passage through France in 1539-40. (See
          note to A7.) Cf. HA85.

          Watts, Margaret Elizabeth: see J32.

HA108   Weber, Henri, *La Création poétique au XVIe siècle en
          France, de Maurice Scève à Agrippa d'Aubigné*, Paris:
          Nizet, 2 vols, 1956.
          Numerous references to CM, in various connections.

HA109   Weber, H., 'A la découverte de Clément Marot', *Lettres
          Françaises*, no. 759 (1959), p. 2.
          Very favourable review of *OC*, I.

*HA110   Wells, Margaret W., 'Aspects of Du Bellay's Treatment of
          Certain Problems Pertaining to the External Structure of
          his Poetry', Ph. D. thesis, Univ. of Southampton, 1975,
          290 pp.
          Deals with the ode, the sonnet, translation, and satire.

HA111   Y. [pseud. of Dussault], '*Œuvres choisies* de Clément Marot',
          Journal des Débats, 2 Frimaire, An X [23 Nov. 1801], pp.
          2-4.
          Occasioned by the publication of E5. Claims that, even though CM's
          poetry is scarcely intelligible any more without the help of a dictionary,
          his style has triumphed over the passage of time and accounts for his
          enduring fame. Reprinted as HA26.

Ballades

HB1   Chamard, Henri, 'Ballade', *DLF*, pp. 80-82.

          Cohen, Gustave: see HA19,20.

HB2   Cohen, Helen Louise, *The Ballade*, New York: Columbia UP,
          1915, xix + 397 pp.

          Lloyd-Jones, Kenneth: see HA54.

HB3   Schunck, Peter, 'Elegie und Ballade: Interpretation einer
       Ballade von Clément Marot', *NS*, LXX (1971), 29-36.
       Analysis of the *Ballade d'une dame et de sa beaulté par le nouveau
       serviteur* (*OC*, IV, pp. 169-70) which, in the 1538 ed. of the *Œuvres*,
       appeared among the elegies with the title *La Dixiesme Elegie en forme
       de ballade*. (N.B. It had already appeared under that title in the *Suite
       de l'Adolescence cl.*)

Blasons

HC1   Chamard, Henri, 'Blason', in *DLF*, pp. 110-11.

HC2   Giudici, Enzo, *Le opere minori di Maurice Scève*, Parma:
       Guanda, 1958, 765 pp.
       Contains a detailed, informative study of the *blasons* (pp. 63-169).
       CM's *blasons* derived partly from a medieval genre, partly − and more
       immediately − from the Italian *capitoli* which owed their popularity
       esp. to Olimpo da Sassoferrato. The latter's poems were known in
       France before 1536, but CM most likely became familiar with them
       in Ferrara. Sassoferrato's influence on him was general rather than
       particular.

       Jacob, P.L. (bibliophile): see F26.

HC3   Kupisz, Kazimierz, 'Des recherches sur l'évolution du blason
       au XVIe siècle', *ZRL*, IX, 2 (1967), 67-81.
       CM's *blason Du beau tetin* (*OC*, V, pp. 156-57) is a rare example in
       the sixteenth century of the objectivity considered such a desirable
       feature of the genre. Increasingly the *blason* was invaded by subjectivism
       which, by introducing a lyrical tone, sowed the seeds for its eventual
       decline and its replacement by other lyrical genres of personal poetry
       which found greater favour with the Pléiade. An interesting art. which
       illumines important aspects not previously considered in such detail.

HC4   Pike, Robert E., 'The *Blasons* in French literature of the 16th
       Century', *RR*, XXVII (1936), 223-42.
       A comprehensive study of the subject. CM must have known the early
       French *blasons*; Pike lists seventeen dating from the period 1484-1530
       (but he does not mention those probably before 1530 by CM himself,
       published in 1532 and not reclassified as epigrams until six years later).
       One section of the art. is devoted to the *blasons anatomiques*. The
       direct inspiration for CM's *Du beau tetin* probably came from Olimpo

da Sassoferrato's two long *capitoli* in praise of Madonna Pegasea's beautiful breasts.

*HC5   Saunders, Alison M., 'The *Blason poétique* and Allied Poetry of the French Renaissance', Ph. D. thesis, Univ. of Durham, 1972, 517 pp.

HC6   Tomarken, Annette and Edward, 'The Rise and Fall of the Sixteenth-Century French *Blason*', *S*, XXIX (1975), 139-63.

*HC7   Vickers, Nancy Jean, 'Preface to the *Blasons anatomiques*: The Poetic and Philosophical Contexts of Descriptions of the Female Body in the Renaissance', Ph. D. thesis, Yale Univ., 1976, 215 pp. *DisA*, XXXVII (1976-77), 4407A.
'The purpose of this study is to define the *blasons* as they were most probably interpreted by those who initiated their publication in France in 1536 ... In the third chapter the composition of Clément Marot's initial *blason*, the *concours* it inspired, and the publication of the original group of poems is discussed.' Cf. J32.

HC8   Wilson, D.B., *Descriptive Poetry in France from 'Blason' to Baroque*, Manchester: Manchester UP, 1967, ix + 262 pp.
Contains an interesting discussion of the *blason marotique*. Agrees with Giudici's conclusions regarding the general rather than particular influence of Olimpo da Sassoferrato (see HC2).

Cantiques

HD1   Heath, Michael J., 'Note on Clément Marot', *BHR*, XXXIII (1971), 615-19.
On lines 49-54 of *La Chrestienté à Charles empereur et à Françoys roy de France* (*OC*, III, pp. 291-94).

HD2   Keil, Erika, *'Cantique' und 'Hymne' in der französischen Lyrik seit der Romantik*, Bonn: Romanisches Seminar, Univ. of Bonn, 1966, 259 pp.
Has a section on CM's *cantiques*, pp. 25-29.

Chansons

*HE1   Baehr, Rudolf, 'Marot's Chanson XII "Tant que vivray" ', in

Romania cantat. Lieder in alten und neuen Chorsätzen mit sprachlichen, literarischen und musikwissenschaftlichen Interpretationen. Gerhard Rohlfs zum 85. Geburtstag gewidmet, ed. by Francisco J. Oroz Arizcuren, Tübingen: Narr, 2 vols, 1980, II, pp. 477-85.

HE2   Chamard, Henri, 'Chanson', in *DLF*, pp. 167-68.

Cocco, Mia: see KA5.

HE3   Colombel, Évariste, 'La Chanson au XVIe siècle', *Annales de la Société Académique de Nantes et du Département de la Loire-Inférieure*, XXIV (1853), 3-20.
Quotations from poems, linked by brief remarks.

Dottin, Georges: see KB10.

Doucet, J.: see HA25.

Françon, Marcel: see KB13, 14, 16.

*HE4   Helm, Everett B., 'The Sixteenth Century French *Chanson*', *Proceedings of the Music Teachers' National Association*, XXXVI (1942, for 1941), 236 ff.

*HE5   Hertzmann, Erich, 'Trends in the Development of the *Chanson* in the Early 16th Century', *Papers Read by the Members of the American Musicological Society* (1946, for 1940), 5 ff.

Lesure, François: see M1, 2.

Morçay, Raoul: see I30.

Rollin, Jean: see M4.

Chants-Royaux

HF1   Chamard, Henri, 'Chant royal', in *DLF*, pp. 168-69.

HF2   Guiot, Jos. André, *Les Trois Siècles palinodiques; ou, Histoire générale des palinods de Rouen, Dieppe, etc.* Publiés pour la première fois, d'après le manuscrit de Rouen, par l'abbé A. Tougard, Rouen: Lestringant, 2 vols, 1898.
On CM, see II, pp. 94-95. Cf. HF3.

HF3   Robillard de Beaurepaire, Eugène de, *Les Puys de palinod de Rouen et de Caen*. Ouvrage posthume publié par Charles de Robillard de Beaurepaire, Caen: Delesques, 1907, xvii +403 pp. On the *Chant royal de la Conception Nostre Dame*, CM's unsuccessful entry at Rouen in 1521 (*OC*, IV, pp. 175-78), see pp. 117-20, where the text is reproduced.

Complaintes

Akiyama, Haruo: see J1.

HG1   Chamard, Henri, 'Complainte ou déploration', *DLF*, pp. 197-98.

Françon, Marcel: see KB15.

HG2   McClelland, John, 'La Poésie à l'époque de l'humanisme: Molinet, Lemaire de Belges et Marot', in *Colloque International de Tours (XIVe stage): L'Humanisme français au début de la Renaissance*, De Pétrarque à Descartes, XXIX, Paris: Vrin, 1973, pp. 313-27. Molinet's *Complainte sur la mort madame Ostrisse* (1482), Lemaire's *Plainte du désiré* (1504), and CM's *Déploration de Florimond Robertet* (1527), though belonging to the same genre, reflect three different attitudes towards traditional medieval rhetoric. In particular, the last two mark a progressive liberation, in accord with the new intellectual currents, from its basic assumptions.

Martineau-Génieys, Christine: see J16, 17.

HG3   Masclé, Thérèse, 'Les Robertet', in *Études Foréziennes*, IX: *Aspects de la vie littéraire en Forez*, Saint-Étienne: Centre d'Études Foréziennes, 1978, pp. 9-24.

Richter, Mario: see J24.

Saulnier, V.L.: see F59.

*HG4   Thiry, Claude, 'Recherches sur la déploration funèbre française à la Prérenaissance', Doctoral thesis, Univ. of Liège, 2 vols, 1973.

Vaganay, Hugues: see KB42.

HG5   Vipper, G., 'Sur un parallèle traditionnel dans l'histoire de la
       poésie française', *Wissenschaftliche Zeitschrift der Humboldt-
       Universität zu Berlin*, XVIII (1969), 565-69.
       Although manifestly influenced by Villon's *Ballade des pendus* (cf. KB5,6)
       CM's elegy XXII *Du Riche Infortuné Jacques de Beaune* is an original
       work, both in its ideology which reflects Renaissance ideas, and in its
       structure and style. (In *OC*, III, this poem is classified as a *complainte*.)

Coq-à-l'âne

HH1   Chamard, Henri, 'Coq-à-l'âne', in *DLF*, pp. 200-01.

HH2   Mayer, C.A., 'Coq-à-l'âne: Définition, invention, attributions',
       FS, XVI (1962), 1-13.
       Opposes the view, recently restated by Meylan (in HH5), that Eustorg
       de Beaulieu's *De l'asne au coq* is the first *coq-à-l'âne*; reaffirms CM's
       precedence. Furthermore disputes Meylan's attribution of certain poems
       to CM: only three *coq-à-l'âne* can be attributed to him with certainty;
       in addition, his authorship of another one is highly probable, that of
       two others possible.

HH3   Mayer, C.A., 'Le Coq-à-l'âne marotique', *RHR*, no. 7 (1978),
       66-67. (Discussion, p. 68.)
       Outline of a paper read at a colloquium. Focuses on sources, and on
       obscurities in the text.

HH4   Mayer, C.A., 'Le Coq-à-l'âne', *Actes du Deuxième Colloque
       de Goutelas, 21-23 septembre 1979, RHR*, no. 11 (Dec. 1980),
       105-16. (Discussion, p. 117.)

       Mayer, C.A.: see also I28.

HH5   Meylan, Henri, *Épîtres du coq à l'âne: Contribution à l'histoire
       de la satire au XVIe siècle*, THR, XX, Geneva: Droz, 1956,
       xxviii + 130 pp.
       Prints several examples of the genre, extending over the period 1536-75:
       some of them previously published but little known, others so far
       unpublished. Of the latter, Meylan attributes two to CM. (These attribu-
       tions will be described as 'insoutenables' by Mayer in HH2; see also *OC*,
       VI, 'Introduction'.) One poem here reproduced, the *Epistre de Pasquille
       de Romme* dating from 1543, provides proof of the link between the
       coq-à-l'âne and the *pasquinade*.

Rev.: .1 Bainton, Roland H., *Church History*, XXVI (1957), 294.
.2 Grève, Marcel de, *RBPH*, XXXV (1957), 87-92.
.3 Mandelsloh, E. Gfn., *Archiv für Reformationsgeschichte*, XLVIII (1957), 273-75.
.4 Screech, M.A., *BHR*, XX (1958), 477-78.

*HH6   Rieux, Charles, 'Le Coq à l'âne en France de 1530 à 1650', Thèse de 3ᵉ cycle, Univ. of Tours, 2 vols, 1979.

HH7   Rossettini, Olga, *Les Influences anciennes et italiennes sur la satire en France au XVIᵉ siècle*, Publications de l'Institut Français de Florence, 1st ser., XIII, Florence: Sansoni, 1958, 422 pp. (Also published under the name of Olga Trtnik-Rossettini.)
On CM's *coq-à-l'âne*, see esp. pp. 46-47, in the chapter on the conception of satire in France.

Trtnik-Rossettini, Olga: see HH7.

HH8   Van Brabant, Luc, 'Analyse analogique de quelques extraits de l'*Epistre du coq à l'asne à Lyon* de Clément Marot: Étude critique dans le cadre de nos recherches sur Louïze Labé', *RLV*, XXXII (1966), 567-86.
Contests some of Mayer's statements (in *OC*, II) on the genre in general and on CM's *coq-à-l'âne* in particular. Claims that this epistle (*OC*, II, pp. 160-67) contains allusions to Louise Labé's affair with the Dauphin, as well as to CM's unrequited love for her (cf. C139, HA100). Reprinted in HA100.
Rev.: .1 Sozzi, L., *SFr*, XI (1967), 525-26.

Van Brabant, Luc: see also HA100.

Zumthor, Paul: see KB45, 46.

Dialogue de deux amoureux

Thiry, Claude J.: see HA98.

HI1   Truffier, Jules, 'Le Théâtre au XVIᵉ siècle: Scènes commentées par M. Jules Truffier. Clément Marot et la farce de *Deux amoureux récréatis et joyeux*', *Conferencia*, XXIX, Pt I (1934-35), 445-52.
Some general remarks about CM and the *Dialogue*, followed by the version

performed at the Comédie Française in 1915 (see E25).

Églogues

Altman, Beulah L.: see KB1.

Bayet, Jean: see KB4.

HJ1   Chamard, Henri, 'Églogue', in *DLF*, pp. 285-87.

Charlier, Gustave: see KB7.

HJ2   Cooper, Helen, *Pastoral: Medieval into Renaissance*, Ipswich: Brewer, 1977, 257 pp.
On CM's eclogues, see esp. pp. 111-14; for brief allusions to their influence on Spenser, see pp. 152-53.

HJ3   Dorangeon, Simone, *L'Églogue anglaise de Spenser à Milton*, Paris: Didier, 1974, 594 pp.
The detailed study of the English eclogue is preceded by important sections on the rise of pastoralism in England, on the classical origins of the eclogue, and on the history of the genre in Italy, Spain, and France. On CM's eclogues, see pp. 119-22; on their influence on Spenser, pp. 141-45.

HJ4   Egger, E., *L'Hellénisme en France: Leçons sur l'influence des études grecques dans le développement de la langue et de la littérature françaises*, Paris: Didier, 2 vols, 1869.
On CM, see I, pp. 378-79. Without any intention of founding a school, CM, through his eclogues, determined the nature of French bucolic poetry for the next two centuries.

Frappier, Jean: see KB19, 20.

HJ5   Gerhardt, Mia I., 'Clément Marot', in her *La Pastorale: Essai d'analyse littéraire*, Assen: Van Gorcum, 1950, pp. 206-15.
CM marks the transition from the medieval tradition to the Renaissance pastoral, the former still being the predominating element in his eclogues. Interesting discussion of CM's poetic technique in the *Eglogue sur le trespas de ... Loyse de Savoye*.

Gmelin, Hermann: see KB22.

HJ6   Greg, Walter W., *Pastoral Poetry and Pastoral Drama: A Literary*

Inquiry, with Special Reference to the Pre-Restoration Stage in England, London: Bullen, 1906, xii + 464 pp.
CM 'was in no sense a great poet', but one of his chief merits 'lies in the power he possesses ... of treating the allegorical pastoral without entirely losing the charm of naïve simplicity and genuine feeling'.

HJ7 Hulubei, Alice, *L'Églogue en France au XVIᵉ siècle: Époque des Valois (1515-1589)*, Paris: Droz, 1938, xxiv + 794 pp.
On CM, see esp. pp. 49-52 (on the tr. of Virgil's first eclogue) and pp. 210-24. Hulubei studies CM's eclogues within the context of the evolution of the genre, and examines their influence. Sheds new light on the sources of the *Eglogue sur le trespas de ... Loyse de Savoye*.

HJ8 Hulubei, Alice, *Répertoire des églogues en France au XVIᵉ siècle (Époque des Valois, 1515-1589)*, Paris: Droz, 1939, xi + 114 pp.
Complements HJ7.

HJ9 Lambert, Ellen Zetzel, *Placing Sorrow: A Study of the Pastoral Elegy Convention from Theocritus to Milton*, Univ. of North Carolina Studies in Comparative Literature, LX, Chapel Hill: Univ. of North Carolina Press, 1976, xxxiv + 238 pp.
On CM's *Eglogue sur le trespas de ,.. Loyse de Savoye*, see pp. 107-12, on Spenser's debt to CM, p. 129 ff.

Martineau-Génieys, Christine: see J17.

*HJ10 Paret-Limardo, L., 'L'Églogue et son développement de Théocrite à Clément Marot', M.A. thesis, Laval Univ., 1946, 80 pp.

HJ11 Spitzer, Leo, 'Zu Marot's *Eglogue au roy, soubs les noms de Pan et Robin* (1539)', *RJ*, IX (1958), 161-73.
Examines CM's technique and poetic inspiration in this poem. Seeks to elucidate the 'mysterious way' in which CM, working in a genre as quintessentially artificial as the eclogue, succeeds in creating a work of rare originality and freshness, by judiciously fusing very different themes and by carefully adapting his sources – notably Lemaire's *Illustrations de Gaule* (cf. KB4, 7) – to his purpose. (Mayer mistakenly believes in C105, p. 456, n. 256, that Spitzer denies CM's debt to Lemaire in this art. But even if he had, it is difficult to understand why this should have provoked such an extraordinary personal attack.)

HJ12 Spitzer, Leo, 'Clément Marot: *Eglogue au roy, soubz les noms de Pan et Robin* (1539)', in his *Interpretationen zur Geschichte der französischen Lyrik*, ed. by Helga Jauss-Meyer and Peter Schunk, Heidelberg: Romanisches Seminar, Univ. of Heidelberg, 1961, pp. 24-43.

Text of a lecture given at the Univ. of Heidelberg in 1958, as part of a series — here published from tape recordings, after his death — on French lyric poetry from the Renaissance to the nineteenth century. The lecture presents essentially the same views and arguments as HJ11, but, due to a certain discursiveness, does so less effectively. The opening remarks contain some factual errors.

Stackelberg, Jürgen von: see KB38.

Voigt, Julius: see HA105.

HJ13   Weidinger, Anton, *Die Schäferlyrik der französischen Vorrenaissance*, Munich, 1893, 67 pp.

On CM, see pp. 24-32. Of little value. Chronology is at sixes and sevens: Weidinger considers the *Eglogue au roy, soubz les noms de Pan et Robin* to be CM's first eclogue, the *Eglogue sur le trespas de … Loyse de Savoye* his last. Cretin is named among the poets who developed the genre after CM.

Élégies

Bambeck, Manfred: see KB2, 3.

HK1   Becker, Philipp August, 'Clément Marots Buch der Elegien: Sein Sinn und seine Bedeutung', in *Romanica. Festschrift … Fritz Neubert … zum 60. Geburtstag*, ed. by Rudolf Brunner, Berlin: Stundenglas, 1948, pp. 9-54.

Becker's interpretations of CM's elegies as reflections of his feelings and experiences produce highly ingenious, but also, on occasion, decidedly dubious, readings. The result, at times, is a veritable historical romance. Cf. HK11.

HK2   Becker, Philipp August, 'Clément Marots Buch der Elegien: Sein Sinn und seine Bedeutung', in his *Zur romanischen Literaturgeschichte: Ausgewählte Studien und Aufsätze*, Munich: Francke, 1967, pp. 604-40.

Reprint of HK1.

HK3   Chamard, Henri, 'Élégie', in *DLF*, pp. 287-88.

HK4   Clark, John E., *'Élégie': The Fortunes of a Classical Genre in Sixteenth-Century France*, Studies in French Literature, XXIII, The Hague: Mouton, 1975, x + 268 pp.
See esp. 'Marot', pp. 23-37. A valuable study. Shows that, apart from the three deplorative elegies, CM's elegies were *épîtres amoureuses* which observed the conventions of that genre, including the tripartite argumentation. Disputes Scollen's thesis of the influence of Ovid's *Heroides* (see HK11, also HK7); CM's elegies are more likely to be distantly related to the *Amores*. Maintains, however, that classical influences are altogether slight and that CM's elegies are essentially modifications, in the simpler style he developed in the later 1520s, of earlier French models. As for the title 'elegy', Clark speculates that, quite apart from reflecting the prestige then enjoyed by classical antiquity, the choice of this term may have been influenced by Alamanni's *Opere toscane* which contained a section of 'elegies'. (The *Opere toscane* were published by Seb. Gryphius in Lyons in 1532-33.)

Cocco, Mia: see KA5.

HK5   Derche, Roland, 'Clément Marot: *Élégie (IX)*', in his *Études de textes français*, new ser., II: *XVIe siècle*, Paris: Société d'Édition d'Enseignement Supérieur, 1965, pp. 47-67.
Analysis of elegy IX (*OC*, III, pp. 232-33) in the text of E26.

Fauchet, Claude: see C54.

*HK6   Forster, Elborg, 'Die französische Elegie im 16. Jahrhundert', Doctoral thesis, Univ. of Cologne, 1959, 220 pp.
Has a short chapter on the elegy prior to the publication of Du Bellay's *Deffence* ...

HK7   Hanisch, Gertrude S., 'Clément Marot and *l'épître amoureuse*', in her *Love Elegies of the Renaissance: Marot, Louise Labé and Ronsard*, Stanford French and Italian Studies, XV, Saratoga: Anma Libri, 1979, pp. 22-52.
The French elegy, which CM created, is a long and serious love letter in the tradition of Ovid's *Heroides* (cf. HK4, 11), its plaintive tone being due to the fact that the love is generally unrequited. It owes little, beyond the title, to the Latin love elegists, but draws heavily on medieval sources. Hanisch is unconvinced by Saulnier's thematic analysis of CM's elegies (in HK10) which she considers no less contrived than earlier critics' attempts to find in each elegy a reflection of CM's love for a particular woman.

HK8 Mahieu, Robert G., 'L'Élégie au XVIe siècle: Essai sur l'histoire du genre', *RHLF*, XLVI (1939), 145-79.
On CM, see pp. 154-55. A few very general remarks, expressing limited admiration for CM's elegies, e.g.: 'nous ne sentons pas chez Marot cet accent ému qui nous fait vibrer à l'unisson ... il ne semble pas souffrir beaucoup.'

Mayer, C.A.: see F45.

Popârda, Oana: see I32.

HK9 Roedel, Alfred, *Studien zu den Elegien Clément Marots*, Meiningen, 1898, 106 pp.
Divides CM's elegies into two main cycles of love letters, the first addressed to an unidentifiable lady, the second to Marguerite de Navarre. However, the existence of this latter cycle does not necessarily imply an actual love affair between CM and Marguerite. Roedel analyzes the content and tone of the elegies and investigates likely sources (Ovid, Tibullus, Propertius). The second part (pp. 66-103) is devoted to a detailed metrical study. Cf. HK11.

HK10 Saulnier, V.L., *Les Élégies de Clément Marot*, Paris: Société d'Édition d'Enseignement Supérieur, 1952, 156 pp.; nouvelle éd. augmentée, 1968, 196 pp.
Deals with the *élégies déploratives* as well as the *élégies amoureuses*. Esp. good on the latter's classical and medieval sources, their emotional content and poetic technique. Rejects idea that they can be arranged into cycles inspired by different mistresses. Instead, proposes division into groups forming 'un roman à cinq épisodes' and illustrating the types of women who cause unhappiness to lovers: 'l'Oublieuse, la Rebelle, l'Intéressée, la trop bien gardée, la Malavisée: tels sont les visages de celles dont on souffre, tels sont les visages du malheur d'amour.' Cf. HK7.
Rev.: .1 Françon, Marcel, *MLJ*, XXXVII (1953), 379.
   .2 Mayer, C.A., *BHR*, XV (1953), 239-41.

Schunck, Peter: see HB3.

HK11 Scollen, Christine M., 'The Elegies of Clément Marot', in her *The Birth of the Elegy in France, 1500-1550*, THR, XCV, Geneva: Droz, 1967, 39-56.
CM's elegies are not intimate poems, as esp. Becker maintains (HA5, HK1, 2), nor do they owe much either to Propertius or to Tibullus, as Roedel, in particular suggests (HK9). However, CM is indebted to Ovid,

whose *Heroides* provide him with a framework of elegiac poetry which is not necessarily personal and which uses the epistolary form. Cf. HK4.

HK12 Thiry, Claude, '*Élégie, elegien, élégiaque* au XVe siècle', in *Hommage au professeur Maurice Delbouille, MRo*, Numéro spécial (1973), 279-92.
An important study. Corrects date of earliest known occurrence of the term *élégie* from 1500 to between 1461 and 1463 (in Simon Greban's *Epitaphes de Charles VII de France*), that of the term *élégiaque*, adjective or noun, from 1480 to 1463 or 1464 (in the anonymous *Exclamacion en la mors pour Marie d'Anjou royne de France*). Furthermore, *elegien* is used in the latter poem both adjectivally and substantivally, apparently as a synonym of *élégiaque*. Thiry also adds examples of the use of *élégie* around 1500 to the previously known ones, thus proving that the term was not as rare by CM's time as has been thought. Moreover, these various terms were consistently applied in the fifteenth century to laments for the dead, and never to love epistles in the manner of Ovid. This fact explains and justifies CM's inclusion of his *élégies déploratives* among the elegies in the 1538 ed. of his *Œuvres*, and invalidates Mayer's theory — applied in *OC* — that they should be classified as *complaintes*.

HK13 Thiry, Claude, 'L'Honneur et l'Empire: À propos des poèmes de langue françaises sur la bataille de Pavie', in *Mélanges ... Franco Simone: France et Italie dans la culture européenne*, I: *Moyen âge et Renaissance*, Centre d'Études Franco-Italien, Universités de Turin et de Savoie, Bibliothèque Franco Simone, IV, Geneva: Slatkine, 1980, pp. 297-324.
CM's elegy (*OC*, III, pp. 211-17) is compared, in particular, with François I's own epistle on the disaster.

Thiry, Claude: see also HG4.

Van Brabant, Luc: see HA100.

HK14 Villey, P., ['Lettre'], *RSS*, IX (1922), 223-24.
Refers to his demonstration, in HA102, 103, that CM's first elegy does not prove his presence at Pavia, since it was composed for a patron. Now invites the reader to identify the latter whose name, Antonius Pastoureau, appears in the margin beside the poem in MS BN f. fr. 1721. (In actual fact, the name in question is spelt 'Pastureau' in the MS.)

Vipper, G.: see HG5.

L'Enfer

HL1 Derche, Roland, 'Clément Marot: *L'Enfer*', in his *Études de textes français*, new ser., II: *XVIᵉ siècle*, Paris: Société d'Édition d'Enseignement Supérieur, 1965, pp. 9-45.
Commentary on lines 367-410, in the text of E26.

Eckhardt, Alexandre: see KB12.

Françon, Marcel: see C58, 59, 61, 62, HA32, 35.

Lerond, Alain: see I25.

HL2 Mayer, C.A., 'Clément Marot et le grand Minos', *BHR*, XIX (1957), 482-84.
'Le grand Minos' (*L'Enfer*, line 47, see also line 92) represents, not the 'bailli de Paris', Jean de la Barre, as Guiffrey believed (E17), but Gabriel d'Allègre, the 'prévôt de Paris'.

Saulnier, V.L.: see L47.

Épigrammes

HM1 Becker, Philipp August, 'Zu Clément Marots Epigrammen', *RF*, LX (1947), 316-62.
Attempts to establish the chronology of CM's epigrams, omitting those printed in E17 which he considers unauthentic. A useful art. in many respects, but Becker's identification of some of the ladies mentioned in the poems is open to doubt.

HM2 Becker, Philipp August, 'Zu Clément Marots Epigrammen', in his *Zur romanischen Literaturgeschichte: Ausgewählte Studien und Aufsätze*, Munich: Francke, 1967, pp. 641-76.
Reprint of HM1.

HM3 Breghot du Lut, C., 'Sur les dames de Lyon, au sujet d'un passage de Marot', in his *Mélanges biographiques et littéraires pour servir à l'histoire de Lyon*, Lyons, 1828, pp. 200-17.
The epigram about Jeanne Gaillarde (*OC*, V, pp. 96-97) has been wrongly interpreted as expressing CM's opinion that almost all Lyonese women are ugly. In any case, 'Lyon a toujours passé pour avoir donné naissance à de belles femmes, autant et plus qu'aucune autre ville du royaume.'

HM4   Chamard, Henri, 'Épigramme', in *DLF*, pp. 296-98.

HM5   Chamard, Henri, 'Dizain', in *DLF*, pp. 231-32.
(This art., like HM6-9, mentions poems by CM which in Dolet's 1538 ed. – and in *OC* – are classified as epigrams.)

HM6   Chamard, Henri, 'Douzain', in *DLF*, p. 238.
See note to HM5.

HM7   Chamard, Henri, 'Madrigal', in *DLF*, pp. 470-71.
The epigram 'Un doux Nenny avec un doulx sourire' (*De ouy et nenny*, *OC*, V, p. 149) is a typical madrigal, though not so called by CM.

HM8   Chamard, Henri, 'Quatrain', in *DLF*, pp. 581-82.
See note to HM5.

HM9   Chamard, Henri, 'Sixain', in *DLF*, p. 645.
See note to HM5.

Cocco, Mia: see KA5.

HM10   Colletet, Guillaume, *L'Art poétique*, I: *'Traitté de l'épigramme' et 'Traitté du sonnet'*. Texte établi et introduction par P.A. Jannini, TLF, CXVI, Geneva: Droz, 1965, xxvi + 270 pp.

Deloffre, Frédéric: see I9.

HM11   Hutton, James, 'Spenser and the "cinq points en amours"', *MLN*, LVII (1942), 657-61.
Suggests that the theme, common in French and English literature and illustrated by CM's epigram *Des cinq poinctz en amours* (*OC*, V, p. 138), represents a secularization of the warnings contained in medieval homilies and instructions for priests, against the dangers which the senses represent for chastity.

HM12   Ito, Susumu, 'Amour courtois et sensualité dans les épigrammes amoureuses de Marot', *BFLACU*, XV (1974), 767-803. (Text in Japanese.)
On the ambivalence characterizing CM's portrayal of love. (See note to A7.)

HM13   Jacoubet, Henri, 'Les Dix Années d'amitié de Dolet et Boyssoné (Toulouse 1532 – Lyon 1542)', *RSS*, XII (1925), 290-321.
Wonders whether the name 'Villars' mentioned in CM's epigram *Il convie troys poetes à disner* (*OC*, V, pp. 196-97) and also in a poem by Boyssoné

designates Étienne Dolet.

Kalwies, Howard H.: see G5.

Laurens, Pierre: see KB29.

HM14 Laurent, M., 'Explication française: Marot, *Du Lieutenant criminel et de Semblançay*', *École (Second Cycle et Propédeutique)* (1962-63), 9-10.

Mayer, C.A.: see E34.

Mehnert, Kurt Henning: see KB32.

HM15 Perrat, Charles, 'Relations de Maurice Scève et de Clément Marot, d'après le manuscrit 524 du Musée Condé', *AIBL* (1962) 81-87.
Suggests that the *Petit œuvre d'amour et gaige d'amytié* (1538) is mainly by Maurice Scève and provides evidence of his close relationship with CM. The latter's epigram *De Anne à ce propos* (*OC*, V, p. 139) seems to be a reply to poem XXV of the *Petit œuvre* which also contains what could be regarded as two variant versions of the *Epigramme qu'il perdit contre Helene de Tournon* (*OC*, V, p. 168).

Rickard, Peter: see I35.

Rigolot, François: see I36-38.

Saulnier, V.L.: see F58.

HM16 Smith, P.M., and C.A. Mayer, 'La Première Épigramme française: Clément Marot, Jean Bouchet et Michel d'Amboise. Définition, sources, antériorité', *BHR*, XXXII (1970), 579-602.
Valuable for the study of the *Cent épigrammes* by Michel d'Amboise (published 'vers 1533'. His original poems in this collection, like the 'epigrams' in Bouchet's *Jugement poetic de l'honneur femenin ...* ('vers 1538'), are typical 'rhétoriqueurs' compositions. Only the poems tr. by Michel d'Amboise from Angeriano's *Erotopaegnion* can be considered true epigrams. Accordingly, CM still retains precedence as the author of original epigrams in France.

HM17 Sozzi, Lionello, 'Marot, Dolet, Des Périers e l'epigramma *Contre l'inique*', *SFr*, V (1961), 83-88.
The play on words 'malheureux-bienheureux-plus heureux' (*OC*, V, p. 265, lines 11-13) appears to be an allusion to Des Périers' first name 'Bonaventure'

Sozzi surmises that CM's hostility towards Des Périers stemmed from his outrage over the *Cymbalum mundi.*

HM18 Thiry-Stassin, Martine, 'Un Dizain de Clément Marot: *D'Anne qui luy jecta de la neige*', CAT, XIII (1971), 54-62.
An interesting close analysis of the poem.

Voltaire: see HA106.

HM19 Williams, Annwyl, 'A Reading of the *huitain* "Plus ne suis ce que j'ay esté" (Clément Marot, 1542): Towards a New Account of Marot's Evolution', *Degré Second*, IV (1980), 1-28.
Argues that the humanist approach to CM's poetry has reached an impasse. Aims to reopen the question of his evolution within a new framework by undertaking two different readings of the poem (*OC*, V, p. 280), 'the first in terms of the ego/classical rhetoric/the logic of the sign, the second in terms of the unconscious/that which undermines the logic of the sign'. Williams's conclusion:'the difference between the early and late periods emerges in this poem firstly in the predominance of the logic of the sign [over the logic of the symbol], and, secondly, though the suggestion is more tentative, in the impression of greater freedom and energy.'

Épitaphes

HN1 Chamard, Henri, 'Épitaphe', in *DLF*, pp. 300-01.

Cohen, Gustave: see HA19, 20.

Martineau-Génieys, Christine: see J17.

HN2 Saulnier, Verdun L., 'La Mort du dauphin François et son tombeau poétique (1536)', *BHR*, VI (1945), 50-97.
Prints various documents relating to the Dauphin's death and to subsequent events. Half the article is devoted to a discussion of the commemorative *Recueil de vers latins et vulgaires de plusieurs poëtes françoys ...*, to which CM contributed an epitaph (*OC*, IV, pp. 229-30).

Épithalames

Leblanc, P.: see KB31.

HO1 Richter, Bodo L.O.,'*Venere pronuba*: The French Renaissance

Epithalamia', in *From Marot to Montaigne: Essays on French Renaissance Literature*, ed. by Raymond C. La Charité, *KRQ*, XIX (1972), Suppl. I, 65-98.

On CM, see pp. 72-76. Contains a brief, unsympathetic appraisal of CM's 'histrionics in favour of his future protectress' in the *Chant nuptial du mariage de madame Renée* ... and some comments on the poem he wrote for the wedding of Madeleine de France.

Épîtres

Akiyama, Haruo: see HA1.

Bambeck, Manfred: see KB2, 3.

Camproux, Ch.: see I5.

HP1   Chamard, Henri, 'Épître', in *DLF*, pp. 301-02.
Touches briefly on CM's transformation of the genre. (On earlier French examples of the genre, see esp. Ph. Aug. Becker, 'Die Versepistel vor Clément Marot', in his *Aus Frankreichs Frührenaissance: Kritische Skizzen* Leipzig, 1927, pp. 47-84.)

HP2   Decriaud, Roland, 'Marot: *A son ami Lion*, La Fontaine: *Le Lion et le rat*', *École des Lettres* (1979-80, no. 7), 15-22, 51.

HP3   Désormaux, J., 'L'Épître de Clément Marot *A un sien amy* (Angelon de Bellegarde, doyen de Notre-Dame de Liesse, professeur de rhétorique au Collège d'Annecy)', *RevS*, LXI (1920), 85-91.
Corrects a faulty reading in E18. Argues that the addressee is not Claude de Bellegarde, as Mugnier believed (HP8), but his younger brother Angelon. Cf. E32, HP4, 5, 8, 11.

Doucet, J.: see HA25.

HP4   Duparc, P. and S., *Vieil Annecy: Scènes et portraits*, Annecy: Gardet & Garin, 1945, 75 pp.
Supports the identification of the recipient of the epistle *A ung sien amy* with Angelon de Bellegarde (see 'Un Chanoine homme de lettres et d'épée', pp. 19-23). Cf. E32, HP3, 5, 8, 11.

Françon, Marcel: see I12.

Galliot, Marcel: see I14.

HP5   Gardet, Clément, 'Sur le séjour de Marot en Savoie', *RevS*,
       XC (1949), 33-39.
       Maintains against Droz and Plan (see E32) that CM's epistle *A ung sien*
       amy is addressed, not to François de Bellegarde, but to Angelon de
       Bellegarde, as Désormaux suggested (in HP3; cf. HP4, 8, 11).

       Giraud, Yves: see J9.

*HP6   Ito, Susumu, 'Clément Marot et le "siècle d'or": Une Lecture
       des vers 1-62 de l'*Epistre au roy, du temps de son exil à*
       Ferrare', *BFLACU*, XVI (1975), 145-70. (Text in Japanese.)
       CM exhorts François I not to bring the Golden Age to a close, despite
       the *affaire des placards*. (See note to A7.)

HP7   Joukovsky, F., 'Voyageurs français dans la Venise du XVIe
       siècle', *RLC*, XLI (1967), 481-507.
       On CM's reflections on Venice in the epistle he sent from there to Renée
       of Ferrara, see pp. 501-03.

       Laurens, Pierre: see KB29.

       Lloyd-Jones, Kenneth: see HA54.

       Mayer, C.A.: see D5.

HP8   Mugnier, François, 'Marc-Claude de Buttet, poète savoisien (XVIe
       siècle): Notice sur sa vie, ses œuvres poétiques et en prose fran-
       çaise, et sur ses amis; *L'Apologie pour la Savoie*; le testament de
       M.C. de Buttet', *Mémoires et Documents publiés par la Société*
       Savoisienne d'Histoire et d'Archéologie, XXXV (1896), 3-232.
       On CM, see pp. 165-70. States that CM's epistle *A ung sien amy* was
       addressed to Claude de Bellegarde, sieur de Montagny. Cf. E32, HP3-5, 11.

HP9   Muller, A., 'Explication française: Marot, *Épître aux dames*
       de France (1543)', *École (Second Cycle et Propédeutique)*
       (1962-63), 11-12.
       Brief comments on lines 1-22 of this poem (*OC*, VI, pp. 314-16).

       Natori, Seiichi: see HA63.

HP10   Paret-Limardo, Lise, '*Épître au roi pour avoir été dérobé*',
       Amérique Française (Oct. 1946), 17-21.
       Clearly intended for the general reader.

HP11   Pérouse, Gabriel, 'Marot en Savoie', in his *Causeries sur l'histoire littéraire de la Savoie*, Chambéry: Dardel, 2 vols, 1934, I, pp. 104-07.

Repeats – presumably after Désormaux (HP3), and evidently not after Mugnier (HP8), as stated by Droz and Plan in E32 – that the epistle *A ung sien amy* was addressed to Angelin [sic] de Bellegarde. See also HP4, 5.

Plattard, J.: see G11.

Rickard, Peter: see I35.

HP12 Saulnier, V.L., 'Marguerite de Navarre aux temps de Briçonnet: Étude de la correspondance générale. Première partie', *BHR*, XXXIX (1977), 437-78.

On CM's *Epistre du camp d'Atigny* (*OC*, I, pp. 105-12), see pp. 469-71.

HP13 Tiemann, Barbara, 'Clément Marot: *Épître XI*', in *Die franzö-sische Lyrik von Villon bis zur Gegenwart*, ed. by Hans Hinter-häuser, Düsseldorf: Bagel, 2 vols, 1975, I, pp. 35-48.

Commentary on *Marot, prisonnier, escript au roy pour sa delivrance* (*OC*, I, pp. 132-35).

HP14 Tomarken, Annette, 'Clément Marot and the Grands Rhéto-riqueurs', *S*, XXXII (1978), 41-55.

Argues that CM's *Petite epistre au roy* (*OC*, I, pp. 97-98) represents a brilliant continuation of a specific type of writing, namely the request for patronage. Examines two previous examples: a letter written by Jean Robertet ca 1464, and a poem by Jean Marot composed in 1507 or 1508 It would be a mistake to regard CM's epistle simply as a parody of such earlier requests. 'Marot's reader must be simultaneously conscious of the writer's poetic heritage, historical situation and humorous manner of presenting both rhetoric and reality.'

Van Brabant, Luc: see HA100.

HP15 Vianey, J., 'Marot: *Le Lion et le rat*', in his *L'Explication française*, Paris: Hatier, 3 vols, 1912-14, III, pp. 4-11.

Analysis of the *Epistre à son amy Lyon*, beginning at line 14.

HP16 Vianey, Joseph, *Les Épîtres de Marot*, Grands Événements Littéraires, Paris: Société Française d'Éditions Littéraires et Techniques, 1935, 176 pp.

Shows how CM turns an essentially impersonal and formal genre into a model of personal poetry, full of charm and wit. Good discussion of the epistles, considered in groups: 'Les Épîtres du dépourvu', 'Les Épîtres du prisonnier', etc.

Rev.: .1 Jourda, P., *RHLF*, XLIII (1936), 303.

Villey, Pierre: see KB43.

*HP17   Walter, Ernst, 'Die Epistel in der französischen Literatur des Mittelalters und der Frührenaissance bis zu Clément Marot's Zeit', Doctoral thesis, Univ. of Leipzig, 1925, iv + 134 pp.

*HP18   Yamazaki, Yoichiro, 'Notes sur Clément Marot: A propos des épîtres de son premier exil', *Bulletin of the Faculty of Letters of Gakushuin University*, II (1954), 267-303. (Text in Japanese.)

Analysis of these poems, in their chronological order. (See note to A7.)

Étrennes

HQ1   Becker, Ph. Aug., 'Clément Marots *Estreines aux dames de la court*, 1541', *ZRP*, XLI (1921), 1-14.

Identifies the ladies to whom CM offered *étrennes* on 1 January 1541. Often provides more information on their families than can be found in *OC*, IV. However, where identifications differ, Mayer's suggestions usually seem the more likely ones. The most notable divergence of views concerns 'Madame Marguerite' (*Étrenne* III), in whom Becker sees Marguerite de France (the daughter of François Ier and future duchesse de Savoie), while Mayer proposes Marguerite de Navarre.

HQ2   Becker, Philipp August, Clément Marots *Estreines aux dames de la court*, 1541', in his *Zur romanischen Literaturgeschichte: Ausgewählte Studien und Aufsätze*, Munich: Francke, 1967, pp. 677-89.

Reprint of HQ1.

HQ3   Kerlinou, E. de, 'Une Inscription allemande en Bretagne et les *Étrennes* de Clément Marot', *Bulletin de la Société Polymathique du Morbihan* (1885), 146-49.

On *A Cardelan* (*OC*, IV, p. 255). A memorial tablet in a private chapel on an estate once the property of the Kerdelan, or Cardelan, family, in the commune of Baden in Morbihan, reads as follows: 'Got gipt Genot/ Hans von Cardelan/15:17:64'. A sixteenth-century document mentions Jean de Keralbaut, seigneur de Cardelan, who died in 1580. Kerlinou speculates that he may have placed the tablet in the chapel, in memory of his German mother who was born in 1517 and died in 1564 and who was the lady to whom CM offered the *étrenne.*

Rondeaux

HR1   Chamard, Henri, 'Rondeau', in *DLF*, pp. 610-12.

       Cocco, Mia: see KA5.

HR2   Conley, Tom, 'A Last Spending of *Rhetoricque*: Reading Marot's *Par contradictions*', *EsC*, XVIII (1978), 82-91.
An extravagant interpretation of the rondeau 'En esperant, espoir me desespere' (*OC*, IV, pp. 93-95).

HR3   Conley, Tom, 'La Poétique dehors: Autour d'un rondeau de Clément Marot', in *Poétiques: Théorie et critique littéraires*. Textes réunis par Floyd Gray, Michigan Romance Studies, I, Ann Arbor: Department of Romance Languages, Univ. of Michigan, 1980, pp. 47-72.
A highly idiosyncratic reading of *Des nonnes qui sortirent du couvent pour aller se recreer* (*OC*, IV, pp. 104-05), e.g. on the refrain 'Hors du couvent': 'Lorsqu'on récite le poème, *hors* rappelle un passé qui diffère le texte à venir, le reflet de l'*or*, métal en médaille que voudrait figurer la forme du poème en tant que gage d'un valet du roi – *or du couvent*, lieu proprement impropre, *hors*. Ou bien, par homonymie parfaite, le refrain serait le début d'une spéculation sur un échange non de l'or mais du papier qu'est la fausse espèce du poème en sa vérité.'

HR4   Courten, Clementina de, *I 'rondeaux' di Clément Marot*, Milan: Casa Editrice 'Alpes', 1927, 221 pp.
The discussion of the literary value of the rondeaux only rarely forsakes description for critical appraisal. The examination of linguistic features, while providing some useful information on certain aspects, lacks a sufficiently rigorous method. Altogether, a book which leaves more questions unanswered, or even unasked, than it tackles satisfactorily.

       Doucet, J.: see HA25.

HR5   Evans, W. Hugo, 'Marot's *Rondeau à un créancier*', *MLR*, XXXIII (1938), 411-12.
Suggests that in line 3 of the poem (*OC*, IV, p. 68), CM is playing on the double meaning of 'Angloys': an Englishman, and a creditor; and that *baille* in line 4, rather than being a pun on 'good-bye', as editors

have thought, is merely a demand for money. Evans believes that the poem may have been written in 1527 and that lines 3-4 may reflect French irritation at the exorbitant demands made by the English at the discussions which had been held earlier that year in London concerning financial settlements for the proposed marriage of Mary of England to the Duc d'Orléans.

HR6 Françon, Marcel, 'Sur le sonnet du sonnet', *MLN*, LXVII (1952), 46-47.
In his rondeau defining the *rondeau* ('Ma foi, c'est fait de moi'), Voiture is following a tradition of poems defining their genre, to which CM contributed two rondeaux – *Rondeau responsif à ung aultre* ... and *A celluy dont les lettres capitales* ... – (*OC*, IV, pp. 67, 86-87) – and to which the sonnet in Lope de Vega's *Niña de plata* probably also belongs. See also L18.

HR7 Françon, Marcel, 'Sur les poèmes à forme fixe de Clément Marot', *ZRL*, XVI, 2 (1973), 69-75.
Mainly of interest for the discussion of the unusual form of the rondeau 'Qu'on meine aux champs ce coquardeau' (*A ung poete ignorant – OC*, IV, p. 73).

HR8 Françon, Marcel, 'Sur les poèmes à forme fixe de Clément Marot', *RLM*, XXVII (1974), 5-11.
Identical with HR7.

HR9 Hatzfeld, Helmut, 'Clément Marot, 1496-1544: *De l'amour du siècle antique* (1534)', in his *Initiation à l'explication de textes français*, 4ᵉ éd., augmentée, Munich: Hueber, 1975, pp. 18-22.
An analysis of this rondeau (*OC*, IV, p. 129).

HR10 Jourda, Pierre, 'Un Humaniste italien en France: Theocrenus (1480-1536)', *RSS*, XVI (1929), 40-57.
On the humanist extolled in the rondeau *Au seigneur Theocrenus lisant à ses disciples* (*OC*, IV, p. 82).

Rickard, Peter: see I35.

HR11 Saulnier, V.L., 'Documents nouveaux sur Jeanne Gaillarde et ses amis: Clément Marot, Jacques Colin, Germain Colin', *Bulletin de la Société Historique, Archéologique et Littéraire de Lyon*, XVIII (1950-51), 79-100.
Believes that MS BN f. fr. 2335 contains previously unidentified rondeaux

by Jeanne Gaillarde; also that several rondeaux by CM in the MS may be addressed to her, in addition to 'D'avoir le pris en science et doctrine' (*De ma dame Jehanne Gaillarde*: *OC*, IV, pp. 85-86) which is already known to have been written for her and is likewise transcribed in the MS. Furthermore, Saulnier considers that the inclusion of 'S'il est ainsi' among the poems attributed to CM in the MS is a persuasive argument for its authenticity (cf. G3, KA14, L59).

Steiner, Arpad: see KB39.

Sonnets

HS1   Bullock, Walter L., 'The First French Sonnets', *MLN*, XXXIX (1924), 475-78.
Sets out to correct Clement's datings (in HS4), mainly by reference to Villey's art. HS22, but in the process mistakenly amends Clement's date 1546 for the first publication of a sonnet by CM to 1539, instead of to 1538, as indicated by Villey. Argues, with supporting evidence, against the common belief, reaffirmed by Clement, that the Italian sonnet sestet could not be divided into a quatrain and a couplet.

HS2   Cerreta, Florindo V., 'The Italian Origin of the *sonnet régulier*' *BHR*, XXI (1959), 301-10.
The sestet rhymes usually identified with the 'sonnet régulier' can no longer be regarded as exclusively French, for their appearance in Italian poetry antedates the first French examples by two centuries. As for the pattern CCD EED, found, for instance, in CM and Saint-Gelais, it occurs also in the verse of their contemporary Alessandro Piccolomini and even in earlier Italian poets. However, if the Italians were indeed the originator of this pattern, there is as yet insufficient information available to explain its migration to France. A useful art., though not always as clear as one would wish.

HS3   Chamard, Henri, 'Sonnet', in *DLF*, pp. 646-51.

HS4   Clement, N.H., 'The First French Sonneteer', *RR*, XIV (1923), 189-98.
An examination of CM's and Saint-Gelais's sonnets leads Clement to affirm CM's precedence both in composition and in publication, but his unfamiliarity with important bibliographical and critical studies – notably Villey's art. HS22 – results in much wrong dating (see HS1).

Colletet, Guillaume: see HM10.

HS5   Françon, Marcel, 'Notes sur l'histoire du sonnet en France', *It*, XXIX (1952), 121-28.

The rise of the French sonnet corresponds to the *rapprochement* between François I and Pope Clement VII, following the Dauphin's marriage to the latter's niece Catherine de' Medici in 1533. The decline of its great vogue dates from a change of French policy in the early 1550s, when Henri II came to regard the Protestants as potentially more useful allies against Charles V than the pope. Françon accepts Villey's dating of CM's sonnets, but not of Saint-Gelais's *Sonnet faict au nom de madamoiselle de Traves* (see HS22). Contends that this poem was written in late 1533 and thus constitutes the first French sonnet ever composed (CM having precedence in publication). Cf. HS9, 14, 15. The last part of the art. deals with rhyme-schemes in French Renaissance sonnets.

HS6   Françon, Marcel, 'La Date d'un sonnet de Saint-Gelais', *BHR*, XV (1953), 213-14.

Ascribes the composition of 'Voyant ces mons de veue si loingtaine' to the same period as he has proposed for the composition of the *Sonnet faict au nom de madamoiselle de Traves*, namely late 1533 (see HS5), on the sole grounds that this was a propitious time for a courtier-poet to imitate an Italian sonnet – in this case, one by Sannazaro. Cf. HS14, 15.

HS7   Françon, Marcel, 'Sur le premier sonnet français publié', *BHR*, XXXIII (1971), 365-66.

On the statement by Smith and Mayer in HM16 that Michel d'Amboise wrote one of the earliest French sonnets: the poem in question, printed with *Les Anticques Erections des Gaules* ... [1535], is not a sonnet at all, but a *douzain.*

HS8   Françon, Marcel, 'L'Introduction du sonnet en France', *RPh*, XXVI (1972-73), 62-67.

Clear, concise exposition of the main arguments in support of his theses concerning the historical reasons for the rise and decline of the vogue of the sonnet in France, the precedence of Saint-Gelais in the composition and of CM in the publication of sonnets, and the conclusions to be drawn from the use of certain rhyme-schemes. Cf. HS5.

HS9   Françon, Marcel, 'Note sur la diffusion de l'italianisme en France au XVIe siècle', *BHR*, XLII (1980), 658.

Basically the same standpoint as in HS5, 6, but with a slight shift in the dating of Saint-Gelais's poems: the composition of the *Sonnet faict au nom de madamoiselle de Traves* is now ascribed to late 1533 or early

1534, that of 'Voyant ces noms de veue ainsi loingtaine' to 1533 or 1536. Cf. HS14, 15.

HS10 Françon, Marcel, 'Sur l'introduction du sonnet en France', *Fra*, no. 35 (1980), 12-16.
Yet another broadside in the battle of the sonnets. In response to McClelland's reply to his objections to HS13, Françon mostly reiterates arguments set out in HS5, 8, etc.

HS11 Jasinski, Max, 'Le Sonnet lyonnais. Marot', in his *Histoire du sonnet en France*, Douai, 1903, pp. 33-41.
Argues that 'le sonnet a pénétré en France par Lyon, grâce à l'engoue-ment pour la poésie d'une société riche, polie, stimulée par la présence de la cour et des poètes en renom', but the evidence he presents is inadequate to substantiate this statement, at least as far as CM is con-cerned.

HS12 Kupisz, Kazimierz, 'U źródeł dziejów sonetu we Francji' [A la source de l'histoire du sonnet en France], *Zeszyty Naukowe Uniwersytetu Łódzkiego*, 1st ser., Nauki Humanistyczno Społeczne, XLI, Filologia, 1965, 153-66.
At the end, a summary in French.

HS13 McClelland, John, 'Sonnet ou quatorzain? Marot et le choix d'une forme poétique', *RHLF*, LXXIII (1973), 591-607.
A very interesting art. which defines the essential differences between the sonnet and other fourteen-line poems. McClelland accepts CM's precedence over Saint-Gelais in the composition of sonnets in France. Moreover, Bouchet did not write proper sonnets, as Mayer thought (HS14), so CM was the first French poet to compose one.
McClelland's remarks about CM's precedence as well as his statements on rhyme-schemes are challenged by Marcel Françon in a letter in *RHLF*, LXXIV (1974), 347-48. McClelland replies, maintaining his position, pp. 348-49. See also HS10.

HS14 Mayer, C.A., 'Le Premier Sonnet français: Marot, Mellin de Saint-Gelais et Jean Bouchet', *RHLF*, LXVII (1967), 481-93.
Contests Françon's dating at 1533 of Saint-Gelais's *Sonnet faict au nom de madamoiselle de Traves* and the sonnet 'Voyant ces mons de veue si loingtaine' (see HS5, 6). Regarding the former, reproduces Villey's arguments for a later date (HS22). Regarding the latter – which, incidentally, he inclines to attribute to CM rather than to Saint-Gelais (see also HS16) – Mayer concludes that 'il n'est pas possible ... d'accepter la date de 1533.' He adds, however, that the first French sonnet may have

been written by neither CM nor Saint-Gelais, but by Jean Bouchet who published fifteen 'épigrammes' in his *Jugement poetic de l'honneur femenin* ... in 1539; these are, in fact, sonnets and could have been composed before the summer of 1536. (But see HS13 on Bouchet's poems.)

Mayer's arguments concerning the dating of the two above-mentioned sonnets are challenged in separate letters by Yves Giraud and Marcel Françon, *RHLF*, LXVIII (1968), 875-76 and 876-77. In his reply, Mayer maintains his position, pp. 877-78.

HS15 Mayer, Claude Albert, 'Gabriele Simeoni et le premier sonnet français', *SFr*, XVIII (1974), 213-23.

Simeoni's sonnet *Alla signora Helena di Traves sopra la somiglianza di sua madre* was almost certainly written not in 1533, but in 1547 (cf. already Villey's arguments in HS22). Accordingly, Saint-Gelais's sonnet replying in Helen's name (see HS5, 6) must have been composed between then and 1549, when both poems were published. A fairly convincing demonstration.

HS16 Mayer, Claude Albert, 'Du Nouveau sur le sonnet français: Marot, Du Bellay et Castiglione', *SFr*, XX (1976), 422-29.

MS BN f. fr. 2334 contains a previously unknown version — hence not mentioned in *Bibliog. I* or *OC*, IV — of CM's earliest sonnet (*Sonnet à madame de Ferrare*: *OC*, IV, p. 267). Also transcribed, unsigned, in the MS is the sonnet 'Voyant ces mons de veue si loingtaine' — for which Mayer considered CM's authorship 'probable' in *OC*, IV, pp. 48-49 (cf. HS14) — and which he here definitely attributes to him. But curiously, Mayer does not rule out the possibility that the somewhat different versions printed in Saint-Gelais's *Œuvres* in 1547 and 1574 could be by that poet.

HS17 Mönch, Walter, *Das Sonett: Gestalt und Geschichte*, Heidelberg: Kerle, 1955, 341 pp.

On CM, see p. 118. The book, which traces the history of the sonnet in the major European literatures, has a very extensive bibliography.

HS18 Olmsted, Everett Ward, *The Sonnet in French Literature and the Development of the French Sonnet Form*, Ithaca, 1897, 212 pp.

On CM, see pp. 55-57. Olmsted doubts Lenglet-Dufresnoy's dating of *Pour le mai planté par les imprimeurs de Lyon* ... (*OC*, IV, p. 269) at 1529, and wrongly believes it to have been first published in 1545. (According to Villey, HS22, and Mayer, *OC*, IV, p. 269, it was composed in 1538. It first appeared in Dolet's ed. of CM's *Œuvres* that same year.) Olmsted concludes that the first French sonnet was written by Saint-Gelais, but is unable to identify it. The book has a useful tabulation of the rhyme-schemes of 3,390 sonnets from Saint-Gelais to Gautier

HS19 Pflänzel, Max, *Über die Sonette des Joachim du Bellay, nebst einer Einleitung: Die Einführung des Sonetts in Frankreich*, Saalfeld, 1898, 85 pp.

HS20 Vaganay, Hugues, *Le Sonnet en Italie et en France au XVIe siècle: Essai de bibliographie comparée*, Lyon: Facultés Catholiques, 2 vols, 1902-03.

HS21 Veyrières, Louis de, 'Clément Marot', in his *Monographie du sonnet: Sonnetistes anciens et modernes, suivis de quatre-vingts sonnets*, Paris: Bachelin-Deflorenne, 2 vols, 1869, I, pp. 39-40.

Vianey, Joseph: see I44.

HS22 Villey, Pierre, 'Marot et le premier sonnet français', *RHLF*, XXVII (1920), 538-47.
Supports the commonly-held view of CM's precedence over Saint-Gelais as a composer of sonnets, but does so on the basis of dates corrected as follows: (i) CM's *Pour le may planté par les imprimeurs de Lyon devant le logis du seigneur Trivulse* (*OC*, IV, p. 269) does not date 'au plus tard de 1530, puisque Trivulce mourut en 1531', as Jasinski thought (HS11, p. 37), but most probably from 1538, being addressed, not to Théodore but to his nephew Pomponio Trivulzio; (ii) this poem was therefore later than CM's sonnet to Renée of Ferrara (*OC*, IV, p. 267), composed in or soon after June-July 1536, and later than the *Sonnet de la difference du roy et de l'empereur* (*OC*, IV, p. 268), written between Sept. 1536 and March 1538; (iii) Saint-Gelais's *Sonnet faict au nom de madamoiselle de Traves* was not composed in 1533, but almost certainly no earlier than 1547 (cf. HS5, 9, 15); (iv) Molinier's suggestion, in C107, that Saint-Gelais's undated sonnets may have been written as early as 1525, nineteen years before the first dated one, is highly improbable: none of them is likely to have been composed much before 1540, at the earliest. Villey's conclusion: CM's sonnet *A madame de Ferrare* may well be the earliest French sonnet.
An excellent art., meticulous and impeccably argued, which greatly influenced critics. Mayer adopts the same order and dating in *OC*.

Wells, Margaret W.: see HA110.

Le Temple de Cupido

Ito, Susumu: see I20.

Frappier, Jean: see KB19, 20.

Popârda, Oana: see I32.

Translations

Psalms

HUa1 Albaric, M., 'Le Psautier de Clément Marot', *RSPT*, LIV
(1970), 227-43.
Excellent review-art. on E40. Acknowledges the overall interest of
Lenselink's ed., but criticizes various aspects of the introduction, as
well as the establishment of the text. Considers the presentation of the
early eds unclear and incomplete, and gives a far more comprehensive
list (but does not appraise or classify the eds – for this, see F47, 48,
and *OC*, VI). Lenselink's text of the psalms contains numerous errors,
and his critical apparatus is inadequate. Unconvinced by Lenselink's
conclusions regarding the theological and literary sources of CM's tr.,
Albaric offers some interesting remarks on the subject.

HUa2 Baulacre, Léonard, 'Les Psaumes de Marot et de Bèze, qu'on
chante dans l'église de Genève', in *Œuvres historiques et
littéraires de Léonard Baulacre ...*, recueillies et mises en ordre
par Édouard Mallet, Geneva: Jullien, 2 vols, 1857, I, pp. 408-
43.
On the composition and history, including eds and revisions, of the CM-
Beza psalter in the sixteenth and seventeenth centuries. (According to a
note by the editor, the study had previously appeared in the *Journal
Helvétique* in 1745 and the *Nouvelle Bibliothèque Germanique* in 1747.)

HUa3 Becker, Ph. Aug., *Clément Marots Psalmenübersetzung*, Berichte
über die Verhandlungen der Sächsischen Akademie der Wissenschaften, Leipzig, Philologisch-Historische Klasse, LXXII, 1
(1920), Leipzig: Teubner, 1921, 44 pp.
Detailed study of the composition of CM's psalms and their early eds.
Becker argues that there was a now lost 1538 Parisian *editio princeps*
of the *Trente psaumes*. Interesting pages on CM's translating technique.
Particularly important is Becker's demonstration of CM's strong reliance

on Bucer's exposition and summary of the psalms, first published, with Latin psalm translations, in Strasbourg in 1529 and reprinted several times. CM may also have been influenced by Olivetan's tr. of the Bible. Cf. HUa18.
Rev.: .1 Lerber, W. de, *RSS*, IX (1922), 295-301.

HUa4 Bovet, Félix, 'Les Psaumes de Cl. Marot et de Th. de Bèze, au point de vue littéraire', *BSHP*, XV (1866), 324-32.
Points out some felicities and some blemishes of the translations. CM's is generally superior to Beza's, and was certainly so regarded by six-teenth-century writers. This essay, with only minor changes, forms the second chapter of HUa5.

HUa5 Bovet, Félix, *Histoire du psautier des églises réformées*, Paris: Grassart, 1872, 342 pp.
Excellent, very informative study which still remains valuable. One of the most interesting chapters deals with translations of the French psalter into other European languages. The wide-ranging bibliography covers eds in French as well as in other tongues.

HUa6 Bruguier, Jean, *Discours sur le chant des pseaumes*, Nîmes: E. Raban, 1662, 62 pp.
Defends the singing of psalms in the vernacular, and the CM-Beza version. But CM himself has a less than enthusiastic champion in Bruguier: 'un meschant homme peut estre un poëte excellent; ainsi les vers de Marot ne sont pas moins justes, pour avoir esté enfantez par un monstre'. In any case, CM 'n'a fourni, ni le sens, ni les paroles mesmes de ces cantique mais seulement la mesure et l'arrangement des paroles.' (This is presumabl a reference to Vatable's supposed collaboration – see HA67, C119.)

*HUa7 Chaix, Henri, 'Le Psautier huguenot: Sa Formation et son histoire dans l'église réformée', Doctoral thesis, Univ. of Geneva 1907, 115 pp.

Clive, H.P.: see F11.

*HUa8 Coppedge, Elizabeth Catherine Wright, 'The Psalms of Clément Marot and Jean Antoine de Baïf: A Discussion of Translation and Poetry in Sixteenth-Century France', Ph. D. thesis, New York Univ., 1975, 236 pp. *DisA*, XXXVI (1975-76), 2239A.
CM and Baïf, while using 'scholarly translations as guides for their versions, rather than working directly from the Hebrew text', sought 'to imitate the original Hebrew lyric scansion in their versification forms ... [and] developed and expanded the capacities of French lyric

poetry through their attempts to find the closest possible equivalencies for the lyrism and textual expression of the Hebrew psalms.'

HUa9   Couthaud, E., 'La Traduction des psaumes de Cl. Marot et de Théod. de Bèze, et celle de Ph. Desportes', *BSHP*, XIV (1865), 177-84.
Prints side by side, without any critical comment, CM's and Desportes's translations of psalm XXXVIII.

HUa10   Crawford, G.A., 'Clément Marot and the Huguenot Psalter', *Musical Times and Singing-Class Circular*, XXII (1881), 285-87, 346-48, 404-06, 450-53, 505-08, 554-57.
Review-art. on C49. Summarizes the book, including the biography of CM, but pays little attention to Douen's description of CM's religious ideas. Concentrates on the psalms.

HUa11   Désiré, Artus, *Le Contrepoison des cinquante-deux chansons de Clément Marot, faulsement intitulées par luy Psalmes de David*, Paris: Pierre Gaultier, 1560. For a modern ed., see Artus Désiré, *Le Contrepoison ... Marot*. Fac-similé de l'éd. de Paris, 1560, avec introduction et notes par Jacques Pineaux, TLF, CCXXXVIII, Geneva: Droz, 1977, 252 pp.
Désiré's *contrafacta* of CM's psalms (fifty-two because Désiré is basing himself on the *Cinquante-deux psaumes de David* which contained, in addition to CM's forty-nine translations, French versions of psalms XXXIV and XLII by Claude Le Maistre, and of psalm LXII by Étienne Pasquier). See also HUa15.

Douen, O.: see C49.

Droz, E.: see F14.

HUa12   Förster, Margarete, 'Die Psalmen Clément Marots', in her *Die französischen Psalmenübersetzungen vom XII. bis zum Ende des XVIII. Jahrhunderts: Ein Beitrag zur Geschichte der französischen Übersetzungskunst*, Berlin: Ebering, 1914, pp. 41-49.
Some interesting remarks, illustrated by numerous examples, on CM's translation technique, Hebraisms, general faithfulness to the Hebrew text. The question of CM's direct sources is, however, barely broached.

HUa13   Gastoué, Amédée, *Le Cantique populaire en France: Ses sources, son histoire, augmentées d'une bibliographie générale des anciens cantiques et noëls*, Lyons: Janin, 1924, 344 pp.

Includes a discussion of the psalm translations. Unlike most critics, Gastoué considers Beza's versions decidedly superior to CM's.

HUa14   Gérold, Th., 'Le Premier Psautier', *BSHP*, LXXXVII (1938), 370-75.
On the partial psalter published in Strasbourg in 1539 (*Bibliog. II*, no. 82) which contained twelve psalms by CM. The remarks deal mainly with the music.

HUa15   Giese, Frank S., *Artus Désiré, Priest and Pamphleteer of the Sixteenth Century*, Univ. of North Carolina Studies in the Romance Languages and Literatures, CXXXVI, Chapel Hill: Department of Romance Languages, Univ. of North Carolina, 1973, 188 pp.
On the author of the *Contrepoison* (see HUa11), on which see esp. pp. 120-30.

Gutknecht, Dieter: see F21.

Harrab, Thomas: see C75.

Harrisse, Henry: see F23, 24.

*HUa16   Heudier, Jean Pierre, 'L'Esprit de la Renaissance dans les paraphrases des psaumes', Ph. D. thesis, Univ. of Colorado, 1970, 216 pp. *DisA*, XXXI (1970-71), 2900A.
Analyzes psalm versions by eight poets, including CM, 'in order to discover which ideas of the Renaissance influenced these paraphrases, and to ascertain the effect of these ideas on the renditions of the psalms, especially as to vocabulary, imagery, lyricism and philosophy'.

HUa17   Jeanneret, Michel, 'Marot traducteur des psaumes entre le néo-platonisme et la Réforme', *BHR*, XXVII (1965) 629-43.
Concludes, on the basis of a close analysis of CM's two prefaces to his psalm translations – *Au roy treschrestien Françoys ...*(*OC*, VI, pp. 309-14) and *Aux dames de France* (*OC*, VI, pp. 314-16) – that CM remains faithful in both poems to the particular blend of neo-platonism and evangelism associated with the circle of Marguerite de Navarre.

HUa18   Jeanneret, Michel, *Poésie et tradition biblique au XVIe siècle: Recherches stylistiques sur les paraphrases des psaumes de Marot à Malherbe*, Paris: Corti, 1969, 574 pp.
See esp. 'Clément Marot', pp. 51-87. CM used extensively Olivetan's

French tr. of the Bible, and probably also, though to a lesser extent, that of Lefèvre d'Étaples. There is no doubt as to the influence of Bucer's commentaries on the psalms, but it is less considerable than Becker thought (see HUa3). CM also drew on the Latin paraphrase by Campensis (Van Kampen). Some interesting, though rather brief, remarks on CM's efforts to remain faithful to the sense and, wherever possible, the form of the original, and on the general style of his tr. There are also several references to his poetic technique in the discussions of other French versions elsewhere in the book.

Jurieu, P.: see C85.

La Harpe, J.F.: see HA49.

Laumonier, Paul: see I23.

Lebègue, Raymond: see F36.

HUa19 Lelièvre, Matth., 'Le Psautier huguenot', *Revue Chrétienne*, XXX (1883), 33-50, 78-86.
Study of the history of the psalter, based to a large extent on HUa5 and C49.

HUa20 Lelièvre, Matthieu, 'Le Psautier huguenot et son histoire', in his *Portraits et récits huguenots du XVIe siècle*, Toulouse: Société des Livres Religieux, 1895, pp. 283-323.
Reprint, in a slightly revised version, of HUa19.

HUa21 Ligas, Pierluigi, 'Sugli *pseaumes* di Clément Marot', *Culture Française*, XXIV (1977), 113-16.

Maimbourg, Louis: see C99.

Martinon, Ph.: see I27.

Mayer, C.A.: see F47, 48.

HUa22 Monnier, Marc, *Genève et ses poëtes du XVIe siècle à nos jours*, Paris: Sandoz & Fischbacher, 1874, vii + 519 pp.
On CM, see pp. 89-96.

HUa23 Muller, A., 'Les Traductions de psaumes au XVIe siècle: Marot', in his *La Poésie religieuse catholique de Marot à Malherbe*, Paris: Foulon, 1950, pp. 37-53.
Identifies the merits and the shortcomings of CM's translations, with particular reference to psalm XXXIII: great metrical richness and

ingenuity, but these are often ill adapted to the spiritual content; an admirable lyricism, an easily flowing style, but excessively free paraphrases, prolixity of language, undue emphasis on certain details. On the whole, Muller considers the translations more important for their influence on later lyric poetry than in their own right.

HUa24   Pannier, Jacques, 'A propos du IVe centenaire du psautier de 1543', *BSHP*, Soixante-dix-huitième Assemblée Générale, 20 juin 1943 (1943), 18-100.
Consists of 'Calvin et le psautier', pp. 18-29, and 'Le Psautier et l'évolution religieuse de Marot', pp. 30-100. The latter traces CM's life, describes his ideas, and sets out the history of his psalm translations against the religious background of the period. Pannier brings together much pertinent information, but also makes some inaccurate statements.

Pasquier, Étienne: see HA67.

HUa25   Pineaux, Jacques, 'Une Contrefaçon protestante des psaumes de Marot au XVIe siècle: Le *Singulier Antidot* d'I.D.D.C.', *BSHP*, CXXII (1976), 149-65.
The full title is *Singulier antidot contre la poison des chansons d'Artus Desiré, ausquelles il a damnablement abusé d'aucuns psalmes du prophete royal David*. The work, published in 1561, is thus a reply to Désiré's *Contrepoison* (HUa11) and uses the same method of parodying the psalm translations.

HUa26   Plattard, Jean, 'Comment Marot entreprit et poursuivit la traduction des psaumes de David', *RER*, X (1912), 321-55.
Disagrees with Douen's portrayal (in C49) of CM as an apostle of liberal protestantism and with his assertion that CM's purpose in translating the psalms was to forge an instrument of reformist propaganda. Believes that the initial impulse came from Marguerite's evangelical circle. Is doubtful of Vatable's collaboration. Indicates different Latin versions available to CM, but does not attempt to narrow the range of likely sources through textual analyses. Traces the history of the early eds. Illustrates the originality and quality of CM's psalms by comparing them with Gringore's *Heures de Notre Dame* (1527).

HUa27   Pratt, Waldo Selden, *The Significance of the Old French Psalter Begun by Clément Marot in 1532*, Papers of the Hymn Society, IV, New York: Hymn Society, 1933, 16 pp.
Text of a lecture about the 'sturdy and prolific seedling that Marot was moved to plant in 1532'. Unreliable on dates and facts, e.g. states

that CM set himself to the project of translating the psalter towards the end of 1532, and that he took up Hebrew that same year.

HUa28   Pratt, Waldo Selden, 'The Importance of the Early French Psalter', *Musical Quarterly*, XXI (1935), 25-32.
Very brief and partly incorrect notes on the history of CM's psalm translations, followed by some even more cursory remarks about the music, and about psalm versions in other languages, based on the Genevan psalter.

HUa29   Pratt, Waldo Selden, *The Music of the French Psalter of 1562: A Historical Survey and Analysis, with the Music in Modern Notation*, New York: Columbia UP, 1939, 213 pp.
Valuable chiefly for the transcription of the tunes in modern notation. Pratt provides also tabulated analyses of the metres amployed by CM and Beza, and of the Genevan melodies which were used in early English and Scottish psalters.

HUa30   *Le Psautier huguenot du XVIe siècle: Mélodies et documents*, recueillis par Pierre Pidoux, Bâle: Baerenreiter, 2 vols, 1962.
An invaluable reference work, esp. Vol. II: *Documents et biographie.*

Raemond, Florimond de: see C119.

HUa31   R[ead], C., 'Les Psaumes et l'épître dédicatoire de Clément Marot', *BSHP*, I (1852-53), 34-36.
Text of *Aux dames de France* (*OC*, VI, pp. 314-16), preceded by brief remarks on the restoration of the religious character of church music under the Reformation.

HUa32   R[ead], C., 'Les Psaumes et l'épître dédicatoire de Clément Marot au roy, 1541', *BSHP*, II (1854), 417-25.
Brief introduction, followed by the text of *Au roy treschrestien Françoys ...* (*OC*, VI, pp. 309-14).

Regius, Karl: see I34.

*HUa33   Reuben, Catherine Ann, 'Clément Marot: Les Psaumes de David', Ph. D. thesis, Univ. of Liverpool, 1971, iii + 390 + xlii pp.
The thesis focuses, in turn, on eds, sources, and 'Le Poète et le traducteur: la forme, le parallelisme, la répétition, l'image'.

HUa34   Richter, Mario, 'Aspetti e orientamenti della poetica prote-
         stante francese nel secolo XVI', *SFr*, XI (1967), 223-45.

         Rocoles, Jean Baptiste: see C122.

HUa35   Rou, Jean, *Remarques sur 'L'Histoire du calvinisme' de M*^r
         Maimbourg, The Hague: A. Moetjens, 1682.
         Defends CM's psalm translations (pp. 33-37).

HUa36   Saulnier, V.L., 'Marguerite de Navarre, Catherine de Médicis
         et les psaumes de Marot: Autour de la lettre dite de Ville-
         madon', *BHR*, XXXVII (1975), 349-75.
         A thorough study of the letter — its reference to Catherine's former
         sterility, the well-known passage about the vogue enjoyed by the
         psalm translations, etc. Saulnier argues that the letter, which is
         evidently written by a Huguenot, is in fact a pamphlet directed
         against Cardinal Charles de Lorraine and, at the same time, a plea
         for religious tolerance and a call for the return to the Bible. Gives
         details of the various eds of the letter.

         Sleidanus, Johannes: see HA92, 93.

HUa37   Stéphan, Raoul, *Histoire du protestantisme français*, Paris:
         Fayard, 1961, 396 pp.
         Some general remarks, in the chapter 'Explosion du lyrisme religieux',
         on CM's religious inspiration, mainly as manifested in the psalm trans-
         lations.

HUa38   Trénel, J., 'Le Psaume CX chez Marot et d'Aubigné', in
         Mélanges ... Ferdinand Brunot, Paris: Société Nouvelle de
         Librairie et d'Édition, 1904, pp. 323-29.
         A rapid, though not instructive, comparison. But Trénel provides
         no evidence to substantiate his assertions that both versions are
         based on Olivetan's translation, and that D'Aubigné recaptures the
         biblical tone less faithfully than CM, because he is concerned more
         with producing a text suitable for musical setting than with achieving
         high literary quality.

*HUa39   Van Griethuysen, Willem, 'Le Psautier huguenot du 16^e
         siècle: Aperçu historique de la création littéraire et musicale
         du psautier de langue française', Doctoral thesis, Univ. of
         Geneva, 1953, 150 pp.

HUa40   Vianey, Joseph, 'La Bible dans la poésie française depuis

Marot: Première leçon', *RCC*, XXIII, Pt I (1921-22), 485-95.

This opening lecture in a course bearing the above general title is almost entirely devoted to CM's psalm translations. Vianey recognizes certain defects, but stresses above all CM's achievement. 'Le premier auteur lyrique français' of modern times and 'celui qui a guidé les autres' is not Ronsard, as he himself claims, 'c'est l'auteur des *Trente psaumes* de 1542, des *Cinquante psaumes* de 1543. Ce petit recueil contenait en germe toutes les nouveautés ...'

Villemadon: see HUa36.

Voltaire: see HA106.

HUa41 Weber, Édith, *La Musique protestante de langue française*, Coll. Musique-Musicologie, VII, Paris: Champion, 1979, 199 pp.

See esp. 'Clément Marot', pp. 133-35, but there are also numerous references to CM elsewhere in the book.

Weiss, N.: see A10.

HUa42 Woodward, G.R., 'The Genevan Psalter of 1562, Set in Four-Part Harmony by Claude Goudimel in 1565', *Proceedings of the Musical Association* [London], Session XLIV (1917-18), 167-89. ('Discussion', 190-92.)

On the two translators, the melodies, the influence of the psalter in other countries. The biographical sketch of CM is quite unreliable.

HUa43 Young, Thomas, 'The French Psalter', in his *The Metrical Psalms and Paraphrases: A Short Sketch of Their History, with Biographical Notes of Their Authors*, London: Black, 1909, pp. 14-18.

Other Translations

HUb1 Balmas, Enea, 'Prime traduzioni dal *Canzoniere* nel cinquecento francese', in *Traduzione e tradizione europea del Petrarca. Atti del III Convegno sui problemi della traduzione letteraria (Monselice, 9 giugno 1974)*, Padua: Antenore, 1975, pp. 37-54, 118-29.

Contains an extensive and very useful discussion of CM's translations of Petrarch.

Becker, Ph. Aug.: see E27, 28.

HUb2   'Un Bibliophile rémois', 'Deux farces inédites de la reine de Navarre', *Bulletin du Bouquiniste*, III (1859), 307-09.
Correctly identifies the two 'farces' published by Lacour in E11 as colloquies by Erasmus. Suggests CM as the likely translator. See also HUb20 and esp. Mayer's remarks in *Bibliog. I*, p. 87 and *OC*, VI, pp. 41-44.

HUb3   Bost, Ch., '*Agimus* et *Père Eternel*', *BSHP*, LXXVIII (1929), 77-83.
On the saying 'Agimus avait gagné Père Éternel' common in the sixteenth century, which, in thus opposing a Catholic to a Protestant symbol, signified that Catholicism had triumphed over the new heresy (see *BSHP*, XI (1862),325, and A. de Montaiglon in *BSHP*, XII (1863), 245). Montaiglon explained that *Agimus* owed its symbolic function to its position at the beginning of the Latin prayer said by Catholics after a meal. Bost shows that the importance of *Père Eternel* as a Protestant symbol derived from the fact that it opens CM's *Priere apres le repas* (*OC*, VI, p. 108) which, from 1543 onward, appeared in various eds of CM's psalms and, later, of the CM-Beza psalter. In composing it, CM drew on a French prayer written by Calvin.

HUb4   Boulmier, Joseph, 'Salmon Macrin, l'"Horace français"', *BBB* (1870-71), 498-508.
Gives text of Macrin's Latin epigram addressed to François I, and of CM's French tr. (*OC*, VI, p. 225).

HUb5   Carvalho, Alfredo de, 'Os estudos latinos de Clément Marot', *Humanitas*, I (1947), 91-111.
Divides CM's study of Latin authors into three main periods. Reviews, in very general terms, the translations he did during each one.

Dédéyan, Charles: see KA6.

HUb6   Françon, Marcel, 'Sur l'influence de Pétrarque en France au XVe et XVIe siècles', *It*, XIX (1942), 105-10.
Considers CM's tr. of 'Chi vuol veder quatunque puo Natura' (*Canzoniere*, CCXLVIII) far less successful than his tr. of 'O passi sparsi' (*Canzoniere*, CLXI; on the latter tr., see also HUb16). (Both the French and Italian texts are given in *OC*, VI, pp. 220-22.)

HUb7   Françon, Marcel, 'Nicolas Bourbon et l'épitaphe à Laure',

FM, XXI (1953), 179-83.
On the text and meaning of the tr. – printed in Constantin's 1544 ed. of CM's *Œuvres* (*Bibliog. II*, no. 129) – of Bourbon's 'translation' of the epitaph. Cf. G13.

HUb8   Giraud, Yves F.-A., *La Fable de Daphné: Essai sur un type de métamorphose végétale dans la littérature et dans les arts jusqu'à la fin du XVIIe siècle*, Histoire des Idées et Critique Littéraire, XCII, Geneva: Droz, 1968, 574 pp.
On CM's French version of the fable of Daphne in his tr. of Ovid's *Metamorphoses*, see pp. 219-22.

Gmelin, Hermann: see KB22.

Guy, Henry: see KB24.

HUb9   Hennebert, Frédéric, 'Histoire des traductions françaises d'auteurs grecs et latins pendant le XVIe et le XVIIe siècles', *Annales des Universités de Belgique: Recueil contenant des Mémoires ..., Années 1858 et 1859*, 2nd ser., I, Brussels, 1861, 261 pp.
On CM, see pp. 91-104.

HUb10   Holl, Fritz, *Das politische und religiöse Tendenzdrama des 16. Jahrhunderts in Frankreich*, Münchener Beiträge zur Romanischen und Englischen Philologie, XXVI, Erlangen: Deichert (Böhme), 1903, xxvi + 219 pp.
On CM, see pp. 97-98. Very briefly summarizes the plots of two of the three colloquies by Erasmus tr. by CM (*OC*, VI, pp. 247-67, 267-97).

HUb11   Hulubei, Alice, 'Virgile en France au XVIe siècle: Éditions, traductions, imitations', *RSS*, XVIII (1931), 1-77.
On CM's tr. of Virgil's first eclogue, see pp. 33-34. 'La traduction est assez harmonieuse et claire et contient peu de verbiage.' However, 'cette version ... nous paraît aujourd'hui bien défectueuse'.

Hulubei, Alice: see also HJ7.

Hutton, James: see KB25-27.

Lebègue, Raymond: see KB30.

HUb12   Lerber, W. de, 'Clément Marot et Lucien', *RSS*, X (1923),

229-30.
Summary of E27.

*HUb13 Morisset, G.M.M., 'Ovide durant la première moitié du XVIᵉ siècle, 1500-1550', Ph. D. thesis, Univ. of London, 1934, v + 231 pp.

HUb14 Naïs, Hélène, 'Traduction et imitation chez quelques poètes du XVIᵉ siècle', *RSH*, LII, no. 180 (1980), 33-49.
Contains some remarks about CM's tr. of Ovid.

HUb15 Patocchi, Pericle, 'Quando Marot traduceva Petrarca', *C*, II, 4 (1953), 3-26.
Concludes that CM tends to substitute for the essentially spiritual, conceptual, abstract quality of Petrarch's text a more concrete, more rationally explicit, more specifically human tone.

HUb16 Pauphilet, Albert, 'Sur des vers de Pétrarque', in *Mélanges ... Henri Hauvette*, Paris: Presses Françaises, 1934, pp. 113-21.
Compares two French versions of 'O passi sparsi' (*Canzoniere*, CLXI): CM's tr. (*OC*, VI, pp. 220-21) is skilful and close, but faithful to the letter rather than to the spirit of the original; Ronsard's 'O traits fichez jusqu'au fond de mon ame' (*Les Amours*, CLXXIII) is a far freer, but also a more subtle, adaptation. (On CM's tr., cf. HUb6).

Popârda, Oana: see I32.

HUb17 Rocher, Gregory de, 'Une Oraison de Clément Marot et la formation de "l'élégant badinage"', *RLV*, XLIV (1978), 301-07.
In the *Oraison contemplative devant le crucifix* (*OC*, VI, pp. 92-98), CM employs the rhetorical devices of Barthélemy's Latin poem (see KB30) and, in so doing, begins to develop his 'verbosité agréable'. At the same time, the poem provides him with a model which will help him depict emotions and states of mind in his own poems.

Regius, Karl: see I34.

HUb18 Saulnier, Verdun L., 'Virgile en France, au XVIᵉ siècle', in *DLF*, pp. 703-05.

HUb19 Stackelberg, Jürgen von, 'Clément Marot', in his *Literarische Rezeptionsformen: Übersetzung, Supplement, Parodie*,

Schwerpunkte Romanistik (Gen. Ed.: Leo Pollmann),
Frankfurt: Athenäum, 1972, pp. 13-15.
CM's tr. of Virgil's first eclogue is one of the earliest French examples
of a 'naturalizing' translation: the shepherd does not speak a learned
or stilted French, as he did in the tr. by Michel de Tours; the additions serve the purpose of injecting local colour.

HUb20   Turquety, Éd., 'Deux farces inédites de la reine de Navarre',
Bulletin du Bouquiniste, III (1859), 346-47.
Points out that the tr. of Erasmus's colloquy *Virgo misogamos* mistakenly attributed by Lacour to Marguerite de Navarre in E11 appeared
in Lenglet-Dufresnoy's 1731 ed. of CM's *Œuvres* (E4). See HUb2 and
esp. Mayer's remarks in *Bibliog. I*, p. 87 and *OC*, VI, pp. 41-44.

Wagner, Albert: see KB44.

Weinberg, Bernard: see E33.

White, Margarita Klara: see KA22.

Editions

Le Roman de la Rose

HVa1   Baridon, Silvio F., 'Hypothèses et controverses sur l'auteur
de la révision de 1526', in E35, I, pp. 56-80.
Replies at length to the objections raised by Becker (HVa2) and
Weinberg (HVa10) to the attribution of this ed. to CM. Accepts
Sneyders de Vogel's arguments supporting the attribution (HVa9)
and adds some new ones. Concludes that there are insufficient
grounds for denying CM's responsibility for the ed. See further
under HVa3.

HVa2   Becker, Ph. Aug., 'Clément Marot und der *Rosenroman*',
GRM, IV (1912), 684-87.
Contests the attribution of Galliot du Pré's 1526 ed. to CM, because
of (i) the absence of his name from the title page, the privilege, and
the preface; (ii) the appearance of a personal motto different from
CM's beneath the preface in the 1529 reprint; (iii) the style of the
preface; (iv) the orthodox religious ideas expressed in the preface.
Becker suggests that Pasquier, who first named CM as the editor in
a letter (see HA67) may have confused the ed. of the *Roman* with
CM's ed. of Villon. (On this last point, see HVa9.)

HVa3 Bourdillon, F.W., *The Early Editions of the 'Roman de la Rose'*, Bibliographical Society Illustrated Monographs, XIV, London: Bibliographical Society, 1906, x + 203 pp.
Gives detailed descriptions of the 1526, 1529, 1531, and 1537 (or 1538) eds of 'Clément Marot's recension', with notes on the text and illustrations. CM worked from the ed. published by G. Le Roy in Lyons in ca 1487, with occasional recourse to a MS. (This view regarding the sources of the 1526 ed. is shared by Eusebi (HVa7) and by Baridon (HVa1). The latter adds, however, that a passage of 104 lines omitted in the 1487 and 1526 eds was restored in the 1529 ed., the text being taken from an ed. of the original poem which had been published in Paris the previous year by A. Lotrian.)

HVa4 Brüning, Detlef, *Clément Marots Bearbeitung des 'Rosenromans' (1526): Studien zur Rezeption des 'Rosenromans' im frühen sechzehnten Jahrhundert*, Berlin: Schmidt, 1972, 200 pp.
Careful study of the religious and moralizing content of the preface, of the literary features of the revision, and of the condition of the language reflected in the text. The purpose is to illuminate CM's ideas in these different areas, for Brüning declares himself fully convinced by Baridon's arguments in favour of CM's editorship (see HVa1)
Rev.: .1 Dubois, E.T., *E*, XXVI (1974), 796-98.
.2 Schulz-Buschhaus, Ulrich, *RF*, LXXXV (1973), 371-74.

HVa5 Chamard, Henri, '*Roman de la Rose*', in *DLF*, pp. 606-08.
Attributes the 1526 version to CM.

HVa6 Dorgan, Cornelia W., '*Le Roman de la Rose*, 1526', *Boston Public Library Quarterly*, V (1953), 58-61.
Art. prompted by the Library's recent acquisition of a copy of Galliot du Pré's 1526 ed., which is briefly described. Some remarks about CM, 'the young warrior and courtier of Marguerite d'Angoulême', and about the *Roman*. Of little interest.

HVa7 Eusebi, M., 'Saggio sulle edizioni cinquecentesche del *Roman de la Rose* attribuite a Clement Marot', *Istituto Lombardo* [Milan]. *Rendiconti, Classe di Lettere e Scienze Morali e Storiche*, XCII (1958), 527-57.
From a close comparison of the first 4070 lines in the 1487 and the 1526 eds of the *Roman*, Eusebi argues that the lack of linguistic unity and the general carelessness evident in the latter revision speak convincingly against CM's editorship. See also under HVa3.

HVa8   Nichols, Stephen G., 'Marot, Villon and the *Roman de la Rose*: A Study in the Language of Creation and Re-Creation', *SP*, LXIII (1966), 135-43; LXIV (1967), 25-43.
An examination of a few selected passages from the eds of Villon and the *Roman* clearly shows CM's desire to present a text which is at once comprehensible to a sixteenth-century reader and as faithful as possible to the old language, as he conceives it. Nichols then points out some possible reminiscences of the *Roman* in CM's own poems.

Pasquier, Étienne: see HA67.

HVa9   Sneyders de Vogel, K., 'Marot et *Le Roman de la Rose*', *N*, XVII (1932), 269-71.
Discounts Becker's arguments against CM's editorship (HVa2). With regard to the final one, shows that Pasquier mentions CM's role on more than one occasion, which makes the possibility of his having confused the ed. of the *Roman* with that of Villon very improbable.

HVa10   Weinberg, Bernard, 'Guillaume Michel, dit de Tours, the Editor of the 1526 *Roman de la Rose*', *BHR*, XI (1949), 72-85.
Finds Sneyders de Vogel's arguments unconvincing (see HVa9). Rejects attribution to CM, because 'it seems inconceivable to me that Marot should have produced the pedantic and devout preface.' Proposes Guillaume Michel as the possible editor. (On this poet and translator, see Elizabeth Armstrong, 'Notes on the Works of Guillaume Michel, dit de Tours', *BHR*, XXXI (1969), 257-81.)

Weinberg, Bernard: see also E33.

Villon, *Les Œuvres*

HVb1   Cons, Louis, *État présent des études sur Villon*, Études Françaises, XXXVII, Paris: Belles Lettres, 1936, 161 pp.
CM's perception of Villon, according to the preface he wrote for his ed.

*HVb2   Delescluse, Dominique, 'Le *Villon* de Clément Marot', Thèse de Maîtrise, Univ. of Lyons II, 1978, ca 100 pp.
According to HVb5, p. 14, n. 7, Delescluse compares CM's text with those published by Galliot du Pré in 1532 and by A. Longnon in 1892.

HVb3   Green, F.C., 'Marot's Preface to his Edition of Villon's Works', *MP*, XXII (1924-25), 69-77.

The preface is important as one of the earliest attempts at serious literary criticism in France. Moreover, CM's assessment of Villon's poetry is, on the whole, remarkably astute. Green attributes the confident tone of CM's pronouncements to the celebrity he is likely to have enjoyed at the time.

HVb4   Hesnaut, Louis, 'Villon et ses éditions', *BBB* (1923), 116-26.

Half the art. is devoted to an examination of CM's textual changes and his annotations in the 1533 ed.

HVb5   Lazard, Madeleine, 'Clément Marot éditeur et lecteur de Villon', *CAIEF*, XXXII (1980), 7-20.

CM showed a critical spirit attuned to the new humanist ideas and generally performed his editorial task scrupulously and also extremely successfully, esp. given the limited research facilities available to him. Certain good readings point to his having had access either to a printed text beyond Pierre Levet's 1489 ed. – and the eds derived from it – or to a MS different from the three main known ones.

Nichols, Stephen G.: see HVa8.

HVb6   Speer, Mary B., 'The Editorial Tradition of Villon's *Testament*: From Marot to Rychner and Henry', *RPh*, XXXI (1977-78), 344-61.

Believes that CM consulted MSS, in addition to the printed textual tradition (not neccessarily Levet's ed.). In thus basing himself on the printed tradition and verifying it with the help of other sources, CM set a methodological precedent which was followed by later editors.

Weinberg, Bernard: see E33.

(Further observations on CM's preface and editorial actions can be found in certain modern eds of Villon.)

I. LANGUAGE, STYLE, VERSIFICATION

I1   Baldensperger, Fernand, 'Diminutifs amicaux dans la poésie de la Renaissance', *Vie et Langage* (1957), 422-25.

I2   Bastin, J., *Le Participe passé dans la langue française et son histoire*, St Petersburg, 1880, iv + 57 pp.

I3   Bastin, J., 'Le Participe passé avec *avoir*, au XVIᵉ siècle', *Revue de Philologie Française et Provençale*, IX (1895), 237-40.
      CM's rule concerning the agreement of the past participle was generally disregarded by sixteenth-century writers, and even by CM himself. Bastin cites, however, no examples of CM's usage.

I4   Borlé, Édouard, *Observations sur l'emploi des conjonctions de subordination dans la langue du XVIᵉ siècle, étudié spécialement dans les deux ouvrages de Bernard Palissy*, Paris: Belles Lettres, 1927, xx + 261 pp.

I5   Camproux, Ch., 'Langue et métrique: A propos du décasyllabe des *Épîtres* de Marot', *FM*, XXXII (1964), 194-205.
      Rejects as anachronistic the commonly held view that the decasyllable was the ideal vehicle for the 'style marotique', because of its brevity and lightness. The different structure of the sixteenth-century language allowed greater conciseness in the expression of the *signifié* than modern French, a fact which Camproux illustrates by analyzing two epistles of strongly contrasting tone, *Marot, prisonnier, escript au roy pour sa delivrance* and the *Epistre envoyée de Venize à madame la duchesse de Ferrare*. The decasyllable could thus carry more meaning and was felt to be longer than in modern times. An interesting, well-argued art.

      Cerreta, Florindo V.: see HS2.

I6   Chamard, Henri, 'Versification', in *DLF*, pp. 686-97.

I7   Chavannes, Fréd., 'Essai sur l'histoire de la versification au XVIᵉ siècle', *Revue Suisse et Chronique Littéraire*, IX (1846), 793-808; X (1847), 18-39, 176-91, 252-71.

Although its development lacks clarity, this is an important study which offers a host of valuable observations on CM's poetic technique.

I8   Delbouille, Maurice, 'Les Origines du lutin Pacolèt', in his 'Notes de philologie et de folklore', *BSLLW*, LXIX (1953), 105-44 (131-44).

The name – found, for instance, in Rabelais, and in CM (*Epistre à la damoyselle negligente de venir veoir ses amys*, *OC*, I, pp. 112-14, line 38) – designates the owner of a very swift horse. This meaning can be traced back to the fifteenth-century prose romance *Valentin et Orson* which tells of a Saracen dwarf-magician of that name who owns a flying horse. See also I12.

I9   Deloffre, Frédéric, 'Deux poèmes du seizième siècle (Méthode comparative)', in his *Stylistique et poétique françaises*, 2ᵉ éd. revue et augmentée, Paris: Société d'Édition d'Enseignement Supérieur, 1974, pp. 29-58.

Points out differences in style and in the underlying poetics between CM's *Dizain de neige* (*OC*, V, p. 115) and Scève's *Délie*, CLXIV.

I10   Eckerdt, H., 'Ueber Sprache und Grammatik Clément Marot's, mit Berücksichtigung einiger anderer Schriftsteller des 16. Jahrhunderts', *ASNS*, XXIX (1861), 183-204.

Some observations on various aspects of CM's language (e.g. archaisms) and grammar. A far from exhaustive study.

I11   Firmery, J., 'Sur la versification de Marot', *Revue de Philologie Française et Provençale*, VII (1893), 1-18.

Illustrates CM's frequent use of alliteration and of the *rime riche*. The study would be more useful if the data were classified according to genre or period of composition.

I12   Françon, Marcel, 'Mythologie et littérature: A propos de récentes éditions de Clément Marot', *Bulletin de la Société de Mythologie Française*, XXXV (1959), 74-75.

The name 'Astarot' in the *Epistre à la damoyselle negligente de venir veoir ses amys* (*OC*, I, pp. 112-14, line 21) does not refer to the goddess Astarte, but goes back to Astarut, one of the idols worshipped by the Saracens. Françon also cites an occurrence of 'Pacolet' (see I8) in the *Croniques admirables du puissant roy Gargantua*, where it is the name borne by the clerk of the hermit who baptizes Gargantua.

I13   Françon, Marcel, 'Le "monstre ignorance" au XVIᵉ siècle',

SFr, IV (1960), 71-74.

On the connotations of the terms 'ignorance' and 'monstre ignorance', as used by CM in the *Avant-naissance du troiziesme enffant de madame Renée* (*OC*, III, pp. 338-42, line 24) and by the Pléiade.

I14   Galliot, Marcel, 'Marot, *Epistres: "La Maladie de Marot"* ', in his *Études d'ancien français: Moyen âge et XVIᵉ siècle. Licence, CAPES, Agrégation*, Paris: Didier, 1967, pp. 246-57.

A study of the language, style and versification of lines 49-78 of the epistle *Au roy, pour avoir esté desrobé*.

I15   Glauning, Friedrich, *Syntaktische Studien zu Marot: Ein Beitrag zur Geschichte der französischen Syntax*, Nördlingen: Beck, 1873, 50 pp.

Lists differences between CM's syntax (according to E3) and modern usage. Avers that CM and Montaigne differ primarily in their use of articles and pronouns and in word order, but this conclusion is reached on the strength of only very general and unsupported remarks about the syntax of the *Essais*.

Griffin, Robert: see HA40.

Heudier, Jean Pierre: see HUa16.

I16   Huguet, Edmond, *L'Évolution du sens des mots depuis le XVIᵉ siècle*, Paris: Droz, 1934, xi + 346 pp.

I17   Huguet, Edmond, *Mots disparus ou vieillis depuis le XVIᵉ siècle*, Paris: Droz, 1935, 355 pp.

*I18   Ito, Susumu, 'Esthétique de la fantaisie chez Marot', *BFLACU*, XVI (1976), 1017-51. (Text in Japanese.)

Distinguishes three types of 'fantaisie' in CM's poems: 'comme arme de sarcasme et de satire, comme mystification, enfin comme lyrisme' (according to Ito's summary — see note to A7).

*I19   Ito, Susumu, 'A propos des poèmes d'éloge de Clément Marot, du point de vue de la rhétorique', *BFLACU*, XVII (1976-77), 699-718, 963-88, XVIII (1977-78), 571-625. (Text in Japanese.)

On CM's use of *inventio*, *dispositio*, and perhaps also *elocutio*, in these poems. (See note to A7.)

I20   Ito, Susumu, 'Essai de lexique du *Temple de Cupido* de Marot',

BFLACU, XXI (1980), 213-75.
Based on the text in *OC*, III, pp. 87-113. (This text reproduces that printed in Gryphius's 1538 ed. of CM's *Œuvres* – *Bibliog. II*, no. 71.)
Rev.: .1 Bellenger, Yvonne, *RHR*, no. 12 (1980), 84-85.

I21   Kastner, L.E., 'Les Grands Rhétoriqueurs et l'abolition de la coupe féminine', *RLR*, XLVI (1903), 289-97.
Not Jean Lemaire de Belges, as has been traditionally affirmed, but CM was responsible for the abandonment of the epic caesura. As for the exclusion of the lyric caesura, with which CM is credited, this should be ascribed to Cretin whose *Poésies*, in Coustellier's ed. (1723), offer not a single example of it. Cf. I26.

I22   Keuter, D*ʳ*, 'Clément Marots Metrik', *ASNS*, LXVIII (1882), 331-60.
References for the examples cited are given to volume and page of the 1731 ed. (E4), mostly without the poem in question being identified. No attempt is made to trace the development of the metrical features of CM's poetry.

I23   Laumonier, Paul, *Ronsard, poète lyrique: Étude historique et littéraire*, Paris: Hachette, 1909, li + 806 pp.
Many references to CM. In particular, Laumonier praises the metrical variety and excellence of CM's poems, esp. the psalm translations which present no fewer than forty-one different rhythmical combinations (a tabulated analysis is given on pp. 655-57). The total for psalms and *chansons* is seventy-six. Laumonier stresses Ronsard's indebtedness to CM's metres.

I24   Le Hir, Yves, *Esthétique et structure du vers français d'après les théoriciens, du XVIᵉ siècle à nos jours*, Paris: Presses Universitaires de France, 1956, 275 pp.

I25   Lerond, Alain, 'Marot et la *rhétorique*: Le Style du début de *L'Enfer*', in *Mélanges ... Jean Frappier*, Publications Romanes et Françaises, CXII, Geneva: Droz, 2 vols, 1970, II, pp. 631-44.
A detailed description and classification of the stylistic elements of lines 1-20 of *L'Enfer*. A painstaking study which at times threatens to crush the text under its weight.

I26   Martinon, Ph., 'La Genèse des règles de Jean Lemaire à Malherbe', *RHLF*, XVI (1909), 62-87.

Reasserts Lemaire's preeminent role – called in doubt by Kastner (I21) – in the abandonment of both epic and lyric caesuras. CM's fame and authority helped to impose the reform.

I27 Martinon, Ph., 'Marot', in his *Les Strophes: Étude historique et critique sur les formes de la poésie lyrique en France depuis la Renaissance*, Paris: Champion, 1912, pp. 8-20.
Pays tribute to CM's brilliant innovation in his choice and handling of lyric forms in the psalm translations: 'Entre les derniers psaumes de Marot et l'œuvre des Rhétoriqueurs, il y a presque un abîme: entre ces mêmes psaumes et l'œuvre lyrique de Ronsard, il n'y a même pas un fossé.' CM's psalms already contain all the essential elements of modern lyric poetry.

I28 Mayer, C.A., 'La Fantaisie dans l'œuvre de Clément Marot', in *Actes du Colloque tenu à Toulouse, les 23 et 24 mars 1959*, *Annales de l'Institut d'Études Occitanes* (1960), 82-87.
Concentrates almost entirely on the *coq-à-l'âne*, since they offer the richest crop of CM's satirical verve. Their key ingredients: a brilliant imagination, and controlled incoherence.

I29 Mayer, C.A., 'Marot et l'archaïsme', *CAIEF*, XIX (1967), 27-37.
Some interesting remarks, but the definition of what constitutes archaism in CM, and the subsequent distinction between conscious and unconscious archaism, produce some debatable statements.

Mayer, C.A.: see also HA56.

I30 Morçay, Raoul, 'L'Avènement du lyrisme au temps de la Renaissance', *HR*, III (1936), 271-88.
Stresses the influence of earlier popular poetry on versification in CM's *chansons*.

I31 Neuhofer, Peter, *Das Adjektiv als Stilelement bei Clément Marot*, Wiener Romanistische Arbeiten, II, Vienna: Braumüller, 1963, 175 pp.
A sound study, well documented, furnished with lists of significant examples and very useful statistical analyses, e.g. of word-frequencies: at the top of the count, *grand* (467), *beau* (308), *bon* (178). Neuhofer divides CM's adjectives into four main groups: adjectives of dimension and intensity; of emotion; of aesthetic expression; and of qualitative and ethical appreciation. In all these areas, the purpose underlying CM's use of adjectives is shown to be '[die] Steigerung des Substantivinhalts

und Pathetisierung der Aussage'. Discussion of certain aspects – for instance, the noun and its adjective, the significant epithet, hypallage – is juxtaposed with the examination of individual poems.

Rev.: .1 Bar, F., *RPh*, XVIII (1964-65), 515.

    .2 Drost, W., *SFr*, VIII (1964), 534-35.

    .3 Engler, Winfried, *NS*, new ser., XVI (1967), 249-50.

    .4 H[ilty], G., *VR*, XXVI (1967), 294-97.

    .5 Müller, Bodo, *ZRP*, LXXXV (1969), 448-51.

    .6 Richter, Bodo L.O., *RR*, LVII (1966), 128-32.

    .7 Schon, Peter M., *ASNS*, CCIII (1966-67), 234-36.

I32   Popârda, Oana, 'Aspecte cantitative ale stilului poetic al lui Clement Marot', *Analele Ştiinţifice ale Universităţii 'Al. I. Cuza' Din Iaşi*, new ser., Secţiunea III: e. Lingvistică, XXIV (1978), 97-100.

A quantitative analysis of CM's use of nouns in *Le Temple de Cupido*, the elegies, and *L'Histoire de Leander et de Hero*.

Pratt, Waldo Selden: see HUa29.

I33   Radmann, Lieselotte, *Der Stil Clément Marots in seinen Dichtungen*, Frankfurt, 1932, xii + 93 pp.

An interesting analysis which focuses on five aspects – antithesis, *gradatio*, *comparatio*, irony, the desire to surprise – and on their use in furtherance of CM's twin aims: to achieve clear thematic development, and to amuse.

I34   Regius, Karl, *Untersuchungen zum Übersetzerstil Clément Marots*, Schwarzenbach, 1951, 218 pp.

A brief survey of CM's translations, in their chronological order, is followed by a rapid stylistic study of all the translations considered together, with no regard to the nature of the original (i.e. whether prose or verse. Latin or Italian). Nothing on CM's development as a translator. On the whole, a superficial analysis which shows a somewhat uncertain knowledge of the sixteenth-century language and uses an insufficiently rigorous method, e.g. in the discussion of variants, which are, moreover, chosen undiscriminatingly.

Rev.: .1 Leblanc, P., *BSHP*, CI (1955), 39-41.

    .2 Mayer, C.A., *BHR*, XV (1953), 136-39.

I35   Rickard, Peter, 'Clément Marot (1496? -1544)', in his *La Langue française au seizième siècle: Étude suivie de textes*, Cambridge: Cambridge UP, 1968, pp. 92-96, 277-79.

Comments on the linguistic aspects of the epistle *Au roy, pour le deslivrer de prison*, the rondeaux *De celluy qui ne pense qu'en s'amye* (*OC*, IV, p. 111) and *De celluy de qui l'amye a faict nouvel amy* (*OC*, IV, p. 115), and the epigram *A ses disciples* (*OC*, V, p. 155).

I36 Rigolot, François, 'Poétique et onomastique: *L'Épigramme de Semblançay*', *Poétique*, V (1974), 194-203.
A study of onomastic motivation in CM's epigram, using the terminology proposed by Todorov in his 'Introduction à la symbolique' in *Poétique*, III (1972), 273-308. See also I37.

I37 Rigolot, François, 'Diagrammatisme et poésie chez les deux Marot', in his *Poétique et onomastique: L'Exemple de la Renaissance*, Histoire des Idées et Critique Littéraire, CLX, Geneva: Droz, 1977, pp. 55-79.
The section on CM consists essentially of a revised version of I36.

I38 Rigolot, François, 'Pour une critique cratylique des textes poétiques du XVIe siècle', in *Renaissance et nouvelle critique: Quatrième symposium sur la Renaissance, Modern Language Association of America, 16-19 Oct. 1975*, Albany: Institute for Renaissance Studies, State Univ. of New York at Albany, 1978, pp. 21-34.
Several references to the epigram *Du Lieutenant criminel de Paris et de Samblançay* (*OC*, V, p. 129). Discusses CM's play on the sound of the name (= 'semblance est') and the significance of variant spellings of the name in sixteenth-century eds.

Rocher, Gregory de: see HUb17.

I39 Siepmann, Helmut, *Die allegorische Tradition im Werke Clément Marots*, Bonn: Univ. of Bonn, 1968, 226 pp.
An exceedingly rapid survey of allegory before CM, including the medieval tradition; a sound analysis of various aspects of CM's use of allegory; an interesting discussion of the allegorical figures 'La Mort' and 'L'Amour'. The final section examines allegorical personification as a stylistic device in CM's poems. Numerous misprints, some inaccurate quotations.
Rev.: .1 Dierlamm, W., *SFr*, XIII (1969), 332-33.
.2 Giraud, Yves, *BHR*, XXXI (1969), 391-95.
.3 Joukovsky, F., *IL*, XXIII (1971), 37-38.

I40 Strathmann, Franz H., 'Die sprache [sic] des Clement Marot in grammatischer hinsicht [sic]', *ASNS*, XIII (1853), 230-35.
Unsatisfactory presentation: no information as to the ed. used, no line references to the poems; a questionable choice of categories proposed

for investigation.

I41   Vaganay, Hugues, 'De Rabelais à Montaigne: Les Adverbes
       terminés en -*ment*', *RER*, I (1903), 166-87; II (1904), 11-18,
       173-89, 258-74; III (1905), 186-215.

I42   Vaganay, Hugues, 'Quelques vocables pré-rabelaisiens', *RER*,
       VII (1909), 479-80.
       Cites CM's use of the rare *éthéré* in his tr. of the first book of Ovid's
       Metamorphoses, line I32.

I43   Vaganay, Hugues, 'Une Strophe lyrique au XVIe siècle', in
       Mélanges ... Joseph Vianey, Paris: Presses Françaises, 1934,
       pp. 175-86.
       On the use of the six-line stanza 7, 3, 7, 7, 3, 7 by, among others,
       CM who is believed to have been the first poet to compose it on three
       rhymes.

       Van Brabant, Luc: see HA100.

I44   Vianey, Joseph, 'Les Origines du sonnet régulier', *RRen*, IV
       (1903), 74-93.
       Interesting study of rhyme-schemes in Italian sonnets and of the schemes
       adopted by French Renaissance poets, including CM.

I45   Vianey, Joseph, 'L'Art du vers chez Clément Marot', in *Mé-
       langes ... Abel Lefranc*, Paris: Droz, 1936, pp. 44-57.
       Brief notes on different aspects of versification in CM's poems.

       Williams, Annwyl: see HM19.

J. IDEAS

*J1   Akiyama, Haruo, *'Déploration de Florimont Robertet'*, *Bulletin d'Études Françaises de l'Université Chuo*, VIII (1976), 1-20. (Text in Japanese.)
Certain passages reflect Luther's ideas, others those of Lefèvre d'Étaples. Akiyama's interpretations are based on the books by Mayer (J18) and Screech (J27). (See note to A7.)

J2   Argus, Elisabeth, *Clément Marot und Margarete von Valois, Herzogin von Alençon, Königin von Navarra*, Leipzig, 1918, ix + 62 pp.
A rather sketchy attempt to establish, on the one hand, CM's literary influence on Marguerite's poetry and, on the other, his spiritual indebtedness to her.

J3   Atance, Félix R., *'La Complainte d'un détenu prisonnier*: Marguerite de Navarre et son attitude envers les novateurs', *BSHP*, CXVI (1970), 325-31.
Unhesitatingly identifies the prisoner as CM. Argues, however, that in the most significant passages, Marguerite is expressing her own ideas and not those of the prisoner. Cf. J5, 13.

J4   Bailly, Auguste, *La Vie littéraire sous la Renaissance*, Paris: Tallandier, 1952, 299 pp.
The discussion of CM (pp. 105-19) is in the chapter headed 'Les Écrivains et la Réforme' and touches on certain religious aspects of his works.

J5   Becker, Ph. Aug., 'Margareta von Navarra und die *Complainte pour un prisonnier*', *ASNS*, CII (1899), 95-108.
Rejects Lefranc's thesis that the prisoner is CM (see J13) as completely untenable. The main purpose of the art., however, is to dispute the attribution to Marguerite; but Becker's explanation of how a poem by another writer could have been included in the *Marguerites de la Marguerite des princesses* is not entirely convincing. (In a later note, Becker suggests that the 'François' addressed in the *Complainte* is François Ricardot, who was the almoner of Renée of Ferrara from

1541 to 1544 – see 'Kleine Nachträge', *NS*, XXXIV (1926), 125-27.) See also J3.

J6   Boisset, Jean, 'La Religion de Clément Marot (1495-1544)', *BSHP*, CXIV (1968), 487-506.
Some factual errors, some questionable interpretations, and arguments based in part on poems of doubtful authenticity. But the art. makes an interesting and useful assessment of CM's religious views, leading to the well-prepared, though not unusual, conclusion: Calvinist, no; Lutheran, yes, but ...; Evangelical: undoubtedly. Boisset shares Screech's view that CM is sincere in denying, in his epistle to François I from Ferrara, that he is a 'Luthériste' (see J27).

J7   Dettmer, Gustav, *Die Geisteshaltung Clément Marots auf Grund seiner religiös-satirischen Lyrik*, Greifswald, 1940, 106 pp.
Stresses the importance of the spiritual influence of Marguerite de Navarre and indirectly, through her, of Briçonnet's mysticism, on CM. Considers that the effect on CM's religious feelings of his grave illness in 1532 has been underestimated. Concludes that CM cannot really be regarded as a Catholic; nor can he be labelled either a Calvinist or a Lutheran, but he was closer to being the latter than the former. A generally objective art. However, the judgements are not always founded on a sufficiently detailed analysis.

Douen, O.: see C49.

Fontana, B.: see C56.

J8   Françon, Marcel, *Notes sur l'esthétique de la femme au XVIe siècle*, Cambridge, Mass.: Harvard UP, 1939, 195 pp.
Comments on CM's enthusiasm for brunettes, which he places in the context of the sixteenth-century shift away from the traditional aristocratic, literary ideal of the blond woman. Cf. HA44.

J9   Giraud, Yves, 'Le Testament poétique de Marot: L'Épître *A ung sien amy* (LXV)', *RHR*, no. 8 (1978), 3-11.
Examines the ideas – notably about poetry – developed in this epistle (*OC*, I, pp. 272-76). Giraud rightly amends Mayer's date of 1543 for the composition of this poem to 1544. Accepts without discussion the identification of the friend by Droz and Plan with François de Bellegarde (E32; on this subject, see also various entries in section HP).

Griffin, Robert: see HA40.

Heudier, Jean Pierre: see HUa16.

J10   Imbart de la Tour, P., *Les Origines de la Réforme*, III:
      L'Évangélisme (1521-1538), Paris: Hachette, 1914, xi + 628
      pp.
      On CM, see pp. 305-09. Likens CM to 'la libellule qui ne se pose sur
      rien, ne se fixe sur rien, emportée au souffle des événements ou à
      l'imprévu de son caprice'. Influenced by Marguerite de Navarre's
      Evangelism, but never advancing beyond it into open adherence to
      the Reformation, hostile to any strong constraint, whether in the
      matter of dogma or in religious practices, 'ce gamin de génie ne souhaita
      jamais qu'une chose ...: la liberté'.

Jeanneret, Michel: see HUa17.

J11   Joukovsky, Françoise, *La Gloire dans la poésie française et
      néolatine du XVIe siècle (des Rhétoriqueurs à Agrippa
      d'Aubigné)*, THR, CII, Geneva: Droz, 1969, 637 pp.
      See esp. 'Marot et son école: La Nouvelle Gloire', pp. 162-77. Between
      1526 and 1535, CM, in laying stress on the spiritual nature of 'gloire',
      was increasingly reflecting humanist attitudes. His two major themes
      in this connection are 'la gloire due au lettré' and 'virtus domitrix
      fortunae'. An interesting discussion, which also shows how certain
      contemporary poets followed CM's lead.

J12   Leblanc, P., *La Poésie religieuse de Clément Marot*, Paris:
      Nizet, 1955, xx + 391 pp.
      The study is not confined to CM's religious poems, but examines
      religious aspects of all his works, considered in chronological order.
      Interesting discussion of certain poems. Leblanc distinguishes different
      stages in CM's religious inspiration. Stresses its overall Evangelical
      character, in accord with Christian humanism. The textual analysis is
      based on Guiffrey's ed. (E17).
      Rev.: .1 F[élice], Ph. de, *BSHP*, CII (1956), 46-48.
            .2 Giudici, Enzo, *SFr*, I (1957), 299.
            .3 Jourda, Pierre, *RHLF*, LVII (1957), 421-23.
            .4 Mayer, C.A., *BHR*, XVIII (1956), 330-35.
            .5 Will, Samuel F., *RR*, XLVII (1956), 303.

J13   Lefranc, Abel, 'Les Idées religieuses de Marguerite de Navarre
      d'après son œuvre poétique (les *Marguerites* et les *Dernières
      poésies*)', *BSHP*, XLVI (1897), 7-30, 72-84, 137-48, 295-311,
      418-42.
      Argues at length that MN's *Complainte pour un detenu prisonnier* is

manifestly inspired by CM's religious activities before and during his stay at Ferrara. A convinced Protestant and eager proselytizer, an 'apôtre' and 'conducteur d'âmes', CM travelled to Ferrara primarily for the purpose of preaching the new faith and played a decisive role in the conversion of Renée de France and some of her retinue. This highly debatable view robs Lefranc's arguments for identifying the prisoner with CM of nearly all plausibility. See also J3, 5.

J14　Lefranc, Abel, 'Garasse et Rabelais', *RER*, VII (1909), 492-99.
The Jesuit François Garasse published in 1622 an attack on Étienne Pasquier in which he blames him for excessively praising CM, Rabelais and Beza, 'un athée, un bouffon et un hérétique'. He likens CM to Aretino.

*J15　Lutkus, Anne Daugherty, 'Aspects of Love, Human and Divine in the Poetry of Clément Marot', Ph. D. thesis, Indiana Univ., 1973, 220 pp. *DisA*, XXXIV (1973-74), 6648-49A.
'An examination, based on close readings, of Marot's definitions and views of love. It will stress the essential unity of the love poetry, a unity imposed largely by a broad view of love that ranged from the divine to the human.'

J16　Martineau-Génieys, Christine, 'En suivant le cercueil de Florimond Robertet (1527)', in her *Le Thème de la mort dans la poésie française de 1450 à 1550*, Nouvelle Bibliothèque du Moyen Âge, VI, Paris: Champion, 1978, pp. 439-85.
An excellent study of CM's *Déploration* ... and, through a close analysis of the speech by 'La Mort', of the Evangelicals' attitude to death. The author does not subscribe to Mayer's view that Mathieu Malingre's sermons on St Paul were an important direct source for that speech (see C105, pp. 162-63). Instead, she lays emphasis on the pervasive influence of Briçonnet's ideas: 'le discours ... contient *toutes* les idées de Briçonnet sur la mort ... *et ne contient qu'elles*.' CM would undoubted have been conversant with them, through Marguerite. See also J17.

J17　Martineau-Génieys, Christine, 'Marot et la mort', in her *Le Thème de la mort* ... [as in J16], pp. 487-521.
The *Déploration de Florimond Robertet* (see J16) constitutes a turning-point in CM's poetry and in his religious thought: the Evangelicals' emphasis on the death of death − that life-enhancing attitude so central to their thought which results in the rejection of grief − is leading CM to abandon the traditional *complainte funèbre*. Good discussion of the later *complaintes* and *epitaphes*, so very different in tone, and esp. of

the *Eglogue sur le trespas de ... Loyse de Savoye*, 'une sorte de *Te Deum* sur le mode champêtre. Et antique.'

J18   Mayer, C.A., *La Religion de Marot*, THR, XXXIX, Geneva: Droz, 1960, 186 pp.

Most valuable for bringing together much material bearing directly or indirectly on CM's views and on his experiences at the hands of the authorities: relevant passages, carefully analyzed, from the poems; opinions expressed by various contemporaries; official documents and decrees relating to religious matters.

Mayer's main conclusions: CM's protestations of orthodoxy, whether in the epistle *A Monsieur Bouchart*, in *L'Enfer*, or in the poem sent to François I from Ferrara, are invariably weak, hence may be presumed to be insincere. CM was strongly attracted by Protestantism, just as he was drawn towards humanism and the Renaissance as a whole. He was a fierce, implacable enemy of the Catholic Church. But, like Rabelais and Des Périers, he was not interested in dogma or metaphysics, only in morals. His attitude was essentially one of humanitarian Evangelism: 'La seule foi qu'il exprime constamment tout au long de sa vie, c'est sa foi dans l'homme.' An important study, even though its conclusions have been challenged in part or entirely by some reviewers. See also J27.

Rev.: .1 Françon, Marcel, *MLN*, LXXVI (1961), 467-73; *MLQ*, XXIII (1962), 187-90.
.2 Krailsheimer, A.J., *MLR*, LVI (1961), 425-26.
.3 Pineaux, J., *BSHP*, CVI (1960), 240-42.
.4 Screech, M.A., *FS*, XV (1961), 260-61.
.5 Sozzi, Lionello, *SFr*, V (1961), 494-99.
.6 Telle, Émile V., *RR*, LIII (1962), 286-88.

*J19   Mazaki, Takaharu, 'L'Idée évangélique de Clément Marot', *Meiiji Gakuin Review*, CXCII (1972), 1-18. (Text in Japanese.)

Draws primarily on the books by Mayer (J18) and Screech (J27). Argues that three passages in which CM defends himself against accusations of Lutheranism contain evangelical ideas. (See note to A7.)

J20   Moore, W.G., *La Réforme allemande et la littérature française: Recherches sur la notoriété de Luther en France*, Publications de la Faculté des Lettres de l'Univ. de Strasbourg, LII, Strasbourg: Univ. de Strasbourg, 1930, 512 pp.

On CM, see pp. 179-82. CM's poems suggest that Luther was no more to him than a famous name, a subject for general discussion. Even if he was acquainted with Luther's writings, he did not turn to them for poetic inspiration.

J21   Muller, A., 'La Poésie religieuse en dehors des psaumes au XVIe siècle: 1° Marot, 1497-1544', in his *La Poésie religieuse catholique de Marot à Malherbe*, Paris: Foulon, 1950, pp. 114-25.

Discerns no trace of profound religious feeling in CM's works. Finds no proof of his adherence to the Reformation, but does not seek to determine his standpoint more specifically, as this would be outside the scope of the book whose purpose is to examine poetry inspired by the Catholic faith.

J22   Muller, A., 'Marot, 1496-1544', in his *De Rabelais à Paul Valéry: Les Grands Écrivains devant le christianisme*, Paris: Foulon, 1969, pp. 20-22.

Pannier, Jacques: see HUa24.

*J23   *Proceso inquisitorial contra el escultor Esteban Jamete*. Transcrip ción y notas preliminares por J. Domínguez Bordona, Madrid: Centro de Estudios Históricos, 1933, 75 pp.

According to the undermentioned review, reference was made during the trial to various incriminating passages in books alleged to have been in the possession of Étienne Jamet (known in Spain as Esteban Jamete or Hamete). Two of these passages are attributed to CM (pp. 23, 30). For details, see J25, 26.

Rev.: .1 Castro, A., *RFE*, XX (1933), 401-06.

J24   Richter, Mario, 'L'Evangelismo di Clément Marot: Lettura della *Déploration de Florimont Robertet*', *BHR*, XXXV (1973), 247-58.

The *Déploration* furnishes significant evidence of CM's religious ideas. Without breaking the formal mould of the traditional *complainte*, CM structures the *Déploration* in such a way as to turn it into a proclamation of Evangelism.

J25   Sarrailh, Jean, 'Note sur Clément Marot et l'Inquisition espagnole', *RFE*, XXI (1934), 62-65.

Identifies one of the passages cited in J23 as a paraphrase of two lines in CM's *Aux dames de Paris* ... (*OC*, II, pp. 77-86, lines 83-84). See also J26.

J26   Sarrailh, Jean, 'Note complémentaire sur Clément Marot et l'Inquisition espagnole', *RFE*, XXI (1934), 169-70.

Confirms the tentative identification in J25 of the second 'incriminating' passage mentioned in J23 as a fragment of CM's *Second chant d'Amour fugitif* (*OC*, II, pp. 86-90, lines 47 ff.).

J27   Screech, Michael A., *Marot évangélique*, Études de Philologie
       et d'Histoire, IV, Geneva: Droz, 1967, 122 pp.
       Essentially a response to the study by Mayer (J18), whose conclusions
       Screech contests as taking insufficient account of sixteenth-century
       theology. CM's attitude was not Protestant in 1526, as Mayer stated.
       On the other hand, the *Epistre au roy, du temps de son exil à Ferrare*
       reflects a significant shift in his religious stance: 'avec une étonnante
       hardiesse, Marot s'avoue luthérien', apparently by sincerely proclaiming
       that he is not. But Screech cautions against labelling CM too precisely
       and prefers to consider him an Evangelical Christian, ever mindful of
       Erasmus's ideas – and of the teaching of St. Paul. The book contains
       an interesting analysis of the precise connotations of certain religious
       terms in the sixteenth century, as well as a valuable examination of CM's
       references to the Bible and of his opposition to non-scriptural practices.
       There is much fascinating argument, often very subtle, occasionally
       strained by the underlying polemical intent.
       Rev.: .1 Giraud, Yves F.A., *RF*, LXXX (1968), 574-78.
              .2 Grosclaude, Pierre, *BSHP*, CXV (1969), 147-48.
              .3 Labarthe, O., *BHR*, XXXI (1969), 235-36.
              .4 Phillips, Margaret Mann, *MLR*, LXIV (1969), 422-23.
              .5 Richter, Mario, *SFr*, XII (1968), 131.
              .6 Sage, Pierre, *ÉtLitt*, I (1968), 143-45.
              .7 Siepmann, Helmut, *ZRP*, LXXXVII (1971), 447-50.
              .8 Weber, Henri, *RHLF*, LXIX (1969), 282-83.

J28   Screech, M.A., 'L'Humanisme évangélique du *Riche en pauvreté*,
       poème attribué quelquefois à Marot', in *Colloque International
       de Tours (XIVe stage): L'Humanisme français au début de la
       Renaissance*, De Pétrarque à Descartes, XXIX, Paris: Vrin,
       1973, pp. 241-51.
       Contends that the theology of the poem – supposedly found among
       CM's papers at Chambéry, and first published in 1558 – is clearly
       Calvinist and characteristic of the reformers belonging to the generation
       following CM's. This is an important argument against accepting the
       authenticity of the *Riche en pauvreté*.

*J29   Spiker, Claud Carl, 'The Critical Literary Ideas of Clément
       Marot', M.A. thesis, Univ. of Chicago, 1916, 52 pp.

J30   Stéphan, Raoul, *L'Épopée huguenote*, Paris: La Colombe,
       1945, 294 pp.
       On CM, see pp. 31-34 in the chapter significantly entitled 'L'Âge des

colombes'. 'Avec Marguerite de Navarre le poète ... en qui l'humanisme et l'évangélisme réformateurs se marient, c'est Clément Marot.'

Stéphan, Raoul: see also HUa37.

J31   Tron, Gisèle, 'Clément Marot entre "Symonne" et "Christine"' *Études Évangéliques*, XXXI, 2 (1971), 33-44.
      Asserts that CM's whole life revolved around his faith, 'foi vive, ardente, n'admettant aucune contrainte, ni aucune concession' — the faith of a Protestant who was at the same time a humanist, and whose poems proclaim a firm Christian optimism.

*J32 Watts, Margaret Elizabeth, 'The Representation of Woman in Selected Poetry and Plastic Arts of the Renaissance in France', Ph. D. thesis, Univ. of Toronto, 1977, 493 pp. *DisA*, XXXIX (1978-79), 4312-13A.
      CM is among the poets whose works are examined. See also HC7.

K. SOURCES

Petrarchism

*KA1   Akiyama, Haruo, 'Marot et le pétrarquisme', *Littérature Fran-
        çaise de la Renaissance*, III (1967), 1-20. (Text in Japanese.)
        On the Petrarchist features of CM's love poetry. Akiyama bases his
        interpretations on Mayer's and Bentley-Cranch's art. KA15. (See note
        to A7.)

        Bentley-Cranch, D: see KA14, 15.

KA2   Berdan, John M., 'Wyatt and the French Sonneteers', *MLR*,
        IV (1908-09), 240-49. Followed by comments by L.E. Kastner,
        249-53.
        Reaffirms his thesis — originally advanced in 'The Migrations of a Sonnet',
        MLN, XXIII (1908), 33-36, and attacked by Kastner in *MLR*, III (1907-
        08), 274 — that Mellin de Saint-Gelais translated the sonnet 'Voyant ces
        mons de veue si loingtaine' from Wyatt's 'Like unto those unmeasurable
        mountains'. Tries here to strengthen his position by arguing that Petrarchism
        reached England, through Wyatt, before it began to influence French
        poetry. Consequently denies that CM's verse displayed any significant
        Petrarchist characteristics prior to 1540. In his comments Kastner strongly
        rejects Berdan's assumptions concerning Saint-Gelais's possible indebted-
        ness to Wyatt and the predating of English Petrarchism. (Earlier, esp.
        before Arthur Tilley's identification, in *Modern Language Quarterly*, V
        (1902), 149, of the common Italian source — the sonnet 'Simile a questi
        smisurati monti', possibly by Sannazaro —, it had been assumed that
        Wyatt's poem derived from the French. Berdan restates his thesis in
        'Professor Kastner's Hypothesis', *MLN*, XXV (1910), 1-4, and again in
        L2. On the authorship of the French poem, see HS14, 16.)

KA3   Buşulenga, Zoe Dumitrescu, 'Aspects contradictoires du
        pétrarquisme européen', *Synthesis*, III (1976), 25-33.
        The introduction, into Anglo-Saxon as well as Romance countries, of
        the Italian forms of poetry, with their Platonist and Petrarchist themes,
        fostered in a significant manner the development of national self-aware-
        ness and national schools of poetry. A reference to CM indicates but

scant acquaintance with his works.

KA4 Calcaterra, Carlo, 'Il Petrarca e il petrarchismo', in *Problemi ed orientamenti critici di lingua e di letteratura italiana*, III: Bosco, U. (and others), *Questioni e correnti di storia letteraria*, Milan: Marzorati, 1971, pp. 167-273.
While the art. itself (pp. 167-213) is concerned solely with Italian literature, the bibliography has sections also on other countries. See 'Sul petrarchismo in Francia', pp. 264-66.

KA5 Cocco, Mia, *La tradizione cortese ed il petrarchismo nella poesia di Clément Marot*, Biblioteca dell' *Archivum Romanicum* ser. I, CXXXV, Florence: Olschki, 1978, 314 pp.
An excellent study which provides sound evidence of the presence of both courtly and Petrarchan traditions in CM's poetry. Argues that the profound extent of their influence suggests that CM was more closely acquainted with each than has so far been recognized. While the native tradition is stronger in the elegies, the two currents are so harmoniously fused in the rondeaux that they cannot easily be separated. Cocco calls CM the last of the troubadours and the first true Petrarchist outside Italy, i.e. the first foreign poet to have not only adopted the external features of Petrarchism, but also assimilated its ethos. In a valuable table Cocco lists the elegies, *chansons*, epigrams and rondeaux in which earlier critics discerned Petrarchan influences, and adds further items to each category. See also KB8.
Rev.: .1 Kennedy, William J., *RR*, LXXI (1980), 342-43.
.2 Raffi, M.E., *SFr*, XXIII (1979), 344-45.

KA6 Dédéyan, Charles, 'La Fortune de Pétrarque en France: De Lemaire de Belges et Octovien de Saint Gelais à Marot. Marot, Pétrarque et les pétrarquistes italiens', in *La Pléiade e il Rinascimento italiano: Colloquio italo-francese, Roma, 16 marzo 1976*, Atti dei Convegni Lincei, XXXII, Rome: Accademia Nazionale dei Lincei, 1977, pp. 39-52.
A rather perfunctory discussion of CM's translations of Petrarch and of his Petrarchism; takes no account of recent research.

KA7 Forster, Leonard, W., 'European Petrarchism as Training in Poetic Diction', *ISt*, XVIII (1963), 19-32.
The impact which Petrarchism had on the literatures of Western Europe was related to the efforts made in the various countries to evolve a new poetic diction. See KA8.

KA8   Forster, Leonard, 'European Petrarchism as Training in Poetic Diction', in his *The Icy Fire: Five Studies in European Petrarchism*, Cambridge: Cambridge UP, 1969, pp. 61-83.
Reprint, in a revised form, of KA7.

KA9   Françon, Marcel, 'Une Imitation du sonnet de Pétrarque: "Pace non trovo ..."', *It*, XX (1943), 127-31.
Considers that CM's *Rondeau par contradictions*: 'En esperant espoir me desespere' (*OC*, IV, pp. 93-95), first published in 1532, owes more to the medieval than the Petrarchan tradition. The first French poem directly imitated from a sonnet of Petrarch's is the *Dizain de Petrarque*: 'Ne trouvant paix homme ne me faict guerre' printed in the *Petit œuvre d'amour et gaige d'amitié* – which Françon dates at 1538.

KA10   Françon, Marcel, 'Pétrarque et Clément Marot', *It*, XL (1963), 18-21.
CM's poems offer a blend of the French medieval tradition and Petrarchan influences. (For a more comprehensive and far more richly documented exposition of this thesis, see KA5.)

KA11   Françon, Marcel, 'Clément Marot et le pétrarquisme', *Annali della Facoltà di Lettere e Filosofia dell' Università di Macerata*, V-VI (1972-73), 187-203.
A fairly comprehensive account of the subject, on the lines of Françon's already previously published views (see KA10). Contests the assertions by Mayer and Bentley-Cranch in KA15 that CM's early poems are strongly marked by Petrarchism and that, in his poetry, the rondeau 'est un genre particulièrement lié au pétrarquisme'. Considers that the first certain example in CM's work of Petrarchan influence is the *Chant royal dont le roy bailla le refrain* (*OC*, IV, pp. 183-85). Repeats his theory about the reasons for the rise of the sonnet in France (see HS5).

Giudici, Enzo: see HC2.

KA12   Griffin, Robert, ' "Solo e pensoso": The Context of Petrarchan Melancholy in French Renaissance Poetry', in *Studi di Letteratura Francese,* IV, (1975), Biblioteca dell'*Archivum Romanicum*, ser. I, CXXIX, Florence: Olschki, 1976, pp. 50-84.
A very good study which includes an interesting remark on variants in *Le Temple de Cupido* (e.g. for line 424).

KA13   Magrini, Diana, 'Clemente Marot e il petrarchismo', in
        *Miscellanea di studi critici pubblicati in onore di Guido
        Mazzoni ...*, ed. by A. della Torre and P.L. Rambaldi,
        Florence, 2 vols, 1907, I, pp. 485-502.
        Maintains that CM's Petrarchism predates his stay at Ferrara by
        several years. His poetry shows less the influence of Petrarch him-
        self than of his imitators, esp. Tebaldeo and Serafino. Magrini identi-
        fies a considerable number of CM's poems which display Petrarchist
        ideas and *concetti*, but emphasizes that CM remained original even
        when imitating. An interesting art. which contains already many of
        the ideas championed in the 1960s and 1970s by certain scholars,
        notably Mayer. (The latter, nonetheless, criticizes it with surprising
        and undue severity in C105, p. 71, n. 132.)

KA14   Mayer, C.A., and D. Bentley-Cranch, 'Le Premier Pétrarquiste
        français: Jean Marot', *BHR*, XXVII (1965), 183-85.
        On the rondeau 'S'il est ainsi que ce corps t'abandonne'. For the con-
        tent of the art., see note to L59. On its authorship, cf. G3.

KA15   Mayer, C.A., and D. Bentley-Cranch, 'Clément Marot, poète
        pétrarquiste', *BHR*, XXVIII (1966), 32-51.
        The authors dispute Vianey's view (KA21) that CM's Petrarchism
        dates essentially from his stay at Ferrara. They contend that it is
        already clearly evident in his earlier work, esp. the rondeaux and
        epigrams which show the influence of Serafino d'Aquila, Olimpo di
        Sassoferrato, and Cariteo. Far from attracting CM to Petrarchism, his
        Italian journey in 1535-36 led to his abandoning it. An interesting
        art. which, however, does not give adequate consideration to the
        possible survival of medieval traditions and themes in CM's earlier
        poetry. For a more balanced approach, see KA5. Cf. also KA16, 17.

KA16   Minta, S.M.J., 'A Problem of Literary History: "Petrarchism"
        in Early Sixteenth-Century French Poetry', *FS*, XXX (1976),
        140-52.
        A powerful reply to Mayer's thesis affirming CM's early indebtedness
        to the Italian Petrarchists (KA15, C105). Minta shows that examples
        can be found in French medieval poetry for each of the themes and
        images on which Mayer bases his standpoint. While it is evident that
        Italian love poetry was not unknown in France in the early sixteenth
        century – the existence of translations alone proves it – there are no
        grounds for concluding that such acquaintance was of importance, as
        far as French literary history is concerned. Minta extends his cautionary
        remarks also to the supposed instances of significant early Petrarchism

cited by E.M. Rutson in 'A Note on Jean Marot's Debt to Italian Sources', *MLR*, LXI (1966), 25-28, and by Margarita White in 'Petrarchism in the French *rondeau* before 1527', *FS*, XXII (1968), 287-95.

KA17 Minta, Stephen, ' "Petrarchism" and the Love Poetry of Clément Marot', in his *Love Poetry in Sixteenth-Century France*, Manchester: Manchester UP, 1977, pp. 13-38.
The pages dealing with CM reproduce almost integrally the text of KA16.
Rev.: .1 Françon, Marcel, *Fra*, no. 28 (1978), 73-74.

Pike, Robert E.: see HC4.

*KA18 Tirone, Rosanna, 'Jean Lemaire de Belges, Clément Marot, Maurice Scève e il *Canzoniere* del Petrarca', Doctoral thesis, Univ. of Genoa, 1957.

*KA19 Tracconaglia, G., *Analyse de l'ouvrage de J. Vianey, 'Le Pétrarquisme en France au XVIᵉ siècle', accompagnée de quelques remarques sur l'École lyonnaise*, Genoa, 1910.
On KA21.

KA20 Vianey, Joseph, 'L'Influence italienne chez les précurseurs de la Pléiade', *Bulletin Italien*, III (1903), 85-117.
An important art., esp. for its time. Vianey shows that early French Petrarchism is derived, not directly from Petrarch himself, but from his followers Tebaldeo, Cariteo, and Serafino d'Aquila. As far as CM is concerned, a few of his epigrams echo the *pointes* of Tebaldeo's and Serafino's poems (pp. 102-04). See also KA21.

KA21 Vianey, Joseph, *Le Pétrarquisme en France au XVIᵉ siècle*, Travaux et Mémoires, Montpellier, III, Montpellier: Coulet, 1909, 399 pp.
On CM, see esp. 'Marot et Sainct-Gelays disciples de Tebaldeo et de Séraphin', pp. 45-50. The text of KA20 is reproduced substantially intact in the part of the book dealing with CM, Saint-Gelais, and Scève. The only significant addition to Vianey's earlier remarks about CM is to the effect that he developed particular admiration for Tebaldeo and Cariteo during his stay at Ferrara, and that he may have been indebted to Olimpo de Sassoferrato in his *blasons anatomiques*. (It is presumably to the first of these statements that Mayer and Bentley-Cranch respond in KA15. On Sassoferrato's influence on CM's *blasons anatomiques*, cf. HC2, 4, 8.)

Rev.: .1 Laumonier, Paul, *RHLF*, XVII (1910), 859-63.
.2 Phelps, Ruth Shepard, *RR*, I (1910), 215-16.
.3 Toldo, Pietro, *GSLI*, LV (1910), 406-11.
.4 Tracconaglia, G.: see KA19.

*KA22 White, Margarita Klara, 'Pétrarque et le pétrarquisme en France avant la Pléiade', Ph. D. thesis, Univ. of Liverpool, 1973, xvi + 544 pp.

KA23 Wilkins, Ernest H., 'A General Survey of Renaissance Petrarchism', *CL*, II (1950), 327-42.
A useful *tour d'horizon* of European Petrarchism. But very sketchy in parts, for instance in the account of early French Petrarchism and in the bibliography.

Wilson, D.B.: see HC8.

Other Sources

*KB1 Altman, Beulah L., 'A Comparison of the Eclogues of Marot and Vergil', M.A. thesis, Univ. of Chicago, 1914, 50 pp.

KB2 Bambeck, Manfred, 'Clément Marot, dispensateur d'immortalité: La Source d'une épître du poète', *Annales publiées par la Faculté des Lettres de Toulouse. Littératures: Études de littérature moderne*, II (1953), 268-81.
The passage proclaiming the poet's ability to bestow immortality, in the *Epistre faicte par Marot* (in Mayer's ed. Elegy XXIV, *OC*, III, pp. 269-71), is based on Ovid's *Amores*, I. iii.

KB3 Bambeck, Manfred, 'A propos d'un poème attribué à Clément Marot', *SFr*, V (1961), 14-22.
Apart from some minor changes in the notes, this art. is identical with KB2.

KB4 Bayet, Jean, 'La Source principale de l'églogue de Clément Marot *Au Roy soubs les noms de Pan et Robin*', *RHLF*, XXXIV (1927), 567-71.
Shows that CM drew on chapters I.xxi, xxii, xxvii, xxix of the *Illustrations de Gaule* by Jean Lemaire de Belges. Cf. KB7.

Becker, Ph. Aug.: see E27, 28.

KB5   Chamard, Henri, 'La Poésie française de la Renaissance', *RCC*, XXII, Pt 1 (1913-14), 209-21, 417-28, 521-37, 651-65, 749-64; Pt 2 (1913-14), 28-41, 105-19, 209-23, 313-27, 447-61, 521-36, 729-73.
In lecture on Villon, Chamard points out (p. 40) CM's indebtedness to the *Ballade des pendus* in his elegy XXII *Du Riche Infortuné Jacques de Beaune* ... (placed among the *complaintes* in *OC*). No detailed comparison. Cf. HG5.

KB6   Chamard, Henri, *Les Origines de la poésie française de la Renaissance*, Paris: De Boccard, 1920, viii + 307 pp.
A slightly revised version of KB5. The passage on CM is on pp. 126-27.

KB7   Charlier, Gustave, 'Sur l'enfance de Marot', *RHLF*, XXXIV (1927), 426-28.
On CM's indebtedness to Lemaire de Belges in the *Eglogue au roy, soubz les noms de Pan et Robin*. Cf. KB4.

Cocco, Mia: see KA5.

KB8   Cremonesi, Carla, 'Reminiscenze trobadoriche nella poesia di Clément Marot e di qualche altro poeta francese del '500', *Istituto Lombardo* [Milan]. *Rendiconti, Classe di Lettere e Scienze Morali e Storiche*, XCVI (1962), 124-32.
Cites passages in CM which appear to echo closely certain troubadour poems. This fact, added to the presence of common themes in CM's amatory verse and troubadour love poetry, suggests that he may have been acquainted with the latter. For a more extensive treatment of this subject, see KA5.

KB9   Del Balzo, Carlo, *L'Italia nella letteratura francese dalla caduta dell'impero romano alla morte di Enrico IV*, Turin, 2 vols, 1905-07.
On CM, see I, pp. 143-47. Of little importance.

KB10   Dottin, Georges, 'Aspects littéraires de la chanson *musicale* à l'époque de Marot', *RSH* (1964), 425-32.
Interesting study of the survival of medieval lyrical themes and the concurrent emergence of Renaissance themes in the *chansonniers* of the period. Dottin suggests that the *bergeries* which perpetuated traditional subjects and whose popularity is attested by numerous musical settings, may have influenced – at least by their rhythm –

the light verse of CM, Ronsard, and even La Fontaine.

KB11   [Du Cerceau?], 'Lettre à Monsieur de ***, en lui envoyant la nouvelle édition des *Œuvres* de François Villon', in *Les Œuvres de François Villon*, Paris: Antoine-Urbain Coustelier 1723, Pt III, pp. 1-56.
Stresses CM's debt to Villon: 'Il ne faut qu'avoir lû Clement Marot pour être convaincu que Villon avoit été son premier maître; que c'étoit sur les ouvrages de celui-ci qu'il s'étoit formé; qu'il en avoit pris le tour badin, et le caractère enjoué, et qu'il l'avoit même quelque fois copié de plus près qu'il ne semble qu'il soit permis ... Villon est, pour ainsi dire, le premier inventeur de ce style, auquel on n'a donné le nom de marotique, que parce-que Marot étoit plus moderne ...' (The letter is reprinted, with the same title, in the 1742 ed. of Villon's *Œuvres*, The Hague: Moetjens, Pt III, pp. 11-90.)

KB12   Eckhardt, Alexandre, 'Marot et Dante: L'*Enfer* et l'*Inferno*', *RSS*, XIII (1926), 140-42.
Believes that lines 33-46 of *L'Enfer* were suggested by *Inferno*, iii, lines 22-36, and that CM took the title from Dante's poem.

Erskine, John: see L13.

KB13   Françon, Marcel, 'Poésie populaire et poésie littéraire', *MP*, XXXVII (1939-40), 7-11.
On traces of popular songs in the poems of CM and Ronsard, and of possible echoes of CM in Ronsard in this connection. The same subject is also discussed, with the same quotations, in KB14, 16. See also KB17.

KB14   Françon, Marcel, 'Navagero et Ronsard', *It*, XXV (1948), 296-99.
On Ronsard's ode *Les Dons de Jaquet à Isabeau*, imitated from Navagero, but presenting a reminiscence of a popular song transmitted by CM. See KB13.

KB15   Françon, Marcel, 'Clément Marot and Popular Songs', *Sp*, XXV (1950), 247-48.
Shows that the final lines of the six stanzas of the *Complaincte d'une niepce, sur la mort de sa tante* (*OC*, III, pp. 131-33) reproduce incipit of popular songs. Cf. KB42.

KB16   Françon, Marcel, 'Rappels d'une chanson populaire faits par Marot et par Ronsard', *Bulletin Folklorique d'Île de France*,

3rd ser., XX [not XXI, as numbered on the cover], 4 (1958), 109-10.
See KB13.

KB17   Françon, Marcel, 'Le Thème de l'occasion manquée', *Bulletin Folklorique d'Île de France*, 3rd ser., XXX (1967), 91.
See KB13.

KB18   Françon, Marcel, 'Jean de Meun, Charles d'Orléans, Clément Marot, Ronsard', in his 'Notes de littérature, de musique et d'histoire', *Fra*, nos 19-20 (1976), 52-64 (52).
Notes, as a possible instance of the influence of earlier medieval literature on that of later periods, a reference to 'Faux Dangier' in a rondeau by Charles d'Orléans. Further references occur in poems by CM and Ronsard. Cf. L20.

KB19   Frappier, Jean, 'Sur quelques emprunts de Clément Marot à Jean Lemaire de Belges', in *Mélanges.... Edmond Huguet*, Paris: Boivin, 1940, pp. 161-76.
An important art. Shows that CM's debt to Lemaire is not confined to the *Eglogue au roy, soubz les noms de Pan et Robin* (see KB4, 7), but extends also to *Le Temple de Cupido*, to the *Eglogue sur le trespas de ... Loyse de Savoye*, and to *L'Enfer* where Frappier discerns the influence of Lemaire's *Seconde épître de l'amant vert* in certain passages as well as in the structure of the poem. Nevertheless, CM achieves originality even in his most manifest borrowings.

KB20   Frappier, Jean, 'Sur quelques emprunts de Clément Marot à Jean Lemaire de Belges', in his *Du Moyen Âge à la Renaissance: Études d'histoire et de critique littéraire*, Paris: Champion, 1976, pp. 373-91.
Reproduces KB19.

KB21   Gambier, Henri, 'Clément Marot', in his *Italie et renaissance poétique en France: La Renaissance poétique en France au XVIe siècle et l'influence de l'Italie*, Padua: Cedam, 1936, pp. 36-50.
Credits CM with having created 'ce genre appelé *Blasons*' in Ferrara under Italian influences. Does not mention CM's earlier use of the generic term. No reference to Petrarchism in CM's poems.

KB22   Gmelin, Hermann, 'Marot', in his 'Das Prinzip der Imitatio in den romanischen Literaturen der Renaissance', *RF*, XLVI

(1932), 83-360 (280-325).
Interesting study of CM's borrowings from Lemaire and of his adaptations and translations of classical authors, examined in the light of humanist theories of imitation. The sections on Martial, Ovid, and Virgil are particularly valuable. In Gmelin's view, CM's last two eclogues are landmarks in the history of imitation in France: in the *Eglogue au roy, soubz les noms de Pan et Robin*, CM achieves perfect balance between *imitatio* and personal expression, whereas the *Eglogue sur la naissance du filz de monseigneur le daulphin*, in which he exceeds the bounds of personal inspiration, serves as a pointer to the risks of artistic imitation.

KB23 Guy, Henry, *Les Sources du poète Clément Marot*, Foix: Gadrat, 1890, 30 pp.
Cites examples of Latin influences on CM, but exaggerates his knowledge of classical civilization ('il n'ignorait rien de cette antiquité'). Makes no allowance for possible intermediary French sources, e.g. in the case of the legend of Troy. Underestimates CM's indebtedness to Lemaire de Belges, regards Petrarchan influence as minimal, does not even mention the possibility of Petrarchist sources.

KB24 Guy, Henry, *De fontibus Clementis Maroti poetae: antiqui et medii aevi scriptores*, Foix: Gadrat, 1898, 85 pp.
A more comprehensive study than KB23. Deals also with CM's translations and with the Biblical reminiscences in his work.

Hulubei, Alice: see HJ7.

KB25 Hutton, James, 'The First Idyl of Moschus in Imitations to the Year 1800', *American Journal of Philology*, XCIX (1928), 105-36.
On CM's *Le Chant de l'Amour fugitif* (*OC*, VI, pp. 108-12), the original of which CM wrongly attributes to Lucian. Hutton suggests that CM was translating the anonymous Latin imitation which followed Poliziano's Latin tr. of Moschus's idyll in the *Epigrammata graeca* published by Joannes Soter in Cologne in 1525. (See also E27, KB26, and esp. KB27.)

KB26 Hutton, James, *The Greek Anthology in France and in the Latin Writers of the Netherlands to the Year 1800*, Cornell Studies in Classical Philology, XXVIII, Ithaca: Cornell UP, 1946, xi + 822 pp.
See esp. 'Clément Marot (1496-1544)', pp. 301-03. Since CM knew no Greek, any theme from the Anthology must have reached him

through an intermediary, for instance, Moschus's *Amor fugitivus*
through Gellius Bernardinus Marmita (on this point, see also E27,
KB25, 27). The only certain echo of a Greek epigram in CM's works
is to be found in the *Dizain de l'image de Vénus armée* which is in
part derived from A.P. 16.174. (This *dizain* appeared among some
additional poems printed at the end of the ed. of the *Adolescence
cl.* which Roffet's widow published in August 1534 – *Bibliog. II*,
no. 19. According to Villey – F64, VII, pp. 85-86, or F65, pp. 40-
41 – it was not included in any further eds published in CM's lifetime. It is reproduced by Grenier in E26, II, p. 119, but not mentioned
in Mayer's *OC*.)

KB27   Hutton, James, '*Amor fugitivus*: The First Idyl of Moschus
in Imitations to the Year 1800', in his *Essays on Renaissance
Poetry*, ed. by Rita Guerlac, Ithaca: Cornell UP, 1980, pp.
74-105.

Reprint of KB25 (the passage on CM is on pp. 86-88). In a note added
at the end, Hutton identifies the 'anonymous' version – used by CM –
in Soter's *Epigrammata graeca* as the work of Battista Guarino. He
bases this identification on information provided by Ludwig Bertalot
in his study 'L'Antologia di Epigrammi di Lorenzo Abstemio nelle
tre edizioni Sonciniane', in *Miscellanea Giovanni Mercati*, IV, Studi
e Testi, CXXIV, Vatican City, 1946, pp. 305-26 (item 52).

KB28   Joukovsky-Micha, F., 'Clément et Jean Marot', *BHR*, XXIX
(1967), 557-65.

Compares their poems, with a view to determining the son's debt to
the father. The results are meager and inconclusive: a few analogies
which could be reminiscences, some common themes which are also
found in other poets.

KB29   Laurens, Pierre, '*Le Dizain de neige*: Histoire d'un poème;
ou, Des sources latines du pétrarquisme européen', *Troi-
sième Congrès International d'Études Néo-latines, Tours/
Acta conventus neo-latini Turonensis: Université François
Rabelais, 6-10 sept. 1976*, ed. by Jean-Claude Margolin, De
Pétrarque à Descartes, XXXVIII, Paris: Vrin, 2 vols, 1980,
I, pp. 557-70.

Shows that CM's seemingly Petrarchist epigram *D'Anne qui luy jecta
de la neige* (*OC*, V, p. 115) is in fact based on a Latin poem probably
dating from the Ovidian or post-Ovidian period.

KB30   Lebègue, Raymond, 'La Source d'un poème religieux de

Marot', in *Mélanges ... Abel Lefranc*, Paris: Droz, 1936, pp. 58-74.

A good study of CM's *Oraison contemplative devant le crucifix* (*OC*, VI, pp. 92-98), which Lebègue shows to be a fairly free tr. of *Ennea ad sospitalem Christum* by the neo-Latin poet Nicolas Bathélémy. (On this poem by CM, see also HUb17.)

KB31   Leblanc, P., 'Les Sources humanistes du *Chant nuptial de Renée de France*', *BSHP*, C (1954), 64-74.

Shows that CM, in addition to his important borrowings from Catullus also imitates Erasmus. The fourth stanza of the poem (*OC*, III, pp. 309-13) draws on a passage in the latter's colloquy *Proci et puellae*. It is significant that this passage develops the humanist idea concerning the superiority of Christian marriage over sterile virginity.

Mayer, C.A.: see HA56, HH3.

KB32   Mehnert, Kurt Henning, *'Sal romanus' und 'esprit français': Studien zur Martialrezeption im Frankreich des sechzehnten und siebzehnten Jahrhunderts*, Romanistische Versuche und Vorarbeiten, XXXIII, Bonn: Romanisches Seminar, Univ. of Bonn, 1970, 229 pp.

See esp. 'Martial und Clément Marot', pp. 55-75. An instructive analysis of CM's adaptations. These differ frequently from the originals both in style and in the development of the ideas.

Morçay, Raoul: see I30.

Nichols, Stephen G.: see HVa8.

KB33   Pelan, Margaret, 'The Influence of Villon on Clément Marot', in *Mélanges ... Rita Lejeune*, Gembloux: Duculot, 2 vols, 1969, II, pp. 1469-79.

The evidence presented here scarcely reveals more than a few verbal resemblances and a certain similarity in the tone of certain poems.

KB34   Pelan, Margaret, 'Villon, Marot and the Courtly Tradition', in *Mélanges ... Albert Henry*, *TLLS*, VIII, 1 (1970), 231-39.

Argues that Villon, in posing as a martyr to love in accounting for his precipitate departure from Paris — undertaken, in reality, to escape arrest for theft — was deliberately parodying the courtly theme of a lover's voluntary separation from his cruel mistress. In attributing his arrest and imprisonment in 1526 to a woman, 'Luna',

CM may have been following the precedent set by Villon. (Mayer makes precisely the same suggestion in C104 and C105, p. 91.)

Rocher, Gregory de: see HUb17.

KB35   Rose, Hermann, 'Der Einfluss Villon's auf Marot', in *Programm des Gymnasiums zu Glückstadt, Ostern 1878*, Glückstadt, 1878, 1-34.
While CM did not as a rule borrow directly from Villon, the latter's influence was a decisive factor in the formation of the 'style marotique'. Rose draws attention to certain parallels, such as those existing between Villon's *Requeste à Monsieur de Bourbon* and CM's epistle *Au roy, pour avoir esté desrobé*, and between Villon's *Débat du cœur et du corps* and CM's epigram *A Pierre Vuyard* (*OC*, V, pp. 127-28).

KB36   Ruutz-Rees, C., 'Flower Garlands of the Poets Milton, Shakespeare, Spenser, Marot, Sannazaro', in *Mélanges ... Abel Lefranc*, Paris: Droz, 1936, pp. 75-90.
The floral lists in *Lycidas*, *The Winter's Tale*, *A Midsummer Night's Dream* and the *Shepheardes Calender* can be traced back to Sannazaro, either directly or through CM's *Temple de Cupido* and the *Eglogue sur le trespas de ... Loyse de Savoye* – and, beyond Sannazaro, to the *Culex* of the pseudo-Virgil. This latter poem was translated by Spenser. CM may well have known it, since it appeared in Josse Bade's ed. of the complete Virgil in 1515.

*KB37   Schmidt, Bertrand, 'Influences italiennes et néo-latines sur quelques poètes français de la première moitié du XVIe siècle: Jean Lemaire de Belges, Mellin de Saint Gelays, Maurice Scève, Clément Marot', Thèse de 3e cycle, Univ. of Montpellier III, 1973.

KB38   Stackelberg, Jürgen von, 'Übersetzung und Imitatio in der französischen Renaissance', *Arc*, I (1966), 167-73.
No clear distinction was made between translation and imitation. This is proved, not only by Sebillet's remarks, but also by Du Bellay who, while insisting on the limited value of translation, praised as a model of 'imitation' CM's *Eglogue sur la naissance du filz de monseigneur le daulphin* which is, in reality, little more than a tr. from the Latin – or certainly closer to one than the 'translation' of Virgil's first eclogue by Michel de Tours.

KB39   Steiner, Arpad, 'Propertius, *Laudator temporis acti*', *RR*,

XXI (1930), 145-47.
Suggests that in *De l'amour du siecle antique* (*OC*, IV, p. 129), CM
drew, not on a passage in the *Roman de la Rose* as has been stated,
but on Propertius's elegy III.xiii.

KB40   Stevens, Linton C., 'The Reputation of Lucian in Sixteenth-
Century France', *SFr*, XI (1967), 401-06.

*KB41   Torraca, Fr., *Gl'imitatori stranieri di Jacopo Sannazaro*,
Rome: Loescher, 1882.
Apparently mentions CM's indebtedness to *Arcadia* in his *Eglogue
sur le trespas de ... Loyse de Savoye.*

KB42   Vaganay, Hugues, 'La Chanson *Au bois de dueil* et ses imitations religieuses', *Eurydice* (1934, no. 12), 8 pp. (unnumber
The opening line of this popular song appears as the last line of stanza
2 and the first line of stanza 3 in CM's *Complaincte d'une niepce,
sur la mort de sa tante* (*OC*, III, pp. 131-33; see KB15). Vaganay
prints two versions of the song and of three *noëls* based on it. He
also reproduces a *Chanson de l'Incarnation du Filz* beginning 'Au bois
de pleurs fut le buthor meschant', which was attributed to CM in the
Vie de Nostre Seigneur selon les quatre Evangelistes published in 1541
and was to be sung to the tune of *Au bois de dueil*. (It does not appe
to have been considered authentic by editors of CM's works.)

KB43   Villey, Pierre, 'A propos des sources de deux épîtres de Mar
RHLF, XXVI (1919), 220-45.
Points out CM's considerable indebtedness to Ovid in two epistles
composed in Venice in 1536, *Au roy* and *A la royne de Navarre* (*OC*,
I, pp. 232-39, 243-51). The significant Latin influence on CM's poems,
esp. during his later years, suggests that his knowledge of the language
was greater than has often been thought (cf. C24, KB44).

Vipper, G,: see HG5.

KB44   Wagner, Albert, *Clément Marot's Verhältnis zur Antike*,
Leipzig: Seele, 1906, 100 pp.
CM knew no Greek, but his knowledge of Latin was greater than
Boyssoné acknowledged (see C24). A good discussion of CM's translations of classical texts, and of classical influences on his choice of
genres and on the content of his poems. But apart from his praise
for the beautiful form and style of Ovid's works, his references to
the writers of antiquity do not suggest that he had gained deep insight
into the particular qualities of any of them. He nevertheless became

an enthusiastic supporter of the humanist movement for the revival of antiquity.

Wilson, D.B.: see HC8.

KB45   Zumthor, Paul, 'Fatrasie et coq-à-l'âne (de Beaumanoir à Clément Marot)', in *Fin du moyen âge et Renaissance: Mélanges ... Robert Guiette*, Antwerp: Nederlandsche Boekhandel, 1961, pp. 5-18.
Interesting discussion of probable antecedents of the *coq-à-l'âne*.
See also KB46.

KB46   Zumthor, Paul, *Langue, texte, énigme*, Coll. Poétique, Paris: Éditions du Seuil, 1975, 266 pp.
See the chapter 'Fatrasie, fatrassiers' (pp. 68-88) for a greatly extended discussion of the subject considered in KB45.

L. INFLUENCE

Beaulieu, Eustorg de: see C6.

L1   Bentley-Cranch, Dana, 'La Réputation de Clément Marot en Angleterre', *SFr*, XVII (1973), 201-21.
Notwithstanding the title, the art. deals not so much with CM's reputation in England as with his influence on English writers. It usefully brings together evidence of the indebtedness of Spenser and others to CM. Most, if not all, of the examples cited have already been identified before, but there is very little reference to earlier studies.

L2   Berdan, John M., *Early Tudor Poetry, 1485-1547*, New York: Macmillan, 1920, xix + 564 pp.
On CM, see pp. 440-50. Concludes that French influence is unexpectedly slight. As for Wyatt's possible debt to CM, the resemblances between their poems amount to no more than an occasional similarity in the treatment of conventional subjects. Berdan repeats his theory that Saint-Gelais imitated Wyatt (see KA2).

L3   Borland, Lois, 'The Influence of Marot on English Poetry of the Sixteenth Century', M.A. thesis, Univ. of Chicago, 1913, 101 pp.
Borland's conclusions: (i) of the different genres employed by CM, the elegy left the most notable mark on English and Scottish poetry: Gifford, Spenser, Montgomerie; (ii) CM's rondeaux and *chansons* influenced esp. Wyatt and his contemporaries; (iii) ten of CM's epigrams were imitated by English poets; (iv) no direct influence of CM's pastoral poems is discernible apart from the very significant one on Spenser; (v) further research may well yield evidence of CM's influence on English psalm translations (see L51, 52); (vi) CM's versification and style were undoubtedly responsible for a certain lightness and variety in English poetry; (vii) CM's indirect influence, through Spenser, must have been considerable.

L4   Borland, Lois, 'Montgomerie and the French Poets of the Early Sixteenth Century', *MP*, XI (1913-14), 127-34.
Alexander Montgomerie based an elegy on CM's third elegy, and imitated

CM's epigram *De ouy et nenny* (*OC*, V, p. 149) in the opening stanza of *An Admonition to Young Lassis.*

Bovet, Félix: see HUa5.

L5 Buisman, J.F. Jr., 'Marot en Spiegel', *N*, XXII (1937), 98-108.
On the strong influence of CM's poems, esp. the epigrams, on the work of the Dutch poet Laurenszoon Spieg(h)el (1549-1612).

L6 Buschner, Hans, *Die Bedeutung der antiken Mythologie für die französische Ode bei deren Entstehung*, Weida, 1909, 79 pp.
In tracing the evolution of the genre in France, Buschner cites many examples of CM's influence on the metre of Du Bellay's and Ronsard's odes.

Cooper, Helen: see HJ2.

L7 Coulter, Mary Welles, '*Satyres chrestieñes de la cuisine papale*', *SP*, LVI (1959), 138-49.
In this useful art., whose main purpose is to establish Conrad Badius's authorship of the *Satyres* and to date the different poems, Coulter also suggests that Badius may have been influenced by CM's *coq-à-l'âne*.

L8 Desguine, André, *Étude des 'Bacchanales, ou le folastrissime voyage d'Hercueil. Fait l'an 1549', par Ronsard*, Geneva: Droz, 1953, 367 pp. (+ facsimile of 1552 ed.).
See esp. 'Clément Marot et Ronsard', pp. 45-53. Desguine affirms, but without offering any detailed evidence, that 'par leur rythme, leur régularité strophique, les réminiscences d'inspiration et de vocabulaire qu'elles contiennent, *les Bacchanales* se classent parmi les textes qui subirent indiscutablement l'influence de Clément Marot sur Ronsard à ses débuts'.

L9 Desonay, Fernand, *Ronsard, poète de l'amour*, Brussels: Académie Royale de Langue et de Littérature Françaises de Belgique, 3 vols, 1952-59.
Various references to reminiscences of CM in Ronsard's poems.

Dorangeon, Simone: see HJ3.

L10 Dorveaux, P., 'Notes pour le commentaire: II', *RER*, VIII (1910), 211-12.
Speculates that in his prologue to *Gargantua* Rabelais may have remembered CM's preface to his ed. of the *Roman de la Rose*.

Egger, E.: see HJ4.

L11   Emerson, Oliver Farrar, 'Spenser, Lady Carey, and the *Complaints* Volume', *PMLA*, XXXII (1917), 306-22.
Discusses the *Visions of Petrarch* (in the *Complaints*) which Spenser based on CM's tr. *Le Chant des visions de Pétrarque* (*OC*, VI, pp. 215-19). Comments on the way in which Spenser changed the final lines of CM's version (but Emerson mistranslates those lines). Cf. L32.

Endrődi, A.: see L28.

L12   Eringa, S., *La Renaissance et les rhétoriqueurs néerlandais: Matthieu de Casteleyn, Anna Bijns, Luc de Heere*, Amsterdam, 1920, viii + 258 pp.
Includes a detailed examination of the translations and adaptations made by Lucas de Heere of CM's poems, and discusses his indebtedness to CM in his own poems.

L13   Erskine, John, *The Elizabethan Lyric: A Study*, New York, Gordian Press, 1967, xvi + 344 pp.
Includes some remarks on Spenser's indebtedness in the 'November' eclogue of the *Shepheardes Calender* to CM's *Eglogue sur le trespas de ... Loyse de Savoye*, and on the relationship of both texts to Moschus's lament for Bion.

L14   Eschenauer, A., 'A propos du psautier des églises réformées', *BSHP*, XXIV (1875), 377-80.
On Lobwasser's German tr. (1573) and on an English tr. (1632) of the CM-Beza psalter, both written to be sung to the Genevan melodies.

L15   Eszlary, Charles d', 'Jean Calvin, Théodore de Bèze et leurs amis hongrois', *BSHP*, CX (1964), 74-99.
The Hungarian contacts included Albert Molnár von Szenc who met Beza in Geneva in 1596 and later translated the psalms into Hungarian, using as his model the French psalter and retaining the original melodies (see also L54). Cf. L21, 24, 28, 33.

L16   Fontaine, Charles, *Un poeta della preriforma: Charles Fontaine Epistres, chantz royaulx, ballades, rondeaulx et dixains faictz à l'honneur de Dieu (Cod. vat. Reg. lat. 1630)*, ed. by Raffaele Scalamandrè, *Archivio Italiano per la Storia della Pietà*, VI (1970), 11-255.
In his important introduction to the ed., Scalamandrè describes Fontaine espousing Evangelical ideas under the influence of Marguerite de Navarre

and CM – in particular, the latter's *Déploration de Florimond Robertet.*

L17   Foxwell, A.K., *A Study of Sir Thomas Wyatt's Poems*, London: Univ. of London Press, 1911, 160 pp.
States that CM exercised a considerable influence on Wyatt, but the evidence presented is rather patchy and inconclusive. See also L59.

L18   Françon, Marcel, 'Le Rondeau du rondeau', *Fra*, no. 16 (1975), 53-55.
Very similar to HR6, except that here CM is named as Voiture's direct model.

L19   Françon, Marcel, ' "Douce proye" ', *Fra*, no. 18 (1976), 14-15.
The idea for the theft of birds' eggs in 'Bel aubepin ...' was not taken by Ronsard from the *Description du printemps* by Peletier du Mans, as has been suggested. Both poets drew on the descriptions of children or youths searching for nests in the *Illustrations de Gaule* of Jean Lemaire de Belges and in CM's *Eglogue au roy, soubz les noms de Pan et Robin.* (On CM's debt to Lemaire in this connection, see KB4, 7.)

L20   Françon, Marcel, 'Sur la tradition classique et médiévale', *Fra*, no. 18 (1976), 12-13.
Regarding Ronsard's use of the term 'Faux Dangier', Françon points out that the *Roman de la Rose* employs only 'Danger', but that CM mentions 'Faulx Dangier' in *Le Temple de Cupido* (line 189). Cf. KB18.

Françon, Marcel: see also KB13, 14, 16.

L21   Gáldi, László, *Szenczi Molnár Albert zsoltárverse* [*The Versification of the Psalms of Albert Molnár von Szenc*], Budapest: Magyar Tudományos Akadémia, 1958, 131 pp.
On Molnár's adaptations of the metres of the CM-Beza psalter. Cf. L15, 24, 28, 33.

L22   Giudici, Enzo, *Maurice Scève bucolico e 'blasonneur'*, Naples: Liguori, 1965, 366 pp.
Numerous references to CM, esp. in connection with Scève's *blasons* and his eclogue *Arion.*

L23   Guy, Henry, 'Les Sources françaises de Ronsard', *RHLF*, IX (1902), 217-56.
On CM, see esp. pp. 246-56. Guy believes that CM influenced Ronsard in matters of style, which explains Ronsard's predilection for alliteration and *vers équivoqués*, and in the choice of such genres as the eclogue and

the *blason*. Moreover, Ronsard may have directly borrowed from CM in some passages and derived certain metres in the odes from CM's psalm translations. Guy's remarks mostly amount to speculation based on similarities rather than to clear proof, but the presumption of Ronsard's debt is fairly well established. At all events, Guy shows conclusively that, despite Ronsard's scorn for native French traditions and his sincere effort to escape from them, his poems display their influence and even contain some evident imitations.

L24   Halmy, Ferenc, *A magyar zsoltárformák Francia előzményei* [*The French Sources of the Forms of the Hungarian Psalms*], Bibliothèque de l'Institut Français à l'Univ. de Budapest, XXXVIII, Budapest, 1939, 54 pp.
Cf. L15, 21, 28, 33, 54.
Rev.: .1 S[chöne], M[aurice], *FM*, X (1942), 314-15.

L25   Hanks, Joyce, 'Ronsard's Debt to Marot in *L'Hymne de la mort*', *EsC*, XII (1972), 189-92.
Notes some common themes in the hymn and CM's *Déploration de Florimond Robertet*, which Ronsard may have taken from the latter poem. In any case, he was undoubtedly thinking of the *Déploration* in certain passages expressing the Christian attitude to death.

L26   Hanks, Joyce Main de, 'L'Attitude de Ronsard vis-à-vis de Marot', *Revista de la Universidad de Costa Rica*, XXXVI (1973) 55-61.
Identifies and analyzes three attitudes displayed by Ronsard towards CM: the wish to imitate; rivalry, or even a desire for revenge; criticism. Believe that Ronsard wanted to avenge CM's slighting of Horace in the prefatory poem to his psalm translations. (This is presumably a reference to the proclamation of David's superiority over Horace in lines 129-34 of the poem *Au roy treschrestien François ...* (*OC*, VI, pp. 309-14). But as R. Lebègue points out in his art. 'Horace en France pendant la Renaissance', *HR*, III (1936), 156, this was a commonplace which went back to Boccaccio and even to St Jerome.)

L27   Harvitt, Helen (Hélène) J., 'Eustorg de Beaulieu, a Disciple of Marot', *RR*, V (1914), 252-75; VI (1915), 42-59, 206-18, 298-326; VII (1916), 83-109; IX (1918), 319-44.
See esp. the section on the influence of the Rhétoriqueurs and of CM on Eustorg de Beaulieu.

Hawkins, Richmond Laurin: see C77.

L28   Horváth, C., A. Kardos, and A. Endrődi, *Histoire de la littéra-ture hongroise*. Ouvrage adapté du hongrois par I. Kont, Buda-pest: Athenaeum, 1900, x + 420 pp.
Albert Molnár translated the Genevan psalms after hearing them sung at Frankfurt in 1601. His psalms, published at Herborn in 1607, have the same number of syllables and the same rhythm as the French ones, so that they might be sung to the same melodies. This is the first instance of the influence of French poetry on a Hungarian work. Molnár also trans-lated Calvin's *Institutes*. Cf. L15, 21, 24, 33.

Hulubei, Alice: see HJ7.

L29   Jacoubet, Henri, *Jean de Boyssoné et son temps*, Toulouse: Privat, 1930, 111 pp.

L30   Jones, H.S.V., *A Spenser Handbook*, New York: Crofts, 1930, viii + 419 pp.
On Spenser's indebtedness to CM, see pp. 62-66.

Joukovsky, Françoise: see J11.

Kalwies, Howard H.: see C86.

Kardos, A.: see L28.

L31   Koczorowski, Stanislas Pierre, 'Louise Labé: Étude littéraire', *Revue de Pologne*, I (1923), 469-91; II (1924), 219-50.
Finds evidence of CM's influence only in Louise Labé's first and third elegies, which are inspired by *Le Temple de Cupido*.

L32   Koeppel, Emil, 'Über die Echtheit der Edmund Spenser zugeschriebenen *Visions of Petrarch* und *Visions of Du Bellay*', *Englische Studien*, XV (1891), 53-81.
Shows that the six *Epigrams* (*Visions of Petrarch*) published anonymously in 1569 in Van der Noodt's *Theatre for Worldlings* and in 1591 in Spenser's *Complaints* are clearly based on CM's tr. of Petrarch's *canzone* 'Standomi un giorno' (*OC*, VI, pp. 215-19). Accepts Spenser's authorship of the 1591 versions, but not of the 1569 ones. See also L11.

L33   Kont, J., 'La Littérature hongroise et le protestantisme de langue française aux XVIe et XVIIe siècles', *BSHP*, XLVIII (1899), 393-418.
Hungarian literature begins essentially in the Reformation. The intellectual movement to which it gave rise was considerably influenced by the French reformers. One of the poetic masterpieces of Hungarian literature is the

adaptation by Albert Molnár von Szenc of the CM-Beza psalter. Cf. L15, 21, 24, 28.

Lambert, Ellen Zetzel: HJ9.

Laumonier, Paul: see I23.

L34 Lee, Sidney, *The French Renaissance in England: An Account of the Literary Relations of England and France in the Sixteenth Century*, Oxford: Clarendon Press, 1910, xxiv + 494 pp
A pioneering study, esp. the section bearing on the first half of the century; in its discussion of the Elizabethan age the book overlaps with and complements Upham's (L57). Lee considers French influence on English literature within the wider context of the debt owed by Tudor culture to France – including dress, dancing, and wine. Deals in some detail with Wyatt's imitation of CM and describes the indebtedness to him of Spenser and others. (On the authorship of Wyatt's model 'S'il est ainsi que ce corps t'abandonne', see also G3, HR11, KA14, L59.)

L35 Lerber, Walther de, *L'Influence de Clément Marot aux XVIIme et XVIIIme siècles*, Lausanne: Haeschel-Dufey, 1920, xv + 125 pp.
A study of CM's reputation, as reflected in judgements and the number of editions, and of his influence, esp. through the 'style marotique' (cf. various entries in section HA). Useful, though the coverage is by no means exhaustive.
Rev.: .1 Harvitt, Hélène, *MLN*, XXXVIII (1923), 303-06.
.2 Klemperer, Victor, *ASNS*, CXLIII (1922), 304-07.
.3 Mornet, D., *RHLF*, XXVIII (1921), 453-54.
.4 Plattard, Jean, *RSS*, VII (1920), 171-73.

L36 Leykauff, August, *François Habert und seine Übersetzung der 'Metamorphosen' Ovids*, Münchener Beiträge zur Romanischen und Englischen Philologie, XXX, Leipzig: Deichert (Böhme), 1904, xi + 123 pp.
See esp. 'Habert und Marot', pp. 84-104. Leykauff tabulates complete or close correspondences between their texts with regard to lines, rhymes errors in translation, paraphrases, and divergences from the original and additions to it. Establishes beyond doubt Habert's very considerable debt to CM.

L37 Livingstone, Charles H., 'Un Disciple de Clément Marot: Bertra de la Borderie', *RSS*, XVI (1929), 219-82.

L38   Maiberger, Max, 'Die Ekloge', in his *Studien über den Einfluss Frankreichs auf die elisabethanische Literatur*, I: *Die Lyrik in der zweiten Hälfte des XVI. Jahrhunderts*, Frankfurt, 1903, pp. 50-54.
On Spenser's debt to CM.

L39   Parmenter, Mary, 'Spenser: *Twelve Aeglogves Proportionable to the Twelve Monethes*', *ELH*, III (1936), 190-217.
Spenser's proportionment of Colin Clout's life to the scheme of the seasons – youth in 'Januarie', middle age in 'June', old age in 'December' – is not merely an imitation of CM's *Eglogue au roy*, but also draws on an old conception equally well-known in England.

L40   Pineaux, Jacques, *La Poésie des protestants de langue française, du premier synode national jusqu'à la proclamation de l'Édit de Nantes (1559-1598)*, Bibliothèque Française et Romane, Série C: Études Littéraires, XXVIII, Paris: Klincksieck, 1971, 523 pp.
Cites instances of CM's influence.

L41   Procop, Wilhelm, 'Die Psalmen des Paulus Melissus in ihrem Verhältnis zur französischen Psalmen-Übersetzung des Marot-Beza und zur Vulgata: Eine sprachliche Untersuchung', *Programm des Kgl. Humanistischen Gymnasiums Rosenheim für das Schuljahr 1898-99*, Rosenheim, 1899, 21 pp.
Melissus's German tr. is based partly on CM's version and partly on the Vulgate, and is written to be sung to the melodies of the French psalter. It is, however, considerably less faithful a tr. than CM's.

L42   Rat, Maurice, 'Avec trois rimes et deux vers impairs, Ronsard fonda toute une école ... Mais l'inventeur véritable était Marot', *Figaro Littéraire*, 17 Oct. 1953, p. 4.
The charming rhythm of Ronsard's *Bacchanales* is taken from CM's psalm XXXVIII.

L43   Reamer, Owen J., 'Spenser's Debt to Marot – Re-examined', *TSLL*, X (1968), 504-27.
Prints side by side 'December' from the *Shepheardes Calender* and CM's *Eglogue au roy, soubz les noms de Pan et Robin*, in such a way that the corresponding passages appear as far as possible opposite to each other. Reamer argues that this arrangement clearly establishes that not more than twenty percent of the English lines were borrowed, more or less closely, from the French eclogue. In any case, Spenser was not a

slavish imitator, but took from CM's poem certain ideas or details which
readily fitted into his own preconceived purpose.

L44   Reissert, O., 'Bemerkungen über Spenser's *Shepheards Calendar*
       und die frühere Bukolik', *Anglia*, IX (1886), 205-24.
       Concise but good discussion of Spenser's debt to CM. Maintains that in
       'November' Spenser often slavishly imitates the *Eglogue sur le trespas de
       Loyse de Savoye*, but that in 'December',while closely following the
       Eglogue au roy, soubz les noms de Pan et Robin in the earlier sections,
       he adopts a significantly different tone and viewpoint in the later parts.

L45   Rigolot, François, 'L'Intertexte du dizain scévien: Pétrarque
       et Marot', *CAIEF*, XXXII (1980), 91-106.
       In *Délie* Scève sets out to compose a great French *canzoniere*, in which
       the code of Petrarch's *Rime sparse* – great malleability of form, intended
       to suggest sincere emotion – and the code of CM's *proto-canzoniere*, the
       Second Livre des épigrammes dedicated to Anne – epigrams characterized
       by considerable strophic and metrical variety – was to be replaced by a
       new code constituted by an epigram of fixed form: 'le dizain isostrophiq'
       et isométrique'. An interesting thesis, splendidly argued. Rigolot also
       draws attention to the strong connection between the opening poem of
       Délie and CM's liminary poem *A Anne* (*OC*, V, p. 163), as well as to the
       fact that the decasyllabic *dizain* with four rhymes, which Scève adopted,
       was also the dominant form of CM's *dizains*.

       Ruutz-Rees, Caroline: see C125, 126, KB36.

L46   Salel, Hughes, *Un Précurseur de la Pléiade: Hugues Salel de
       Cazals-en-Quercy (1504-1553): Œuvres poétiques*, publiées
       avec une introduction, des notes et un lexique [par] L.A.
       Bergounioux, Toulouse: Occitania (Guitard), 1930, v + 342 pp
       On CM, see esp. 'Les Sources françaises: Clément Marot', pp. 65-73.
       Stresses CM's strong influence on Salel's early works, esp. the amatory
       poems. But the arguments are vague; the evidence as here presented
       is not always convincing.

L47   Saulnier, V.L., 'Pantagruel au large de Ganabin; ou, La Peur
       de Panurge', *BHR*, XVI (1954), 58-81.
       In mentioning the Conciergerie in the *Quart Livre* (ch. lxvi), Rabelais
       could not have helped thinking of CM and Dolet, both of whom had
       been imprisoned in the Châtelet. Moreover, there are correspondences
       between the passage in Rabelais and *L'Enfer*.

L48   Scanlan, Timothy M., 'An Echo of Marot, Rabelais and Scarron

in Rousseau's *Les Confessions*', *RoN*, XVI (1974-75), 335-37.
Points out that the ironic phrase 'au demeurant, le meilleur filz du monde' in the epistle *Au roy, pour avoir esté desrobé*, which he dates at 1551, is echoed by Rabelais in *Pantagruel*, which he dates at 1552 (both dates are wildly inaccurate), by Scarron in *Le Roman comique*, and by Rousseau in the *Confessions*. Wonders from which of the three earlier authors Rousseau borrowed the phrase, and whether he did so consciously or unconsciously. (Scarron, in any case, used a variant.)

L49   Schweinitz, Margaret de, *Les Épitaphes de Ronsard: Étude historique et littéraire*, Paris: Presses Universitaires de France, 1925, xv + 187 pp.
Ronsard was attracted to this literary form through reading, on the one hand, the epitaphs of CM and the 'Marotiques', and, on the other, the *tumuli* and *funera* of the Neo-Latin poets. He assimilated characteristics of both types. Schweinitz indicates various parallels between Ronsard's and CM's epitaphs.

L50   Shannon, G.P., 'Against Marot as a Source of Marlowe's *Hero and Leander*', *MLQ*, IX (1948), 387-88.
Contrary to Lee's claim (in L34) that Marlowe's poem was among the 'numerous progeny' of CM's *Histoire de Leander et de Hero*, the latter should be removed from the list of possible sources, since it 'fails to show any resemblance to Marlowe in plot, incident, motive, character, or description which does not also exist between Marlowe and the Greek [i.e. Musaeus]'.

L51   Sidney, Philip, *The Poems of Sir Philip Sidney*, ed. by William A. Ringler, Jr, Oxford: Clarendon Press, 1962, lxx + 578 pp.
On Sidney's indebtedness to the CM-Beza psalter in his psalm translations, see pp. 505-16. Cf. L52.

L52   Smith, Hallett, 'English Metrical Psalms in the Sixteenth Century and their Literary Significance', *HLQ*, IX (1945-46), 249-71.
Of the forty-three psalms tr. by Philip Sidney, fourteen directly imitate the metre of the CM-Beza psalter, while others adapt the rhyme-schemes of the French to a different metre. But the overall debt to the French psalms is even greater than that. Cf. L51.

L53   Smith, W.F., 'Sur le Ve livre', *RER*, IV (1906), 235-43.
States that Rabelais borrowed from CM in his first two books and frequently drew on his poems in the *Cinquième Livre* where, in particular, chapters xi-xv – i.e. the 'Grippenaud' and 'Chats fourrés' episodes –

were inspired by *L'Enfer*. Moreover, the number of allusions to CM and of quotations from his poems is so great in this part of the *Cinquième livre* as to suggest that Rabelais wrote the latter shortly after 1538, 'date de l'édition la plus complète des poèmes de Marot, celle qui contenait son *Enfer*'. Smith produces little evidence in support of his affirmations. In any case, his loose argument rests at least in part on wrong dates: the first publication of the *Adolescence cl.* in 1529, of *L'Enfer* in the *Œuvres* of 1538.

L54   Tagliavini, Carlo, 'Influences du psautier huguenot de Clément Marot et de Théodore de Bèze dans la littérature roumaine ancienne', *Cahiers Sextil Puşcuria*, I (1952) 37-48.
The seventeenth-century Rumanian translations of the psalter were based on the Hungarian tr. by Molnár who had mainly followed Lobwasser's German version of the Genevan psalms. Cf. L15, 21, 24, 28, 33, 56.

Théret, Auguste: see HA96.

L55   Tilley, Arthur, 'From Marot to Ronsard', in *Mélanges ... Paul Laumonier*, Paris: Droz, 1935, pp. 131-61.
Rapid survey of poets who wrote in the period between CM's almost total abandonment of secular poetry in the early 1540's and the advent of the Pléiade. Such labels as 'School of Marot', 'School of Lyons' or 'Precursors of the Pléiade' are all, for different reasons, inappropriate. Each poet must be considered on his own merits and his contribution, if any, to the progress of French poetry during this period separately assessed.

L56   Trunz, Erich, 'Die deutschen Übersetzungen des Hugenotten-psalters', *Euphorion*, XXIX (1928), 578-617.
Valuable art. on the translations by Paul Schede Melissus (cf. L41), Ambrosius Lobwasser (cf. L14), and Philipp von Winnenberg und Beilstein. While the first two very closely follow the French text, Von Winnenberg merely reproduces its content, but this he does faithfully, even where it deviates from the Hebrew.

L57   Upham, Alfred Horatio, *The French Influence in English Literature, from the Accession of Elizabeth to the Restoration*, New York: Columbia UP, 1908, ix + 560 pp.
In the chapter on the Elizabethan sonnet, cites some evidence of knowledge of CM in England during the latter half of the sixteenth century and mentions his influence on Barnabe Googe and on Spenser, among others.

L58 Visscher, Roemer, *Uit Roemer Visscher's 'Brabbeling'*, door
Nicolaas van der Laan, Utrecht: Oosthoek, 2 vols, 1918-23.
A selection of poems from *Brabbeling* (published 1612, augmented ed.
in 1614), preceded by an essay on Visscher (1547-1620) and accompanied
by notes. (From these it appears that the complete collection contains
twenty-seven poems tr. from Marot; a poem entitled *Van den os op den
esel* which presents some minor reminiscences of CM's first and second
coq-à-l'âne; and, among the Martial translations, seven poems which
were previously rendered into French by CM, but it is not made clear
whether Visscher was influenced by the French versions.)

Wiat, Thomas: see L59.

Woodward, G.R.: see HUa42.

L59 Wyatt, Thomas, *The Poems of Sir Thomas Wiat* [sic], ed.
from the MSS and early eds by A.K. Foxwell, London: Univ.
of London Press, 2 vols, 1913.
In her commentary on the rondeau 'Yf it be so' (II, pp. 18-22), Foxwell
shows that Wyatt is indebted to the Italian sonnet 'Se questo miser corpo
t'abandona', presumed to be by Serafino, as well as to the French tr. 'S'il
est ainsi que ce corps t'abandonne' which she attributes to CM. Foxwell
points out that the theme of the exchange of hearts, which is a feature
of the poem, goes back at least to troubadour poetry, and that a fine
example can be found in early French literature in Chrétien de Troyes's
Cligès. Foxwell prints both the Italian and French poems imitated by
Wyatt. (Another, practically identical, demonstration of the French
poet's indebtedness to Serafino and of Wyatt's debt to both, with a
brief reference to the presence of the exchange-of-hearts motif in *Cligès*,
is provided fifty years later by Mayer and Bentley-Cranch in KA14,
where the French rondeau is attributed to Jean Marot. On the latter
point, see also G3, HR11.)

L60 Wyatt, Thomas, *Collected Poems of Sir Thomas Wyatt*, ed.
by Kenneth Muir and Patricia Thomson, Liverpool: Liverpool
UP, 1969, xxvi + 479 pp.

M. MAROT AND MUSIC

Baehr, Rudolf: see HE1.

M1   Lesure, François, 'Autour de Clément Marot et de ses musicien
Revue de Musicologie, XXXIII (1951), 109-19.
Convincing rejection of Rollin's thesis (see M4). A few interesting remark
on CM and contemporary composers of *chansons*, followed by a valuable
list of musical settings of his poems. (Information on some further items,
supplied by Lesure, is included by Saulnier in A8, 9.) See also M2, 3.

M2   Lesure, François, 'Autour de Clément Marot et de ses musicien
in his *Musique et musiciens français du XVIᵉ siècle*, Geneva:
Minkoff Reprint, 1976, pp. 37-49.
Reprint of M1, with an enlarged list of musical settings which incorporat
the items mentioned by Saulnier in A8, 9, and adds some further ones.
This new list contains 253 settings by 65 composers of 122 poems or
parts of poems. See also M3.

*M3   Mills-Pont, Jeanne Dorothée, 'Clément Marot: The Union of
Poetry and Music', Ph. D. thesis, Univ. of Arizona, 1972, 359
pp. *DisA*, XXXIV (1973-74), 327A.
'The three-fold purpose of this dissertation is: 1° to refute the Ronsardia
notion of *vers mesurés* as a prerequisite of musical setting; 2° to present
Marot as the true restorer of the ancient union of poetry and music by
Ronsardian standards, though, in the final analysis, by Greek standards
no such restoration is possible; 3° to provide for the researcher the most
complete tabulation possible of Marot's secular [verse] set to music in
the sixteenth century.'

M4   Rollin, Jean, *Les Chansons de Clément Marot: Étude historiqu
et bibliographique*, Publications de la Société Française de
Musicologie, 3rd ser., I, Paris: Fischbacher, 1951, 379 pp.
Provides much valuable information on the music of CM's *chansons*..
But attributes excessive importance to CM's references to music. Argues
that his remarks could have been written only by a person of great
musical sensibility who had received extensive musical training. CM
clearly intended poems entitled *chansons* to be set to music. Moreover,

he may well have himself composed the first monodic settings which preceded the polyphonic versions: CM 'a manifesté parallèlement une activité de chansonnier et de poète'. (The weaknesses of Rollin's thesis are exposed in the two reviews cited below.)

Rev.: .1 Lesure, François: see M1, 2.
     .2 Saulnier, V.L., *BHR*, XV (1953), 130-36.

M5   Saulnier, V.L., 'Dominique Phinot et Didier Lupi, musiciens de Clément Marot et des marotiques', *Revue de Musicologie*, XLIII (1959), 61-80.

Describes the song-collection, with music by Phinot and Lupi, which was published in 1548 and contained settings of twelve poems by CM.

M6   Silver, Isidore, 'The Marriage of Poetry and Music in France: Ronsard's Predecessors and Contemporaries', in *Poetry and Poetics from Ancient Greece to the Renaissance: Studies in Honor of James Hutton*, ed. by G.M. Kirkwood, Cornell Studies in Classical Philology, XXXVIII, Ithaca: Cornell UP, 1975, pp. 152-84.

On CM, see pp. 167-72. While hesitant to accept Rollin's thesis (see M4), Silver suggests that CM's relationship to the music of his time was probably a close one, if only because his *chansons* 'were ideally adaptable to the requirements of the composers and public taste'. In his psalms, moreover, CM anticipated Ronsard in an even more important association of poetry with music.

M7   Silver, Isidore, 'The Marriage of Poetry and Music in France: Ronsard's Predecessors and Contemporaries', in his *Ronsard and the Hellenic Renaissance in France*, II: *Ronsard and the Grecian Lyre*, Pt 1, THR, CLXXXII, Geneva: Droz, 1981, pp. 57-81.

Reprint of M6 (the passage on CM is on pp. 68-72).

M8   Thibault, G., 'Musique et poésie en France au XVIe siècle avant les *Amours* de Ronsard', in *Musique et poésie au XVIe siècle*, Colloques Internationaux du Centre National de la Recherche Scientifique, Sciences Humanies, V, Paris, 30 juin-4 juillet 1953, Paris: Éditions du CNRS, 1954, pp. 79-88.

Esp. interesting on Claudin de Sermisy's settings of poems by CM.

N. MAROT IN FICTION

N1   Barnouw, A.J., 'T nieuwsgierig aagje van Enkhuizen', *TNTL*, XX (1901), 291-301.

Gives title of 1655 ed. of N12. Suggests that Jan Zoet may have derived the idea of making CM the hero of comic tales from a collection of farces published in Amsterdam in 1654 under the title *De gaven van de milde St. Marten*: 'milde' suggests 'clement', and it is only a short step from 'clemente Marten' to 'Clément Marot'.

N2   Barré, [Pierre Yon], [Jean Baptiste] Radet, and Desfontaines [pseud. of François Georges Fouques], *Les Trois Saphos lyonnaises; ou, Une Cour d'amour. Comédie-vaudeville en deux actes*, Paris: Fages, 1815, 46 pp.

First performed at the Théâtre du Vaudeville, Paris, on 14 January 1815. Marguerite de Navarre presides over a *cour d'amour*. Among the other principal characters are Rabelais and CM, exiled in Lyons, but who receives permission from François I at the end of the play to return to the Court.

N3   Bolte, Johannes, 'Beiträge zur Geschichte der erzählenden Literatur des 16. Jahrhunderts', *TNTL*, XII (1893), 309-19; XIII (1894), 1-16, 85-94.

Describes eds of N12 (pp. 88-89): one published between 1717 and 1740, the other ca 1786; and of N10: 1660, 1665, and 1667.

N4   Bolte, Johannes, 'Zur Schwankliteratur des 16. und 17. Jahrhunderts', *TNTL*, XXXIX (1920), 75-96.

Describes the 1655 ed. of N12, as well as listing four other Amsterdam eds mentioned by Muller (see N12): 1660, ca 1725, two undated ones (p. 94).

Desfontaines: see N2.

N5   Duvergie, J., *L'Hérésie de Clément Marot, 1524-1527, contée par J. Duvergie, d'après Clément lui-même*, Chartres, 1924, xvi + 44 pp.

Having established in the preface 'd'une façon absolument précise et

peut-être irrécusable' that 'Luna' = 'Isabeau' = Diane de Poitiers,
Duvergie tells the story of her relationship with CM in fictional form.
At the same time, each step in the drama is documented with the help
of appropriately interpreted poems by the infatuated lover, who eventually
becomes the victim of Diane's denunciation, following his public proclamation of her fickleness: 'et si il fut hérétique ... il ne le fut pas contre la
religion, mais contre l'inconstance amoureuse d'une haute et noble Dame,
dont les charmes et les coquetteries avaient allumé en lui un sentiment
violent, qu'elle se refusa à satisfaire.'

N6   Flögel, Karl Friedrich, 'Clement Marot', in his *Geschichte der
      Hofnarren*, Liegnitz, Leipzig: Siegert, 1789, pp. 345-46.
      'Wenn auch dieser berühmte französische Dichter und Kammerdiener
      Franz I. kein eigentlicher Hofnarr war, so gehört er doch unter die Lustig-
      macher des französischen Hofes ...' Flögel then tells some − apocryphal −
      anecdotes about CM (he had already very briefly described CM's life
      and made a few cursory remarks about CM's satirical poems in his
      Geschichte der komischen Litteratur, Liegnitz & Leipzig: Siegert, 3 vols,
      1784-87, II (1785), pp. 467-70).

      Fouques, François Georges: see N2.

N7   Francis, Claude, 'Chez le roi François Ier: A Fontainebleau en
      1540', in her *Divertissements littéraires*, I: *Moyen âge et Renais-
      sance*, Trois-Rivières: Éditions Trifluviennes, 1954, pp. 239-73.
      The well-illustrated volume is intended for use in schools. Imaginary
      dialogues between historical persons are interspersed with texts from
      contemporary works. In the course of this particular *divertissement*, CM
      recites passages from two of his epistles.

N8   Giraud, Yves, 'Une Apparition de Clément Marot dans la littéra-
      ture populaire', *BHR*, XXXIII (1971), 620-24.
      Very detailed description of N12, from an ed. dated 1678.

N9   Hugo, Victor, *Le Roi s'amuse*, in his *Œuvres complètes*. Éd.
      chronologique publiée sous la direction de Jean Massin, Paris:
      Club Français du Livre, 18 vols, 1967-69, IV (1967), 513-641.
      First performed at the Théâtre Français, Paris, on 22 Nov. 1832. In the
      play, CM sides with the courtiers against François I's fool Triboulet.
      (CM does not, of course, appear in Verdi's opera *Rigoletto* whose plot,
      while very closely following Hugo's, has been set at the court of the
      Duke of Mantua.)

N10   *Das kurtzweilige Leben von Clement Marott; oder, Allerhand lustige Materi für die kurtzweil-liebende Jugend. Aus dem Französischen ins Niederländische und aus demselben anitzo ins Hochdeutsche gebracht*, 1660, 185 pp.

Presumably a tr. of N12. Augmented eds were published in 1663, 1665, and 1667 (see N3, 15, 17).

N11 Laroussilhe, F. de. 'Ode à Clément Marot', *BSEL*, LXXXIII (1962), 110-11.

N12 *'T Leven en bedrijf van Clement Marot. Uit het Fransch in het Nederduyts vertaalt door Jan Soet. Dezen laatsten druk meer als een derden vermeerdet.* Dordrecht: Abraham Andriessz 1665. (Title from N4, p. 94.)

In this collection of anecdotes CM is described as the famous court jester of François I and is portrayed as a crafty and irreverent, but appealing, rapscallion in the Till Eulenspiegel mould. He is featured in a series of amusing incidents, many of which he relates himself. Most of them are in no way authenticated by CM's known experiences or by his poetry, but one story paraphrases the epistle *Au roy, pour avoir esté desrobé*; others refer, though in the main fancifully, to his troubles with the Catholic authorities. On CM in popular literature, see N17.

The success of this work is attested by the several further eds, and by its tr. into German (see N3, 9, 15, 17). According to Frederik Muller's catalogue, *Nederlandsche letterkunde. Populaire prozaschrijvers der XVIIe en XVIIIe eeuw*, Amsterdam, 1893, *'T Leven* reached its fifth ed. in 1660. Moser-Rath (N17) lists eight eds after 1660. The French original referred to in the title has not yet come to light; perhaps it never existed (cf. N1). The earliest known ed. of the Dutch version is that described above, but it is clear from the title that it was not the first. The name of the Amsterdam actor Jan Soet (or Zoet), who is mentioned as the translator, does not reappear in the later known eds.

N13 Lottin de Laval, V., *Marguerite de Navarre et Clément Marot. Comédie-vaudeville en un acte*, Paris: Dondey-Dupré, 1832, 35 pp.

First performed at the Théâtre de l'Ambigu-comique on 8 Sept. 1832. An amusing plot, set against the sombre background of contemporary religious strife and jumbling various true and imaginary incidents, with no regard for the established chronology of known events. CM is loved by Marguerite, and not only by her; is denounced by Diane de Poitiers, supposedly 'pour se venger de ce qu'il ne savait faire l'amour qu'en paroles'; is pursued by the Sorbonne; is saved from arrest and worse by the intercession of La Belle Ferronnière; and is appointed by François I to the position formerly held by his father. Solos all round, and even a duet between CM and Marguerite. A charming piece of historical nonsense.

N14 Luchet, Auguste, and Félix Pyat, *Ango. Drame en cinq actes, six tableaux, avec un épilogue*, Paris: Dupont, 1835, xi + 112 pp.
First performed at the Théâtre de l'Ambigu-comique on 29 June 1835. A strongly republican play. The authors state in the preface: 'nous avons posé la royauté insouciante, débauchée, spirituelle, mais vile et couarde même dans François Ier, et le peuple au contraire emprisonné, jugé, déshonoré, mais énergique et grand dans la personne d'Ango' (based on the Dieppe ship-owner Jean Ango (1480-1551) — cf. N18). It is furthermore asserted that 'le pouvoir ... commet toujours les mêmes énormités contre l'opposition qu'elle s'appelle protestante ou républicaine'. Accordingly, Dolet, Calvin, Paré, CM 'et quelques autres protestants' are shown eating meat on a Friday, and CM is subsequently condemned to exile from Paris, while the others receive varying sentences for this and other acts of heresy.

N15 Mayer, C.A., 'Notes sur la réputation de Marot aux XVIIe et XVIIIe siècles', *BHR*, XXV (1963), 404-07.
Prints, from MS BN f. fr. 25568, the *Épître de Clément Marot aux dames réformées de la cour de France*, a satirical poem against the bull *Unigenitus* issued by Pope Clement XI in 1713. Quotes a passage from Gaillard, part of which is reproduced in the note to HA37. Describes the 1660 and 1663 eds of N10.

N16 Mégret, Jacques, 'La *Déploration de France sur la mort de Clément Marot*', *BBB* (1926), 85-89.
Describes four eds of the anonymous *Deploration* (the last two eds add '*de France*') *sur la mort de Clement Marot, souverain poete françoys*, three of them dated 1544, the fourth undated but presumably published the same year.

N17 Moser-Rath, Elfriede, 'Clément Marot als Schwankfigur', *Fa*, XX (1979), 137-50.
Important art. examining CM's reincarnation as a prankster in popular literature, esp. in N12 and its German version N10. Mentions also several other German and Dutch works which feature him in that role.

Pyat, Félix: see N14.

Radet, Jean Baptiste: see N2.

N18   Touchard-Lafosse, G., *Jean Ango, histoire du seizième siècle,*
       Paris: Dumont, 2 vols, 1835.
       A historical romance relating the adventurous life of the famous Dieppe
       ship-owner Jean Ango (cf. N14) and describing, with many dramatic
       details, the love felt by François I for Ango's wife. CM, acting on
       instructions given him by his mistress Diane de Poitiers, plays a leading
       role in the affair (there is also a strong hint at an earlier, decidedly non-
       platonic, attachment to Marguerite de Navarre who likewise appears in
       the novel). CM, referred to as 'le traducteur burlesque des psaumes de
       David', is sympathetically portrayed as an amusing and astute person,
       with an endearingly malicious tongue: 'C'est la physionomie de Socrate,
       sur laquelle s'épanouit le sourire d'Anacréon ... [Il] aidait les digestions
       royales de toutes les malices rimées qu'inspiraient journellement au malin
       critique les galanteries peu voilées des dames de bon lieu.'

N19   Voron, Benoist, *Comédie françoyse intitulée 'L'Enfer poétique',*
       publiée à Lyon en 1586 par Benoist Voron. 3ᵉ éd. conforme
       à la première, Société Forézienne de la Diana, Vienne: Savigné,
       1878, 68 pp.
       CM is not a character in this play; but among the heretics condemned
       to eternal torment whom Minos points out to a terrified Mahomet, are
       'Luther, Calvin, Viret, Melancthon et Marot, / Et bref tous ceux qui sont
       de leur secte et complot' (lines 633-34).

N20   Ward, H.L.D., *Catalogue of Romances in the Department of*
       Manuscripts in the British Museum, I, London, 1883, xx + 955
       MS BM Additional 11,153 (late seventeenth century) contains, on fol.
       207, a story in Icelandic about CM and the merchants of Venice (p.
       858). In it CM is described as the French King's jester.

INDEX OF PERSONS

197

Clément Marot

Del Balzo, Carlo, KB9

Delbouille, Maurice, I8

Delescluse, Dominique, HVb2

Deloffre, Frédéric, I9

Delpit, Jules, C106

Denais, Joseph, C39, 45

Denis, Philippe, F72

Derche, Roland, HK5; HL1

Deschamps, P., F13

Desfontaines, N2

Desfontaines, P.F. Guyot, HA23

Desguine, André, L8

Desiré, Artus, HUa11, 15, 25

Desonay, Fernand, L9

Désormaux, J., HP3, 11

Des Périers, Bonaventure, C35; HM17; J18

Desportes, Philippe, HA74; HUa9

Després, M^r, E8

Dettmer, Gustav, J7

Diane de Poitiers, C2, 51, 69, 79, 96, 110, 120; E3, 4.5, 7; N5, 13, 18

Dide, Auguste, C46

Dierlamm, W., I39.1

Diller, Georges, C47

Dimier, Louis, B7, 8

Dolet, Étienne, C34bis, 36, 37; E12, 16; F4, 5, 10, 18, 40, 41, 53, 71; HA102; HM5, 13, 17; HS18; L47; N14

Domínguez Bordona, J., J23

Donaldson-Evans, Lance K., C133.4; HA40.1

Dorangeon, Simone, HJ3

Dorgan, Cornelia W., HVa6

Dorveaux, P., L10

Dossi, Dosso, B10

Dottin, Georges, KB10

Doucet, J., HA25

Douen, O., C20, 46, 48, 49, 66, 80, 94, 108; HUa10, 26

Doumergue, É., C50

Draudius, F26

Dreu du Radier, J.F., C51

Drost, W., I31.2

Droz, Eugénie, E10, 32; F14, 15; G7, 8; HP5, 11; J9

Du Bartas, Guillaume de Saluste, HA80

Du Bellay, Cardinal, F18

Du Bellay, Joachim, HA14, 15, 42, 66, 78; HK6; HS16, 19, 23; KB38; L6, 32

Dubois, E.T., HVa4.1

Dubosc, Georges, D9

Du Cerceau, KB11

Dufour, Théophile, C49.3

Du Lin, Hélouin, F18

Du Moulin, Antoine, C32

Duparc, P., HP4

Duparc, S., HP4

Duplessis, Georges, F16

Du Pré, Galiot, E35; HVa2, 6; HUb2

Du Puy-Herbault, Gabriel, C47

Dussault, J.J.F., HA26; see also 'Y'.

Duval, François, HA27

Du Verdier, Antoine, F17

Duvergie, J., N5

Eckart, Jean, HA26

Eckerdt, H., I10

Eckhardt, Alexandre, KB12

Egger, E., HJ4

Elizabeth I, Queen of England, L57

Elsen, Claude, HA28

Emerson, Oliver Farrar, L11

Endrődi, A., L28

Engler, Winfried, I31.3

Enschedé, E13

Erasmus, E11; HUb2, 20; J27; KB31

Eringa, S., L12

Ernouf, B., C49.4

Erskine, John, L13

Eschenauer, A., L14

Escoffier, Maurice, F18

Eskrisch, Pierre, B13

Espiner-Scott, Janet Girvan, C52, 53

Eszlary, Charles d', L15

Étampes, duc d', HA54; see also La Barre, Jean de

Eusebi, M., HVa3, 7

200

Index of persons

Evans, W. Hugo, HR5

Faguet, Émile, HA29
Farel, Guillaume, C49
Fauchet, Claude, C52-54; HA10
Félice, Ph. de, J12.1
Féret, Ch. Th., HA71
Ferronnière, La Belle, N13
Firmenich-Richartz, Eduard, B6
Firmery, J., I11
Flögel, Karl Friedrich, N6
Fontaine, Charles, C77; HA78; L16
Fontana, Bartolommeo, C55, 56
Forcadel, Étienne, C38
Formey, Jean H.S., HA30
Forster, Elborg, HK6
Forster, Leonard W., KA7, 8
Förster, Margarete, HUa12
Fouques, François Georges, N2
Fournier, Édouard, E16
Foxwell, A.K., L17, 59
Francis, Claude, N7
François Ier, King of France, C33, 34,
   44, 57, 64, 84, 87, 97, 117, 121;
   E11; G11, 13; HA4, 37, 63, 67, 79,
   86, 106; HK13; HP6; HS5; J6, 18;
   N2, 6, 7, 9, 12-14, 18, 20
François, the Dauphin, HN2
François, Alexis, C57
François, L., HA31
Françon, Marcel, C58-62, 83.3, 128,
   133.5; E37.4, 38, 43.1; G3; HA32-
   36; HK10.1; HR6-8; HS5-10, 13, 14;
   HUb6, 7; I12, 13; J8, 18.1; KA9-11,
   17.1; KB13-18; L18-20
Frappier, Jean, KB19, 20
Frère, Henri, C63
Fréville, E. de, C64, 65
Fromage, R., C66, 74, 112; E10, 23,
   32; G9; HA102

Gaiffe, Félix, HA90
Gaillard, G.H., HA37; N15
Gaillarde, Jeanne, HM3; HR11

Gairdner, James, C145
Gáldi, László, L21
Galland, Claude, E34
Gallet, Georges, C120
Galliot, Marcel, I14
Gambier, Henri, KB21
Garasse, François, J14
García de la Fuente, Arturo, F40
Gardet, Clément, HP5
Gastoué, Amédée, HUa13
Gaubert (second wife of Jean Marot),
   C30
Gaudu, F., F12, 19
Gautier, Théophile, HS18
Gendre, André, HA38
Génin, F., C97
Gérard, Jean, F31
Gerhardt, Mia I., HJ5
Gérold, Th., HUa14
Giese, Frank S., HUa15
Gifford, Humphrey, L3
Giono, Jean, C67
Giraud, Jeanne, A3-5
Giraud, Yves F.A., C133.6; E37.5, 42;
   HA39, 100.1; HS14; HUb8; I39.2;
   J9, 27.1; N8
Giudici, Enzo, C68; HC2, 8; J12.2; L22
Glauning, Friedrich, I15
Gmelin, Hermann, KB22
Googe, Barnabe, L57
Goosse, Marie Thérèse, E40.2
Goudimel, Claude, HUa42
Goujet, Claude Pierre, C69, 79
Goulart, Simon, C13, 15
Graesse, Jean George Théodore, F20
Graham, Victor, E37.6
Grau, Lucien, F60
Gray, Floyd, C133.7; E37.7; HR3
Greban, Simon, HK12
Green, F.C., HVb3
Greg, Walter W., HJ6
Greil, Louis, C70
Greiter, Matthaeus, E40
Grenet, Gilbert, E10, 32

201

96, 110; E1, 4, 6; HA23; HS18; HUb20
Lenient, C., HA52, 53
Lenoir, Albert, C64
Lenselink, Samuel Jan, E40; F47; HUa1
Le Petit, Jules, F37
Le Prévost, Robert, HA93, 95
Lerber, Walther de, HUa3.1; HUb12; L35
Lerond, Alain, I25
Le Roux de Lincy, E9, 16
Le Roy, G., HVa3
Lesure, François, M1, 2
Levet, Pierre, HVb5, 6
Leykauff, August, L36
Lifraud, Yvonne, E25
Ligas, Pierluigi, HUa21
Livingstone, Charles H., L37
Lloyd-Jones, Kenneth, HA40.3, 54
Lobwasser, Ambrosius, L14, 54, 56
Longnon, A., HVb2
Lotrian, A., HVa3
Lottin, de Lanval, V., N13
Lotto, Lorenzo, B10
Louis XIV, King of France, HA4
Louise de Savoie, C93
Luchet, Auguste, N14
Lucian, E27, 28; HUb12; KB40
Lupi, Didier, M5
Luther, Martin, B7; J1, 20; N19
Lutkus, Anne Daugherty, J15

McClelland, John, HG2; HS10, 13
Macdonald, Iain, C83.6
McFarlane, I.D., C98; E37.13
Macon, Gustave, E22
Macrin: see Salmon, Jean
Madeleine de France, HO1
Magny, Olivier de, HA74
Magrini, Diana, KA13
Mahieu, Robert G., HK8
Mahomet, N19
Maiberger, Max, L38
Maillard, P^r, F39
Maimbourg, Louis, C4, 85, 99, 122; HUa35

Malherbe, François de, HA22, 29, 49; I26; J21
Malingre, Mathieu, C18; E13; J16
Mallet, E., HA55
Mallet, Édouard, HUa2
Mandelsloh, E. Gfn., HH5.3
Marchand, Prosper, C5
Marguerite de France, duchesse de Savoie, C111; HQ1
Marguerite de Navarre, C2, 32, 69, 79, 82, 91, 93, 96, 97, 110, 140; E4.5, 7, 11; F23, 28, 63; G14; HK9; HP12; HQ1; HUa17, 26, 36; HUb2, 20; HVa6; J2, 3, 5, 7, 10, 13, 16, 30; L16; N2, 13, 18
Marichal, Robert, C116.2
Marlowe, Christopher, L50
Marmita, Gellius Bernardinus, KB26
Marnet, Jeanne de, F56
Marot, Jean, C27, 30, 65, 88, 124, 134; E4; HP14; I37; KA14, 16; KB28; L59
Marot, Michel, E1, 4
Martial, F58; HA75; KB22, 32; L58
Martineau-Génieys, Christine, J16, 17
Martinon, Ph., I26, 27
Mary Tudor (future Queen of England), HR5
Marye, Édouard, C101
Masclé, Thérèse, HG3
Massin, Jean, N9
Mayer, Claude Albert, C8, 48, 57, 62, 83.7, 91, 102-05, 109, 133; D5; E10, 11, 16, 23, 32, 34, 37, 38.1, 43, 44; F4, 29, 31, 36, 40-49, 60, 64, 71; G1, 3-6, 8, 11-13; HA33, 56-59, 85, 98, 100, 102; HH2-5, 8; HJ11; HK10.2, 12; HL2; HM16; HQ1; HS7, 13-16, 18, 22; HUb2, 20; 128, 29, 34.2; J1, 9, 12.4, 16, 18, 19, 27; KA1, 11, 13-16, 21; KB25, 34; L59; N15
Mazaki, Takaharu, J19
Mégret, Jacques, N16
Mehnert, Kurt Henning, E37.14; KB32
Meigret, Laurent, 'Le Magnifique', C57

["

Index of persons

INDEX OF WORKS BY MAROT
AND OF WORKS ATTRIBUTED TO HIM

a)   Poems printed in *OC*

Ballades

A ma dame la duchesse d'Alençon laquelle il supplie d'estre couché en son estat
(IV, pp. 145-47), HA54

Ballade d'une dame et de sa beaulté par le nouveau serviteur (IV, pp. 169-70), HB3

Contre celle qui fut s'amye (IV, pp. 162-64), C58; HA32

Des enfans sans soucy (IV, pp. 139-40), HA19

Blasons

Du beau tétin (V, pp. 156-57), HC3, 4 7

Cantiques

Clement Marot sur la venue de l'empereur en France (III, pp. 302-04), HA85

La Chrestienté à Charles empereur et à Françoys roy de France (III, pp. 291-94),
HD1

Le Dieu gard de Marot à la court de France (III, pp. 284-87), HA70

Marot à l'empereur (III, pp. 366-67), HA85

Chansons

'Changeons propos, c'est trop chanté d'amours' (III, pp. 200-01), HA25

'Tant que vivray en aage florissant' (III, pp. 184-85), HE1

Chants-royaux

*Chant royal de la Conception Nostre Dame que maistre Guillaume Cretin voulut
avoir de l'autheur ...* (IV, pp. 175-78), HF3

Chant royal dont le roy bailla le refrain (IV, pp. 183-85), KA11

Complaintes

*Clement Marot ... sur le trespas de feu messire Florimont Robertet [Déploration
de Florimond Robertet]* (III, pp. 140-61), E31; HG2; J1, 16, 17, 24; L16, 25

Complaincte d'une niepce, sur la mort de sa tante (III, pp. 131-33), KB15, 42

La Complaincte du riche infortuné messire Jaques de Beaune, seigneur de Samblançay
(III, pp. 134-39), F59; HG5; KB5

211

(II, pp. 77-86), E43; J25

Clement Marot aux dames de France ... (VI, pp. 314-16), HP9; HUa17, 31

Clem. Marot, au roy treschrestien Françoys ... (VI, pp. 309-14), HUa17, 32; L26

Epistre de Maguelonne à son amy Pierre de Prouvence ... (III, pp. 114-24), E43

Le Balladin ... (III, pp. 382-90), G2

Le Riche en pauvreté ... (III, pp. 399-406), J28

Le Second Chant d'Amour fugitif ... (II, pp. 86-90), J26

Le Valet de Marot contre Sagon ... [*L'Épître de Frippelippes*] (II, pp. 93-109), D5, 6, 8; E43; HA100

Translations

Psalms (VI, pp. 317-472), C14, 15, 43, 49, 54, 75, 85, 99, 119, 122, 123; E30, 37, 40; F2, 5, 10, 11, 14, 21, 23, 24, 27, 31, 36, 43, 47, 48, 53, 70, 72; HA49, 67, 79, 92, 106; HUa1-43; I23, 27; L14, 15, 21, 23, 24, 28, 33, 41, 42, 51, 52, 54, 56; M6; N18

Other Translations

Epigramme de Salmonius mise de latin en françoys ... (VI, p. 225), HUb4

Le Chant de l'Amour fugitif ... (VI, pp. 108-12), E27; KB25-27

Le Chant des visions de Petrarque translaté de italien en françoys (VI, pp. 215-19), L11, 32

Le Jugement de Minos ... (VI, pp. 79-92), E27; HA98

La Premiere Eglogue des Bucoliques de Virgile (VI, pp. 73-79), HA98; HJ7; HUb11, 19

Le Premier Livre (Le Second Livre) de la Metamorphose d'Ovide ... (VI, pp. 112-214), E33; F12, 16, 19, 38, 40, 60; I42; L36

Les Colloques d'Erasme (VI, pp. 247-308), E11; HUb2, 10, 20

L'Histoire de Leander et de Hero (VI, pp. 230-47), F44; I32; L50

Oraison contemplative devant le crucifix (VI, pp. 92-98), HUb17; KB30

[*Priere*] *apres le repas* (VI, p. 108), HUb3

Six sonnetz de Petrarque ... (VI, pp. 219-25), HUb1, 6, 15, 16

b) Poems not printed in *OC*

Au connétable Anne de Montmorency: 'Ce roy qui doit mieux estre que Pompée', G11

Aultre epistre familiere d'aymer chrestiennement, G1

Aultre espitre de la poule à baudet: 'Tu m'as tant bien au long escript', E32

Au roy: 'Cuydant avoir receu, Sire, la somme', G11

Autre epistre: 'Amy, pour ung peu t'esjoyr', E32

Autre epistre de Clement Marot: 'Coquelicon, je te suplie', E32

Autre epitre du coq à la coquette: 'Ma sœur coquette, au bruict qui court', E32

Chanson de l'Incarnation du Filz, KB42

Index of works

Coq à l'asne de Marot à Me Guillaume le Coq: 'Le coq, mon amy et mon frere',
   E32; G8
Dieu gard de l'autheur à la ville et aux citoyens de Geneve [by Eustorg de Beaulieu]
   G7
Dizain de l'image de Venus armée, KB26
D'un monstre nouvellement baptizé, C74
'En petit lieu compris vous povez veoir', G13
Epistre de complainte, à une qui a laissé son amy [by Jacques Colin], E24
Epistre familiere de prier Dieu, G1
Épître de Clément Marot aux dames réformées de la cour de France, N15
France à l'empereur à son arrivée [by Hugues Salel], HA85
L'Adieu de France à l'empereur, HA85
Le Sermon du bon pasteur, E39; G6
'Que gaignes tu, dy moy, chrestien' [by Mathurin Régnier], G4
'S'il est ainsi que ce corps t'abandonne', G3; HR11; KA14; L34, 59

c)   Editions

Guillaume de Lorris and Jean de Meung, *Le Roman de la Rose*, E33, 35; HA67;
   HVa1-10; L10
Lemaire de Belges, Jean, *Épîtres de l'amant vert*, F22, 46, 68
Villon, François, *Les Œuvres*, E33; HVa2, 9; HVb1-6

d)   Other Works

Briefve doctrine pour deuement escripre selon la proprieté du langaige françoys,
   F63; G1, 12

RESEARCH BIBLIOGRAPHIES & CHECKLISTS
Edited by
A.D. Deyermond, J.R. Little and J.E. Varey